CW00732736

Sir Samuel Meyrick

and Goodrich Court

Sir Samuel Meyrick
and Goodrich Court

by
Rosalind Lowe

Logaston Press

LOGASTON PRESS
Little Logaston, Woonton, Almeley
Herefordshire HR3 6QH

First published by Logaston Press 2003
Copyright © Rosalind Lowe 2003

All rights reserved. No part of this publication
may be reproduced, stored in a retrieval system,
or transmitted, in any form or by any means,
electronic, mechanical, photocopying, recording
or otherwise, without the prior permission,
in writing, of the publisher

ISBN 1 873827 88 1

Set in Garamond, Gill Sans and Baskerville by Logaston Press
and printed in Great Britain by
Cromwell Press, Wiltshire

Front Cover: Original portrait of Sir Samuel by H.P. Briggs 1826, by kind permission of Torre
Abbey Historic House & Gallery, Torquay & descendants of Augustus Meyrick
Rear Cover: Richard Beauchamp, Earl of Warwick: Plate XLVII from *Critical Inquiry into
Antient Armour*, 1842 edition

Contents

Acknowledgements

This work has been a number of years in gestation, and my progress has not always been smooth and or my enthusiasm constant. I have been encouraged to continue by many people who have given their time and expertise with openness, patience and generosity. A friendly smile or a warm reply has been the almost invariable response to my enquiries, and I hope that those kind people not mentioned by name below will accept my heartfelt thanks. To preserve their privacy I have been careful to conceal the identity of some of the private individuals who have helped me in my quest, but they should be in no doubt of my gratitude.

The staff at Hereford Library have carried heavy books without complaint up and down to the strongroom; Ross Library has supplied an endless reading list and Herefordshire Record Office has been a pleasure to visit. In spite of their idiosyncratic systems the service at our great national libraries and repositories has never been less than friendly: thank you to the British Library; the Public Record Office; the National Library of Wales; the British Museum and especially the Bodleian Library. Many institutions have happily allowed me access to their archives, including the College of Arms; the Society of Antiquaries; the Royal Armouries; Queen's College and Christchurch College, Oxford; Eastnor Castle.

I would like to mention particularly those institutions and their representatives who have been most generous with regard to illustrations: Michael Rhodes at Torre Abbey; Neil Barrow of Saddleworth Family History Society; Andrew Benton at the National Museum of Wales, Cardiff; Dinah Birch at Trinity College, Oxford; Chetham's Library; Southampton University Library; Jon Whiteley at the Ashmolean Museum; English Heritage.

Claude Blair has given most generous advice, and copies of letters and photographs. Peter Parsons of the Meyrick Society has furnished me with many items from the Society's archives. Both Sarah Barter-Bailey and Bridget Clifford were most helpful on my visits to the Royal Armouries library while it was still at the Tower, and Charlotte Chipchase now that it is in Leeds. Jeremy Warren at the Wallace Collection has been enthusiastic, supportive and generous in allowing the use of the Collection's material—I am very happy that my research notes will find a home in the library there. Thank you also to Andrea Gilbert and Carmen Colomer for supplying me with material from the Wallace Collection archives.

Although Sir Samuel's direct line died with him, the heir to Goodrich Court and its riches had four daughters whose descendants survive today. Those I have been able to contact have been very generous with their time and their family information, and I regret that it has not been possible to include more of their material in this book. Without the help of the current representatives of the Moffatt and Trafford families much interesting information would have been unavailable.

Many local people bought bits of Goodrich Court when it was demolished, or have stories to tell about it, and they have been very helpful. I wish there was more room in the book for pictures of their souvenirs. I am especially grateful to the purchaser of the Breda Room, for his generosity and hospitality. I must thank the Woolhope Naturalists' Field Club both for the use of their excellent library. This book would not have been written without the initial suggestion of Ron Shoesmith of Logaston Press, and I am grateful to him, and especially to Andy Johnson of Logaston for bearing with my idiosyncracies. Thank you to Michael of MYST for his work on the illustrations.

For more than five years friends and family have been imposed upon, often ignored and frequently inconvenienced, but they have never wavered in their support. Thank you to Jean and Stuart for their hospitality on my visits to London; to Roland for his friendliness and open generosity; to Heather for her strong hands and sympathetic ear; to John Simmons for his expert photography; to Heather and Jon Hurley for their encouragement; to Shirley Preece; to my many friends in Herefordshire who have passed on useful tit-bits.

The members of my family have had to bear with the inevitable ups and downs of a novice author tackling such a major project. If they sometimes felt that they would never see the finished book they concealed it very well. Thank you to my mother and my late father, to my daughter Zeffa and to Tim, Mandy, Lawrie, Stephen and other relatives who have nobly offered to buy copies. The person who has had to bear the brunt of my lack of attention to him, the house and the garden for a number of years is my husband Lawrie. He has borne patiently with the ups and downs of my deep involvement with Sir Samuel, but his help and support have been essential, and they are greatly appreciated.

Lastly, thanks to Sir Samuel himself. He has given me much fun and amusement over the last five years, as well as emotions which range from admiration to dislike. I hope he will forgive me for exposing his sins as well as his virtues.

List of Illustrations

The source of illustrations used in this book is generally noted in the caption, the text or the endnotes. Those from journals such as the *Gentleman's Magazine* and *Archaeologia* and early printed works or engravings will not be separately acknowledged here. Many illustrations are taken from the author's collection of Sir Samuel's works and memorabilia, and those of his fellow antiquarians. I am particularly indebted to the private owners of works of art or photographs that have been used as illustrations. For security and privacy reasons they have not been named, but I am very grateful for their generosity.

Black and White illustrations

The following figures are reproduced by kind permission of the copyright owners and/or current holders of the source material:

Introduction

Every year thousands of tourists come to a small village in the Welsh marches to visit Goodrich Castle, one of the jewels in the crown of English Heritage. Only a few will notice the giant cedar tree almost engulfed by encroaching sycamores on a nearby headland. Yet hardly more than fifty years ago they would have gazed upon a turreted and castellated mansion, which in its heyday eclipsed the attractions of the castle. The name of this exotic building was Goodrich Court.

Doubtless even fewer of the tourists at the castle know the name of Goodrich Court's builder—Sir Samuel Rush Meyrick—and his claims to fame outside Herefordshire. Only in the world of armour does the name of Meyrick still merit instant recognition, an ever widening world thanks to the activities of battle re-enactment societies and the makers of Hollywood epics. Yet in its day Sir Samuel's collection of arms and armour was renowned, and the treasures of Goodrich Court drew visitors from all over the western world during the middle years of the 19th century.

Goodrich Court went the way of many another country mansion in the 1950s, and only the older inhabitants of the surrounding villages remember it at all. The story of the extraordinary man who built it has never been told, despite the fact that he was the first person in Britain to set the study of arms and armour on a regular footing. Today, our attitude towards the accoutrements of war is rather more ambivalent than it was in his time, and only the committed will wax truly enthusiastic about chanfrons and glaives and all the other strange-sounding pieces.

This book is not written principally for the armour expert, but for the ordinary person who wishes to know more about Sir Samuel, his times, and the wonderful treasure house of Goodrich Court. Whilst there is much included about the armour, his life and achievements are so widely spread that it cannot be allowed to dominate his story. His writings range from works for the stage to those on ancient costume, from

Welsh history to the politics of reform, from archaeology to ancient religions. By turns snobbish, impulsive, liberal, pompous, kind, tight-fisted and romantic, he is not an easy person to know or even to like at all times. I have veered from admiration and respect through contempt and dislike, and back again. His personal life was a similar roller-coaster of disaster and triumph.

For all this he *was* an extraordinary man, and is entitled to be better appreciated. His philosophy foreshadowed the gradual change in the 19th century from the 'cabinet of curiosities' mentality towards the more purposeful and instructional *rationale* of today's museum curators. Sir Samuel was not motivated in his acquisitions by the usual considerations of his day. What distinguishes him from any other is that his collection of arms and armour was primarily designed for *instruction*. When he was young, the Linnean system of classification of living things by their differences of form had already been published. He applied the same principles to arms and armour, and in a modern manner supported his conclusions with evidence contemporary with them. He stands at the turning point to the Darwinian age.

His story starts, and ends, in the beautiful county of Herefordshire. It is entirely appropriate that it should be written by someone who lives in a house he once owned in Goodrich, and that it should be published locally.

Rosalind Lowe
Goodrich
March 2003

View of Goodrich Court through an arch at Goodrich Castle, 1840.
(From a private collection by kind permission)

1   Early Days

In 1726 in a remote parish of north Herefordshire, a small boy of seven crossed the threshold of an elegant red-brick building, so different from the local timber-framed farmhouses and hovels. Fifty years later he died in another elegant brick-built house in London, leaving to his numerous issue an estimated six million pounds in modern terms.[1] Perhaps his six years at Lucton School gave James Meyrick an ambition to enjoy the finer things of life, but without such a fortunate start this book would have remained unwritten, for he was Sir Samuel Rush Meyrick's grandfather. Sir Samuel died in 1848, seventy years after his grandfather, full of honours. James would have been pleased but not too surprised, for he had started his rise to riches from rather unlikely beginnings.

Sir Samuel would have said that his grandfather had done no more than retrieve his family's fortunes, for he believed that they were descended from yet another archetypal adventurer—the Elizabethan Sir Gelly Meyrick. Sir Gelly's father was Rowland Meyrick, Bishop of Bangor in North Wales in 1559, and his grandfather was Meuric ap Llewellyn, esquire of the body to King Henry VIII of England.[2] Meuric ap Llewellyn in his turn boasted a distinguished lineage including a descent from Owain Gwynedd, Prince of North Wales. Bishop Rowland's generation was the first to use the English-style family name of Meyrick. The Meyricks had acquired the estate of Bôdorgan in Anglesey and it was still held by their descendants in Sir Samuel's day.

Sir Gelly had tied his fortunes to those of Robert Devereux, the Earl of Essex, and while these were in the ascendant Sir Gelly had prospered. He was knighted by Essex after the daring raid on Cadiz in 1596, and was granted manors in many parts of the country, including Wigmore Castle in north Herefordshire. Unfortunately Essex overreached himself and was condemned for rebellion. Sir Gelly was attainted and executed on 13 March 1601, and his estates became vested in the Crown. He had an only son Rowland by his wife Elizabeth Lewis, who came from Gladestry in Radnorshire. Rowland was succeeded in turn by his son, another Gelly.

In 1828 the historian Nicholas H. Nicolas reviewed a transcription by Sir Samuel of a long letter from Sir Gelly Meyrick,

Fig. 1   Lucton School

which had been published by the Society of Antiquaries.[3] His perceptive, if tactless, comment was 'In this article, not a single fact occurs worthy of preservation, and it was not until we arrived at the conclusion that we could even guess at the cause of its insertion. The following is however a sufficient explanation "These details ... concern my own family". In what way Sir Gelly Meyricke was connected with Dr. Meyrick's family, it would, we believe, be difficult for him to show'.

What is certain is that the family name Meyrick, pronounced 'Merrick', has its origins in the Welsh forename 'Meuric' or 'Meurig'. The Welsh system of nomenclature meant that Meuric, son of Llewellyn, would be called Meuric ap Llewellyn, and Meuric's son, if another Llewellyn, would be called Llewellyn ap Meuric ap Llewellyn. The Welsh adopted the anglicised system of a single family name progressively through the centuries, the relatively limited number of first names explaining the ubiquity of Welsh surnames such as Price (ap Rhys) and Bevan (ab Evan). By the sixteenth century the family name Merrick and its variations such as Meyrick, Meuric, and Myricke were common in the English border counties. As there is no single 'Meuric' ancestor, different Meyrick families need not be related.

The earliest printed pedigree for Sir Gelly and Sir Samuel Meyrick which was widely circulated is in the first edition of Burke's *Landed Gentry*, published in 1838. Almost certainly the details of Sir Samuel's pedigree were obtained or at least verified by Burke in correspondence with him, in which case it is to Sir Samuel that any factual errors must be ascribed. By the time that the *Landed Gentry* was published, Sir

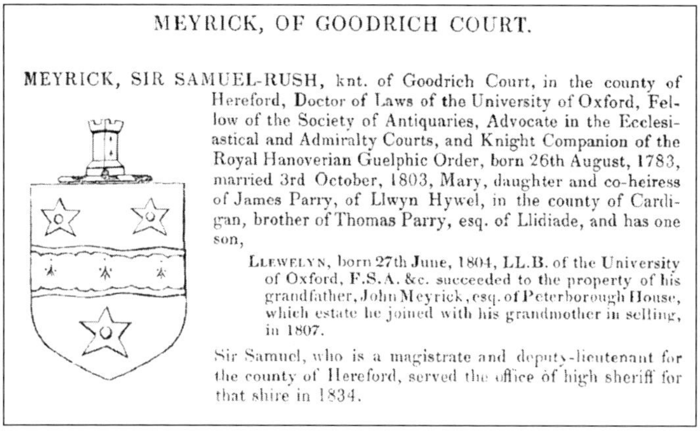

MEYRICK, OF GOODRICH COURT.

MEYRICK, SIR SAMUEL-RUSH, knt. of Goodrich Court, in the county of Hereford, Doctor of Laws of the University of Oxford, Fellow of the Society of Antiquaries, Advocate in the Ecclesiastical and Admiralty Courts, and Knight Companion of the Royal Hanoverian Guelphic Order, born 26th August, 1783, married 3rd October, 1803, Mary, daughter and co-heiress of James Parry, of Llwyn Hywel, in the county of Cardigan, brother of Thomas Parry, esq. of Llidiade, and has one son,

LLEWELYN, born 27th June, 1804, LL.B. of the University of Oxford, F.S.A. &c. succeeded to the property of his grandfather, John Meyrick, esq. of Peterborough House, which estate he joined with his grandmother in selling, in 1807.

Sir Samuel, who is a magistrate and deputy-lieutenant for the county of Hereford, served the office of high sheriff for that shire in 1834.

Fig. 2   Samuel Meyrick's entry in Burke's *Landed Gentry*

Samuel's claimed descent had already been lodged at, but not ratified by, the College of Arms. Two of his closest friends, Francis Martin and Thomas William King, were heralds at the College, but this had not helped the Meyrick cause. After Sir Samuel's death his heir, Augustus Meyrick, asked the College to investigate the pedigree. By this time King had become York Herald and he annotated the descent as supplied (in red ink) as 'not proved'.[4]

The reason for Sir Samuel's pursuit of Gelly Meyrick is not hard to find. As a teenager he fell passionately in love with a Welsh girl, and out of this passion grew another, greater one—for Wales and everything Welsh. Longing to establish Welsh credentials, it must have seemed fortuitous that Sir Gelly Meyrick shared his surname, and that he had lived, or at least owned property, not many miles from Sir Samuel's family home in north Herefordshire. Add to that the fact that Sir Gelly was descended from Welsh royalty and that he had led a highly romantic life, and his attraction to someone of Sir Samuel's character is obvious. However, between the children of Sir Gelly Meyrick and the first certain ancestors of Samuel Meyrick lay a hiatus of just two or three generations in the seventeenth century. This seems a surprisingly short time for any family to have lost track of so notable a potential forbear as Sir Gelly, whose children were restored on the accession of James I and married into leading families. The true Meyrick ancestry, which Sir Samuel had pursued until Sir Gelly took possession of him, has not been proved back to Sir Gelly's time in spite of extensive research. The descent as given in Burke can be proved to be incorrect, however.[5]

Samuel's great-grandfather, the father of the James Meyrick who went to Lucton School was another James, who died in 1749. He had pretensions to gentility, as he described himself in his will as a 'gentleman', a will proved in the Prerogative Court of Canterbury. This implied a certain affluence, yet he did not call himself 'esquire', a term applied in Burke to all Sir Samuel's immediate presumed ancestors. By birth right, only the eldest sons of knights are entitled to call themselves esquires, and though this was

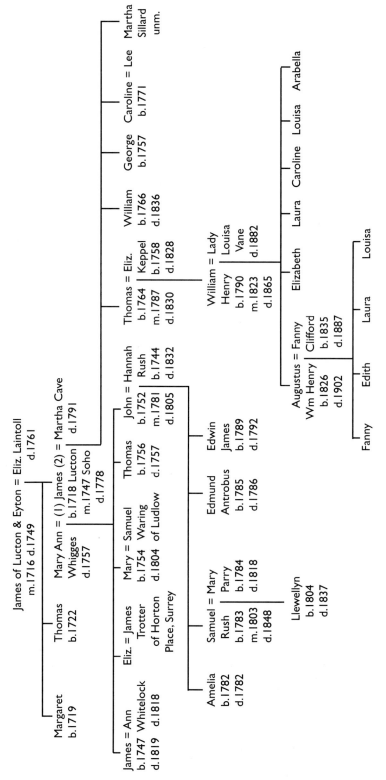

Fig. 3   Simplified Meyrick Family Tree

honoured more generally in the early part of the eighteenth century, by Sir Samuel's time the upwardly mobile preferred 'esq'. to 'gent'., whether deserved or not.

Also according to Samuel's chosen pedigree, his great-grandfather James Meyrick, whom Samuel had included, was 'of Eyton Court', though he described himself as 'of Eyton in the County of Hereford', and left freehold and leasehold land in the parish of Lucton, not Eyton. Eyton Court is a handsome black-and-white building, and the present owners fortunately have a comprehensive set of deeds going well back into the seventeenth century. There is no trace of the Meyricks as tenants or owners, so this may be another of Sir Samuel's assumptions.

There is a reason for labouring the point about Sir Samuel's ancestry, and his lack of a convincing descent from Gelly Meyrick. In general, Sir Samuel was pedantic in the extreme about his historical research—in fact, much of the reputation of his knowledge about armour rests on his rigorous attention to detail. How ironic, then, that his wishful thinking should have led him to overcome any scruples he may have had as to his lineage. Yet it wasn't the first or last time that his heart over-ruled his head.

When Sir Samuel's grandfather James entered Lucton School in the mid 1720s he may not have realised his good fortune. The school was the foundation of John Pierrepoint, a rich vintner who lived in the parish of St. Botolph's without Aldgate in the City of London. The vicar there was Dr. White Kennett, a fervent supporter of the Society for the Promotion of Christian Knowledge (SPCK). Pierrepoint was a bachelor who was considering retiring to his native Lucton, and his friend Kennett encouraged him to fulfil the Society's objectives by founding a school there. In 1708 Pierrepoint paid for the school to be built, and purchased tithes worth £2,500 to support it. When he died in 1711 he left the residue of his estate to the school, a residue somewhat diminished as he had provided for mourning rings and clothes for one hundred and seventy-eight friends and relatives.

The maximum capacity of the school was eighty, and boys from all the surrounding villages were eligible to attend. Provision was made for the 'meaner sort' as well for those who could afford the annual fee, initially ten shillings. They had to be aged between seven and thirteen, and able to read from the Bible.[6] For the boys there was not even the lure of a fire in the schoolroom at the end of a cold, muddy trek, but their parents had the valuable incentive of an apprenticeship when school funds permitted.

The Governors and Assistant Governors met six-monthly, and when they inspected the attendance register on 15 December 1730 J(ames) Meyrick and six other boys were dismissed for non-attendance, but as he was twelve and a half by then his education was virtually complete. His younger brother, Thomas, attended the school between 1729 and 1736.[7] Pierrepoint had wished the school to teach religion, Latin, Greek and mathematics, against Kennett's advice, but in practice writing and arithmetic replaced the Latin and Greek. James Meyrick owed his elegant handwriting and financial skills, if not his moral code, to Lucton School.

Between 1730 and 1747 James Meyrick disappears from view, and yet these were the years when he moves to inhabit the shadier reaches of the political stage of the nation. The trail instead leads to John Calcraft who was to help James make his fortune, as well as a much more considerable one for himself.

Calcraft was born in 1726, and so was eight years younger than James Meyrick. The eldest son of the town clerk of Grantham in Lincolnshire, from an early age he enjoyed the considerable patronage of Henry Fox, later Lord Holland, one of the greatest political manipulators of the age. The suspicion has always been that Calcraft was Fox's son, but it seems equally possible that they were related via Calcraft's mother.[8] Until he broke with Fox in the 1760s, Calcraft was part of an inner circle of Fox's cronies, renowned for intrigue and loose living. Fox himself was called 'the most corrupt in a corrupt age'.

The Fox connection enabled Calcraft when aged only nineteen to become deputy paymaster to the Duke of Cumberland's army engaged in suppressing the 1745 rebellion. There can be no doubt that in spite of his tender age he was exceptionally able, travelling the north of England and managing the transmission of large sums of money from Excise collectors to the troops.[9] After the rebellion was over, he was appointed to increasingly powerful positions in the Pay and War Offices, which he held until the 1760s. Henry Fox was Secretary at War until late 1755, exerting his influence on behalf of Calcraft until

Fig. 4   Henry Fox

6

their breach over politics in 1763. It is as a clerk in the War Office that James Meyrick makes his first appearance in London.

Even in the light of the lax morals of the eighteenth century, Calcraft's set of well-connected young men were renowned for sexual licence, profligate gambling and political chicanery. Among his friends were Richard Rigby and Charles Hanbury Williams, always keen to entice to their card games wealthy young pigeons for plucking. In the early 1740s the brothers John and Herbert Lloyd of Peterwell in Cardiganshire, bored after returning to Wales from lively times in Oxford and London, came to their attention. Their riches were sufficient to tempt Fox, Rigby and Hanbury Williams to the nearby home of Thomas Johnes of Llanfair.[10] The pigeons were duly plucked, as was Johnes himself, his fortunes only rescued by his marriage in 1746 to Elizabeth Knight, the daughter of Richard Knight of Croft Castle in Herefordshire. From then on Johnes lived in Croft, and it is possible that he used his influence with Calcraft on Meyrick's behalf, as the Knight family had bought the Meyrick's home manor of Lucton some years earlier.[11]

The Calcraft-Meyrick association prospered in another direction.[12] At some stage Calcraft took James Meyrick on as a clerk when he established an army agency business in 1748. This ran in tandem with their government employment, a breath-taking conflict of interests only explainable by the standards of the day. The opportunity for an army agent to make a fortune was due to the system for funding the army which obtained at that time. The government always wanted to minimise the cost of the military, whether in nominal peacetime or in war, and the population as a whole were keen to avoid a large standing army as they would be taxed to pay for it. A flexible solution was to raise and disband regiments as conflicts waxed and waned. The troops needed to be paid, fed and equipped, but an expensive bureaucracy was a political non-starter. The solution which had been followed for many years was for the man appointed as colonel of a regiment to receive a sum of money based on the (notional) strength of his regiment, plus various allowances. It was his responsibility to manage the finances, and to account for the strength of his regiment.

Colonels were usually aristocratic by birth and uninterested in the minutiae of accounting and purchasing. Many were Members of Parliament because of the ideal opportunity this gave for securing further promotion from those in power. It was unlikely that they had the time or the inclination to administer the release of their funds from the War Office or to ensure the payment of suppliers nearer to home, and the task was impossible for those posted overseas. Therefore the business of a professional army agency had grown up to service this need, and indeed to act on behalf of officers in their private affairs. The government even acknowledged the value of the agents by allowing a rate for them in the calculation of funds due for the regiment. Colonels appointed their own agents, often leading to unseemly touting for income, and an agent who could show himself efficient, trustworthy and reliable could amass a considerable proportion of the total agency revenue. At the peak of Calcraft's business in 1762, during the Seven Years War, he was agent to sixty-three regiments, with a legitimate income from agency allowances alone of well in excess of £16,000 annually.[13]

An agent acted in some respects very like a bank—money came to them for payments to a regiment from the government, and they reimbursed suppliers, as well as sending the money to pay the troops. The agent was also obliged to deposit a large sum of money as security for the colonel in case he should die suddenly and leave the regiment's funds in limbo. From Calcraft's cash books[14] enormous amounts of money passed through his agency's hands—in 1760 for example, the subsistence he earned for thirty regiments for a month was about £25,000 or £2,000,000 in today's terms.[15] As long as an agent was efficient in keeping a steady flow of money through his accounts, it was quite possible for him to also issue loans or organise lotteries, and accumulate a substantial fortune. None of this was illegal, but army agents had a bad reputation as vultures feeding on the bodies of the poor soldiers, and Calcraft himself was known as Crafterio.[16] Most of his circle bought themselves seats in Parliament, and vast country estates to match.

There was just one area where agents were vulnerable, and that was in the sale of commissions in the army. The Hanoverian monarchs disapproved of the practice, and royal warrants had been issued in the early 1720s to establish regulation prices for commissions.[17] Officers regarded their commissions as an investment, however, and wished to sell them at as high a price as possible when they wanted to move on. An army agent was in a good position to know where a post was becoming available, and bring purchaser and seller together, earning a percentage of the increased sale price. An attempted clamp-down by the Secretary at War in the late 1750s nearly led to James Meyrick returning to the obscurity from whence he had come.[18]

James had married a girl called Mary Wiggs in 1747, in a somewhat clandestine way, by licence outside their home parish of St. Margaret's, Westminster. By 1757 he had five children: James, John, Mary, Elizabeth and Thomas. Tragedy struck in August when the eighteen-month-old Thomas died. It was then that a young man called Jacob Grose, in search of an ensigncy, had contacted an associate of Calcraft and Meyrick called Kidgell, who found Grose a commission for the price of £315. Meyrick advised Grose that the cash should be paid to one Taylor, another Calcraft colleague. When Grose turned up at his regiment[19] he found that he should have been offered the commission for nothing.[20] The ensuing scandal led to Meyrick being sacked from his position in the Widows' Pay Office, a prime position for acting as bankers to officers' widows and their families.[21]

Although it may seem surprising that Calcraft kept his clerk after this lack of adroitness, Meyrick had been hit by a second blow when his wife Mary died at the beginning of October. Calcraft's sympathetic support was repaid by devoted service over the next six years, and Meyrick was rewarded by becoming a junior partner in 1763.[22] In May 1761 the first independent agency taken by Meyrick was for one of the transient companies of foot which had been raised at the time.[23] During this period he began to manage Calcraft's network of military and political contacts, as the latter became increasingly absorbed in politics. Calcraft died in 1772, leaving seven children by two mistresses, large estates in Dorset and Kent, and an immense fortune.

An army agency business, of necessity, had to be situated close to the seat of Government. Calcraft had rented a newly built house, 43 Parliament Street, from 1758 for which James Meyrick had taken over the payment of rates in 1766. After Calcraft's death he and then his elder son James continued at that address until 1792.[24] Remarkably, the house still exists, one of only two of the early houses in the street to do so, and has now been restored and incorporated in the Palisades building opened in May 1991, which houses apartments for Parliamentary officers. James Meyrick senior had housed his increasing family between 1763 and 1772 at another house which still exists—19 Queen Anne's Gate, which was then 6 Queen Square.[26]

Calcraft had probably decided to quit the agency business after the fall-off in business due to the Treaty of Paris of 1763, which had ended the Seven Years War. Although it must have taken some time for James Meyrick senior to build up his income again, he took into partnership a Robert Porter, who gave him a valuable entrée into the North American army business.[26] The outbreak of the American War of Independence thus led to a vastly increased turnover, and the opportunity for the Meyricks to feather their nest once again, though by now government controls had tightened considerably. They still acted as private bankers for the officers: for example, releasing General Robertson's funds in payment for furs another General (Haldimand) had bought in Canada. Numerous letters exist to show the wide range of the activities of the Meyricks' agency. Apart from the standard operations concerning pay, clothing, provisions and the like for the British forces stationed in many parts of the world, there is constant gossip about the political situation.

Their most famous client was Benedict Arnold, a commander in the American Independence forces from 1775 until he changed sides in 1779. Arnold was courageous, but regarded as rash by Congress, and not promoted as quickly as he wished. Often wounded, he was eventually rewarded with the command of Philadelphia, but mixing with those of Loyalist sympathies which included his wife, he secretly approached the British. He betrayed the American plans to attack Canada, and leaving his British contact to be hanged as a spy, he escaped on a British ship. A letter written by James Meyrick in January 1781 to Arnold was exposed when the ship carrying it was captured at sea. When it was published in the *Annual Register*[27] it was clear that the Meyricks were investing the £5,000 that Arnold had earned for his betrayal under their name, against the time he should claim it. Arnold left for England at the end of 1781, and lived for another twenty years ostracised by both sides in the conflict.

James Meyrick senior's two elder sons James (born 1747) and John (born 1752) must have been familiar figures to all the military calling at the Parliament Street offices and well equipped to take over the business on Meyrick senior's early death in 1778, the other sons being still too young. James senior had married again, and his fortune of £100,000 was now divided between ten children, his widow Martha being left with a miserly pension of £100 a year. In his will, he specified that James and John should have the use of the ground floor then employed in the business of agency, and of their two bedchambers.[28]

James Meyrick senior had made the giant leap from rural

Fig. 5 43 Parliament Street is the house on the right

10

obscurity to middle-class affluence, a typical eighteenth-century success story in the new world of finance and administration. It could have been the start of a Meyrick dynasty, like those of Fox and Calcraft, but it is remarkable that although he was survived by five sons—James, John, Thomas, William and George—only two grandsons lived to carry on the Meyrick name, and one was John's son, Samuel Rush Meyrick.[29]

When the younger James died in 1818 he left £180,000, in addition to 'an estate of 300 acres surrounding a palace at Wimbledon'.[30] He had married Ann Whitelock, but the marriage was to prove childless. When he first applied to become a fellow of the Royal Society of London in March 1781, he was supported by a number of distinguished fellows with military backgrounds, including the Earl of Loudon and Sir James Napier.[31] However, he was blackballed, perhaps in consequence of the captured Benedict Arnold letter having been recently published. It had been forgotten by 1800, when among the fellows proposing him was Leonard Morse, an old associate of his father from the Calcraft days.[32]

Long before this James had been elected as a fellow of the Society of Antiquaries. In 1788 he was made Esquire to Sir Charles Grey, a most distinguished military commander, when Samuel asserted that 'instead of troubling himself to prove his title to the Bôdorgan arms [he] took a fresh grant'.[33] Probably he had no thought of being entitled to them. Grey, a stout Tory, was the father of the Earl Grey who became a member of the Radical Whigs under Charles Fox. After many attempts to introduce reform legislation, Earl Grey was the prime minister who was instrumental in the Reform Bill becoming law in 1832, and as such, he was surely one of Samuel's heroes, as shall be seen later.

Of John Meyrick's three remaining half-brothers, two—Thomas and George—had distinguished military careers, and the third, William, became an attorney. George and William remained bachelors, and Samuel seems to have been on very affectionate terms with them, perhaps because they were only seventeen or eighteen years his senior. General George Meyrick outlived Samuel, but he visited Goodrich Court, and Samuel stayed with him in Devon a number of times.

Thomas Meyrick made a most advantageous marriage, as his wife was Elizabeth Keppel, the illegitimate daughter of Lord Augustus Keppel sometime first Lord of the Admiralty. Lord Keppel was the second son of the Earl of Albemarle by Anne Lennox, daughter of the Duke of Richmond, and hence great-grandson of Charles II by Louise de Kéroualle. Keppel, an experienced naval commander, had been a bitter opponent of the American War of Independence and was regarded with antipathy by George III.

Popular with the Navy, Keppel was given the command of the Channel fleet in the event of a European war. In 1779, after an inconclusive battle with the French off Brest in July the previous year, he was court-martialled on a trumped-up charge of misconduct and neglect of duty. He was acquitted to great scenes of rejoicing and riotous disorder, and although the king managed to oust him from his parliamentary seat at Windsor, he was soon returned for Surrey. Lord Keppel had never married, and on his death in 1786 as his main heir Elizabeth Keppel brought Thomas Meyrick a not inconsiderable fortune.[34]

The Keppel name, and the Meyrick-Keppel money gave Thomas Meyrick's only child, William Henry Meyrick yet another leg up the social scale. In 1823 he married Lady Laura Vane, third daughter of the Duke of Cleveland, another descendant of Charles II but by Barbara Villiers. Their only son Augustus William Henry Meyrick, born in 1826 and perhaps named after his great-grandfather, appears later in the story.

John Meyrick's sister Elizabeth had married James Trotter, son of a Scot called John Trotter, who had been the executor of James Meyrick senior's will. The Trotter family moved in the same circles as the Meyricks—the army supplier Alexander Trotter who was James's cousin was called 'the most improper person that Lord Melville [Treasurer of the Navy] could have selected in the whole kingdom for his agent'.[35] The Trotters were connected by marriage to Thomas Coutts the banker, who had as partner Edmund Antrobus. Coutts had gained sole control of the great banking enterprise in 1778, and was one of the richest commoners in the country.

Given Thomas Coutts' great wealth, society was not too surprised when he married the actress Harriet Mellon within a few months of his first wife's death. At that time (1815), he was 74 and she was 28. In spite of her antecedents, she was so kind and unassuming that she was accepted by many people, including Sir Walter Scott. After Coutts' death in 1822 she married the Duke of St. Albans, and they were early visitors to Goodrich Court, though Samuel was rather condescending—'she came in full splendour, expressed her admiration in extravagant terms, and he faintly echoed her words'.[36]

In 1785 Samuel Rush, an affluent jeweller, appointed as executors of his will his 'good friends', Coutts and Antrobus. Thus it may have been that John Meyrick was introduced to Samuel Rush, whose two surviving children were both daughters. Jane was already married, but Hannah, in her late thirties, was almost past her prayers. John Meyrick was ready to overlook the eight years difference in their ages, given that Samuel Rush had already made his fortune. The stage was now set for Samuel Rush Meyrick's entry on the scene.

2 An Extraordinary Boy

John Meyrick and Hannah Rush were married from her father's house near Chislehurst, Kent on 3 May 1781. Just a week earlier their marriage settlement had been drawn up, giving Hannah about £10,000[1] immediately, with another £9,000 in trust and her father's jewels eventually.[2] Those ubiquitous bankers, Coutts & Antrobus, were trustees as were James Meyrick and James Trotter.

Samuel Rush was a jeweller at Ludgate Hill, in the City of London,[3] but he also owned estates in Great and Little Hadham, Hertfordshire as well as in Chislehurst. His first wife Jane had been of Welsh ancestry,[4] and it was from her that Jane and Hannah descended. After his first wife died leaving him with a young family, he married a toy shop owner[5] called Susannah Passavant in 1759, a marriage that proved childless. The Passavant family, with members in Exeter and London, was part of the large French Protestant community. Philip Passavant who died aged eighty-eight in 1790 was 'an eminent jeweller in the City',[6] and Susannah's nephew John was jeweller to the King of Sardinia.[7] The French connection continued some years later when Jane, Samuel Rush's elder daughter, married Philip Devisme, a merchant of Dowgate Hill.

John Meyrick had leased a town house in Westminster in 1782—No. 1 Great George Street—

Fig. 6   Silhouette of John Meyrick

13

soon after his marriage which he held until 1796.[8] In spite of Hannah Meyrick's comparatively advanced age, the marriage was quickly fruitful—Amelia was born in April 1782, but only lived until October.[9] Samuel Rush Meyrick was born on 26 August 1783, but the baptism at St. Margaret's, Westminster, was delayed until December—perhaps Hannah had returned to the quieter environs of Chislehurst for the birth. Edmund Antrobus Meyrick followed in March 1785, but he died in May 1786.[10] Hannah was almost forty-five when her last child was born in 1789, but Edwin James died when he was three and a half,[11] and his death must have made a great impression on the nine-year-old Samuel. Nearly fifty years later another Edwin James Meyrick would cause Samuel to grieve again.

It cannot be denied that however affluent the environs of Westminster and Parliament Street may have been, they ran cheek by jowl with areas of filth and poverty. Tothill Fields was an open area between Westminster Abbey and Millbank which had been used for pasture and horticulture. It also accommodated burial pits, archery practice grounds, militia parades, bear and bull baiting, and prostitutes, along with rubbish dumps and other nuisances. The increasingly insalubrious character of the West End no doubt influenced John Meyrick to seek a country residence in Fulham, at that time a beautiful district of nurseries and orchards. It had the advantage of being only half an hour's ride from London using the 'King's Private Road', originally Charles II's private way leading from London via Chelsea to Hampton Court. It was possible to use the road on purchase of a metal ticket but it was not thrown open to the general public until 1830.[12]

The village of Fulham itself clustered around the Bishop's Palace, and the ancient bridge across the Thames. Although there were still large common fields in the parish, the area around the King's Road had become a favourite place of resort for affluent Londoners. One of the most aristocratic hamlets, and one to which John Meyrick was attracted, was Parson's Green. In 1705 it was 'inhabited mostly by Gentry and Persons of Quality' who resided in 'several very Handsome Houses all standing very airy upon a dry, clean Green'.[13] Towards the south-east corner of the green was a large sheet of water, now long filled in, one corner of which was very deep. Although the atmosphere was usually refined, the annual August fair brought three days of merriment with puppet shows, acting booths, whelk and oyster stalls and the like. No doubt the publicans of the White Horse and the new Peterborough Arms did a roaring trade.

The old houses around the green had seen a number of illustrious inhabitants. There was Richardson's Villa, the home of Samuel Richardson, author of *Clarissa* and

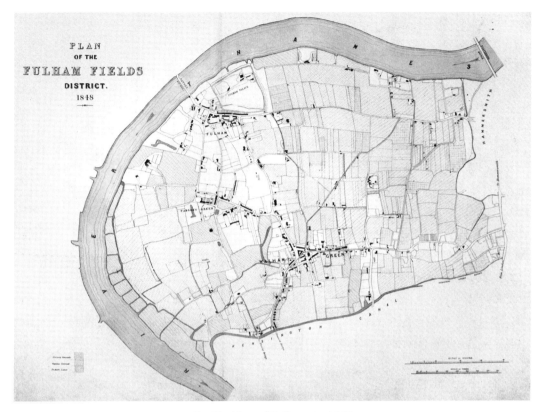

Fig. 7   Map of Fulham in 1848

Pamela, who had died in 1761. Belfield House was supposedly occupied at one time by Mrs. Jordan, the mistress of the Duke of Clarence, later William IV.[14] East End House, originally built for Sir Francis Child, Lord Mayor of London in 1699, later became the residence of Mrs. Fitzherbert who was visited there by George IV when Prince of Wales.[15]

When John Meyrick first moved to Fulham in 1778, he leased Westfield House from the Dupuis family. Just north of Parson's Green at Purser's Cross, it was later to become the Fulham Library and reading room. Although Hannah came to the marriage generously dowered and the Meyricks could have afforded a bigger property, they were to stay in this house for some considerable time even after Hannah's father died in 1787 and his large estate was divided between his daughters. Jane received the Hertfordshire estates, and Hannah those in Chislehurst and Mottingham, with £2,688[16] in addition to bring her inheritance up to the same value as Jane's.[17]

On his way to his London office, John Meyrick would have passed a property in a desirable location at Parson's Green. This was Peterborough House, an ancient mansion originally called Brightwells. It had been the residence of John Tamworth, Privy Councillor to Elizabeth I, but was refurbished[18] in the time of Charles II, when it was lavishly decorated by Francis Cleyne.[19] It descended to Charles Mordaunt, the great Earl of Peterborough, who was renowned for his energy, atheism, and the literary parties which he held there. Writers

Fig. 8   Westfield House, Fulham

and wits such as Addison, Swift, Pope, Voltaire and Locke enjoyed his hospitality, and the gardens were said by Swift to be the finest he had seen about London. One of the earl's habits was to cook for his guests personally. After his first wife died, the earl took up with Anastasia Robinson, the celebrated opera singer, and later married her, but did not introduce her to society as his wife until a short time before his death in 1735.

The Peterborough family put the house up for sale in 1779, when it was described in the *London Argus* as 'A Freehold capital mansion house called PETERBOROW HOUSE, with the spacious and convenient outhouses, offices, stabling for 12 horses,

Fig. 9   Old Peterborough House

16

dairy, dog kennell, very extensive pleasure grounds tastefully laid out, and large kitchen-garden, well-cropped and planted with the choicest fruits, hot-houses, green-house, ice-house and fruit-house, with exceeding rich meadow lands, close adjoining; the whole containing above 40 acres'. There were also large ponds in the garden. It was eventually purchased in 1782 by Richard Heaviside, a timber merchant. John Meyrick began to cultivate Heaviside's friendship,[20] and eventually the property was sold to him in 1797 for £6,500.[21]

John Meyrick was a fellow of the Society of Antiquaries, but his regard for the antique did not extend to old Peterborough House. The design for its replacement was ready even before the old building had been sold to him.[22] His chosen architect was Aaron Hurst, who had designed Wimbledon Lodge for Gerard de Visme, a relative of his sister-in-law. Hurst was young and very talented and had already designed the church of St. James Pentonville, although he was now only thirty-three. Unfortunately, his early promise was cut short by his death in 1799.

By the time that Daniel Lysons wrote about Fulham in his *Environs of London* in 1798 a great part of the historic old building was already pulled down, no doubt to the regret of many. The new Peterborough House (see plate 2) was elegantly symmetrical, but rather bloodless. Built of stuccoed Suffolk brick, the entrance steps rose to an enormous pair of Corinthian columns. The house was a box, relieved only at the back by a double-height bay. It was 'built in the French style prevailing at the time of its erection, nearly all the rooms having their corners rounded'.[23] The large drawing room (45 feet by 20 feet) had a painted ceiling and moiré silk walls, and Hannah's circular boudoir had blue walls and another painted ceiling. The rear of the house led to a lawn which had replaced the ancient garden maze. Fortunately many of the garden features such as the great gateway were allowed to survive.

The house was apparently stuffed with antiquities and more importantly, John Meyrick had an armoury in the garden. In the Guildhall Library there is a portfolio of drawings by Frederick Fairholt made to illustrate Crofton Croker's *A Walk from London to Fulham*.[24] Not all the drawings were used in the book, and one of these is a picture of a conservatory, with the words 'originally built by Meyrick for an armoury'. From the style it was probably built much earlier as an orangery. This is the first intimation that the Meyrick collection of armour was founded by Samuel's father.

By the time that the new house was finished, Samuel was in his mid teens, and his schooling was coming towards its end. It's not known definitely where he was educated, but in Parson's Green there was a school with a high reputation. Originally called

High Elms House, it came to be known as Fulham Park House, where a school was established in 1784 by the Rev. Thomas Bowen, chaplain of Bridewell Hospital. He died in 1800, but his widow continued the school until 1818 with the help of the Rev. Joshua Ruddock. Samuel certainly sent his own son Llewellyn to school at Parson's Green—firstly to that of the Rev. William

Fig. 10 Sketch of the armoury at Peterborough House

Pearson at Elm House. He planned that Llewellyn should then go to the Rev. Ruddock,[25] and presumably he did so, as there's a sketch of Fulham Park School by Llewellyn in the Wallace Collection, dated 1816.[26] Hopefully Llewellyn was happier at the school than his near contemporary, Lord Lytton, who was so badly treated that he was taken away after a fortnight.[27] Since the Meyrick family was living in Chelsea by this time, it seems possible that Samuel's experience of the school was so favourable that he wished his son to follow him there.

Although there is every reason to believe that Samuel had a natural inclination to scholarship, his time was not all spent with his books, and his earliest hands-on experience of arms was due to his father. John Meyrick had been an officer in the Honourable Artillery Company, the earliest regiment in the British Army and the second most senior of the Territorial Army. Founded in 1537 as a guild for defending the realm but also for the 'maintenance of the Science and Feat of shooting Long Bows', the Company has always had strong ties with the City of London. It also had connections with the Finsbury Archers, a body founded some time in the sixteenth century that had organised shooting competitions from the mid seventeenth century. In later life Samuel recalled having seen as a child Philip Constable, the last captain of the Archers, whose bow was in the Meyrick collection.[28]

In 1781 a society called the Toxophilites was set up by a group of enthusiastic bowmen, including the last members of the Finsbury Archers. They practised at butts set up in the garden of Leicester House in London, where Sir Ashton Lever had his

Fig. 11   Fulham Park School from Llewellyn's sketch book

Museum of Curiosities or 'Holophusicon'.[29] This was a typical miscellaneous collection of items, ranging from seashells to suits of armour. Sir Ashton was the first president of the Toxophilites, remaining so until his death in 1788. When the Holophusicon was put up for sale in 1784, a group of the Toxophilites led by the Earl of Effingham approached the Honourable Artillery Company for permission to shoot in the Artillery ground. In July 1784 it was agreed that an Archers Division of the Company should be set up, Effingham being the first Captain, and this relationship continued for twenty years.

John Meyrick joined the Company on 4 March 1789, and was elected as First Serjeant of the Archer's Division on 25 April 1792.[30] He succeeded Robert Fielden as Captain on 30 April 1794, but had left by 1798. In the British Library there is a child-hood scrapbook on archery belonging to Samuel,[31] in which a notice from the Society of Toxophilites for 1794 describes their uniform as 'a Green Cloth Coat, with Gilt Arrow Buttons, White Waistcoat, White or nankeen Breeches, a Black Round Hat, a Gilt Button with the Prince of Wales's Crest, a double Gold Loop, and a black cock Feather'. Thomas Barritt painted a portrait of Sir Ashton Lever in this uniform, wearing on his breast the Gold Medal of the Society presented to him by the members.

Samuel himself says in the scrapbook that he was 'always possessing from my Childhood a great Penchant for Archery, and having frequently practised that Amusement with the greatest Pleasure, I had often wondered why such a valuable Weapon as the Bow should be neglected'. There were many archery societies in the late eighteenth century, all with their own uniforms. One mentioned in the scrapbook was the 'ARCHERS of ARCHENFIELD [from] near Hereford [which] have been much spoken of, both for their dexterity and hospitality'.

When Samuel was nearly eight, he may have attended the Grand Annual Meeting of the Societies of Archers which took place on Friday, 27 May 1791 at Blackheath. Present were: The Honourable Artillery Company, in two divisions; Surrey Bowmen 1st & 2nd divisions; Hainault Foresters; Toxophilites 1st & 2nd divisions; Northumberland Archers; Sherwood Foresters; Kentish Rangers; Kentish Bowmen; Loyal Archers; Woodmen of Arden; Robin Hood Society; Yorkshire Archers and the Woodmen of Hornsey. They were all dressed in green, with half-boots. Numbers of ladies were likewise dressed in the uniform of the Societies. Thirty-two targets were placed on the ground, and about a dozen archers appointed to shoot at each. At twelve o'clock the shooting for the prizes commenced, and continued without intermission till three, when they retired to their tents and partook of some refreshments. After which the contest was renewed, and after examining the targets at six o'clock, Mr. Rickard of the Toxophilites Society appeared to be entitled to the Gold Medal, and Mr. Rush of the Woodmen of Hornsey to the Silver Medal. Two people were slightly wounded by standing too near the targets.[32]

While the Meyricks were still living at Westfield House, the country was thrown into agitation by the prospect of an invasion by the French. The Volunteer Act of 1794 authorised the raising of volunteer companies for the defence of the realm. These were in addition to the militia, and had the advantage that service with them exempted a man from militia service which could be onerous. In 1797 Pitt suggested that local armed associations could be set up, and an Act was passed in 1798, again giving exemption from militia duties. The volunteers were granted a small amount of money for their uniforms, but as the companies were set up by wealthy citizens who had a fancy to dress up but not to join the army, money was donated to the fund. Consequently, they were usually impressively clad, as witness the illustrations in Thomas Rowlandson's *Loyal Volunteers … in their respective uniforms* (see plate 3).[33]

John Meyrick himself set up the Fulham Association on 25 June 1798. It consisted of eighty men, with a Captain (himself), two lieutenants and an ensign—

Samuel Rush Meyrick. The Rev. Graham Jepson preached a sermon in Fulham Church before the assembled corps on Sunday, 5 August,[34] and a Mr. Hussey wrote a poem in honour of the inauguration day of the corps—which must have been 26 August, Samuel's fifteenth birthday—when Hannah Meyrick presented them with their colours. A few lines will suffice:[35]

> Ye envy'ed Corps! By far and near,
> Around your banners stand;
> By freedom's chart you're sure to steer
> While MEYRICK takes command:
>
> Let this your Ensign's natal day
> With manly mirth be crown'd;
> Let ev'ry heart be blithe and gay,
> With martial music sound.
>
> In memr'y see this day record
> Wishing him health and years;
> He's brave, and worthy the regard
> Of Freedom's Volunteers.

Before a year had passed Captain John Meyrick had promoted himself to Colonel, and by September Samuel was a lieutenant, when on behalf of the volunteers he presented a flag to Fulham church 'for their use on Public Rejoicing days'.[36] There was a paved area in front of the old Swan Inn near Fulham Bridge which the Volunteers used as a parade ground.[37] An important annual event for the Fulham Association must have been the parade held in honour of George III on his birthday—4 June. In 1799 this took place in Hyde Park, in front of an estimated hundred thousand spectators. The volunteers taking part must have been up before dawn in order to be in place when the king arrived at nine o'clock. From engravings made showing the disposition of the different corps of volunteers, it seems that the Fulham Association (with fifty-six men one of the smaller contingents) was stationed with its back to the Grosvenor Gate on Park Lane.[38] After the king had made his inspection, the whole body of some 8,000 troops marched past.

The volunteers were subjected to some ridicule, much as the Home Guard was in World War II, and John Meyrick held shooting competitions in the grounds of Peterborough House with the hope of improving his troops' performance. In 1900

Nathaniel Chasemore's grandson still treasured a silver medal donated by John Meyrick, his grandfather having won it in a shooting competition for the volunteers a hundred years earlier. This had been held in the grounds of Peterborough House, when he shot with 'the old brown Bess'—the muzzle-loading flintlock

Fig. 12   Shooting medal

which had long been the standard issue for British troops.[39]

The Association seems to have fallen into limbo, because the renewed alarm over a possible invasion by Bonaparte in 1803 led to the formation of the Fulham Volunteer Corps of Light Infantry. Graham Jepson as the rector of Fulham was also the chairman of the organising committee, and he wrote to Lord Titchfield on 5 August 1803 to tell him that the parishioners had met in the church and had raised funds for a corps of three hundred men.[40] By 3 September John Meyrick had been appointed Major Commandant with Samuel Rush Meyrick as one of his captains.

John Meyrick was a stern disciplinarian judging by the rules of the corps and the regular punishment of the men for insubordination. More evidence of his domineering character appeared when he replaced the committee run by the parish with his own military committee. Not only did this lead to financial difficulties for him, as he had to subsidise the men's pay to avoid a mutiny, but caused considerable ill-feeling in the parish. Eventually he had to ask for the parish committee to re-form, and by early August 1804 he had resigned.

It was a sad end to John Meyrick's period of service to his community. After settling into Peterborough House, he had been elected as churchwarden of Fulham church in 1800, and served for a year. He may already have had an eye to the armour and armorial brasses in the church, as at some time the Meyricks acquired various pieces: an 'armet from the charnel house in Fulham church'[41] and 'iron helmets of different forms from Fulham church ... with iron spikes on top and visors'.[42]

The church also lost some monumental brasses to the Meyrick collection, for they were in John Meyrick's library at the time of his death and included in its sale catalogue. The brasses had already been illustrated in a book by Thomas Faulkner.[43] Although only those for Samson Norton and Margaret Cheyne are specifically named, those of William Harvey and William Butt are also missing from the church—there were sixteen altogether in the sale. Once separated from their inscriptions, it becomes difficult to identify who is represented by a monumental brass, and the location of these is now unknown. Norton and Butt were wearing armour, and thus the style of the armour can theoretically be dated accurately by the inscription—an early example to Samuel which gave him one of his dating methods. How John Meyrick extracted these items from the church is not recorded in the vestry minutes.

Meantime the family agency business had continued to prosper—in lieu of any conflicts at home it supported regiments in far-flung locations such as India.[44] Whilst Samuel's schoolmasters would have detected his natural turn for scholarship, John Meyrick must also have had great hopes that his clever young son would make a mark in the higher reaches of politics or the law. The next step was for Samuel to attend Oxford or Cambridge universities where he would in theory make friends with the best in the land. On 27 June 1800, when nearly seventeen, he matriculated at Queen's College Oxford as a Commoner, one of only seven boys to enter the College that year.[45]

Fig. 13   Brass of Norton from Fulham Church

Queen's College was founded in 1340 by Robert Eglesfield, chaplain to Queen Philippa, the wife of Edward III, since when it had had a long association with the counties of Cumberland and Westmorland. By the later eighteenth century, the original scholarly aims of the university as a whole had been lost in a scramble for income, which saw a huge increase in fee-paying commoners.[46] The Cumbrian schools which had supplied Queen's with bright but poor boys had fallen behind in the range of subjects taught, and did not attract the *nouveau riche*. At the other end of the social scale, by the late 1700s fewer of the nobility and gentry were sending their sons to Queen's College—they preferred Christ Church and other colleges with strong public school connections. The middle classes were also wary, there being a general perception that a young man could be ruined by the extravagant company he would meet there, another that in spite of the investment a young graduate may not even recoup the outlay by an increased income. The major increase in students came from those seeking holy orders, for which a degree was a necessity.

The academic reputation of the college had been low for some time, the fellows concerning themselves with infighting rather than learning. Jeremy Bentham, one of Queen's more noted graduates, was only twelve when he matriculated in 1760. In later life he was to dismiss his education there: 'They were all stupid or dissipated. I learnt nothing. I played at tennis once or twice. I took to reading Greek of my own fancy'.[47] John James from Cumberland came up in 1778, and he is quite clear that as well as the 'farce of discipline and the freezing indifference of this College and its governors' he had to suffer sharp practice by the College servants.[48] Matters were to change soon after 1800 when new regulations meant that undergraduates had to undergo a nerve-wracking public examination to obtain their degree.

At the time that Samuel matriculated in 1800, Dr. Septimus Collinson had been the college's Provost for four years, and was to remain so for another twenty-seven, becoming Lady Margaret Professor of Divinity. According to one undergraduate he had such a thick Cumbrian accent that his sermons were barely comprehensible.[49] Samuel thought highly of Collinson, as he dedicated his first published work to his old provost with this encomium:

> The ancient Britons were of the opinion 'that there are three men whom all ought to regard with affection: he that with gratitude surveys the face of the earth; he that is delighted with rational works of art: and he that with loving kindness looks on infancy.' This sketch of a history of part of their descendants cannot be more affectionately dedicated than to the man in whom such qualifi-cations are united.

Normally a boy as well-off as Samuel would have entered as a gentleman commoner, but besides the extra cost of entrance John Meyrick may have been keen to depress pretensions in his son. Certainly the gentleman commoners were more likely to spend extravagantly, and were under less academic supervision.[50] The essential expenses[51] of a commoner's Oxford education were numerous: entrance fees; gown and cap; thirds (paid to the previous occupant of a student's room or rooms in college, the amount depending upon the estimated value of the furnishings they had acquired in their tenancy); cautions (a deposit in case of failure to pay dues); tuition fees; table dues; batells or board (due to the college for board and lodging); rentals (rentals of rooms depending on their size and location); fuel and lights; together with all kinds of minor charges. This was in addition to drink and any extra food, books, amusements or clothes.

With luck and enough money, a suite of three rooms could be had in one of the less crowded colleges, otherwise a garret might be the only option. From the Queen's College records Samuel's 'caution' was £10, finally repaid in December 1809. The batell and rental books show the amounts due from each member of the college, not what was actually paid, but from them it seems that his charges ranged from about £7 to £18 a term. Table dues were about 1 guinea a year. It was calculated that it would cost a commoner between £600 and £800 to obtain his degree.[52] Samuel's long gown was a simple affair of black stuff, with no sleeves but streamers from each side of the yoke, decorated with black braid, and a cap without a tassel.

The daily routine at Queen's College was described by Francis Jeffrey, a Scottish undergraduate in 1791.[53] Locking themselves in their rooms at night, the students were roused by the bell for chapel at seven o'clock. After an hour there, they could take some fresh air before returning for breakfast about nine, when it was the custom to take their 'George'—a penny bun—with butter, and their own tea and sugar to a friend's room. Unless they had to attend a lecture, their time was their own until three, when the bell proclaimed dinner in the Hall. As they passed through the kitchen they selected their preferred dishes from those on offer. It seems they had a clean tablecloth every day, and that the food at Queen's was acceptable, unlike some other colleges. The time of 'dinner' had gradually advanced from noon earlier in the century until three and even four at some colleges.[54] It was expected that the members of college should dress for dinner in the Hall, black or dark suits were worn with breeches and hair was dressed. Their place at the long tables was governed by status and seniority.

After dinner was over, the undergraduates were free to follow their own inclination. Although their supper was paid for and could be claimed later, many chose to venture out into the town or to other colleges. Regulations were constantly put forward to try to stop the supply of food to private dinners in college rooms, but they were never successful. Few commoners would have risked coming back to Queen's after 11 p.m., when they would be fined one shilling.[55]

One of the most historic traditions in Queen's is the feast held in Hall on Christmas Day, when a boar's head is brought in on a salver. A carol, partly in English and partly in Latin is sung to a tune possibly dating from 1521 by Wynkyn de Worde.

It is believed to be the oldest surviving secular carol. The feast commemorates the legend that a scholar of the college was attacked by a wild boar on Christmas Day, and escaped by ramming his only weapon (a volume of Aristotle) down the boar's throat.

> The boar's head in hand bear I,
> Bedeck'd with bays and rosemary;
> And I pray you, my masters, be merry…

Some years later Samuel described the scene in a letter to his friend Douce: 'on every Christmas day when all are assembled in hall ready for dinner four men enter holding a large pewter dish on which is a boar's head with a lemon in its mouth and decked with bay leaves and rosemary. The six tabarders being three on each side sing one verse of the carol - then proceed to the middle of the hall and the second is sung - and lastly on the dish being placed on the high table the concluding stanza'.[56]

When Samuel was at Queen's, there were theoretically four terms in the academic year starting in October—Michaelmas, Christmas, Easter and Trinity—although Easter and Trinity ran directly into each other. This system was not abolished until World War I. Until a student graduated and severed his connection with the university, it was possible for him to pay a small fee as a retainer to keep his membership of the college. From the batell books we know that Samuel was present for all the terms from Michaelmas 1800 until Trinity 1803, though he seems not to have been there for the whole of that last summer term.

For all undergraduates (from time immemorial) one of the greatest benefits of a university education is the new found-privacy and freedom from family constraints. No doubt it was now very easy for Samuel to send, and more importantly to receive, letters from whoever he pleased. Indeed, it wasn't out of the question to make a private visit or two without being discovered by his parents. As Samuel approached his twentieth birthday in the summer of 1803, he must have been the envy of many. He was the only child of a very rich man, he was clever, healthy and good-looking. His flaws, such as they were, were in his proud and passionate personality which was concealed under a layer of strict control. Throughout his life, the passion was liable to break out as unfettered and unwise actions. The adored only child was about to find the truly enduring love of his life, but in the process to deal his father a blow from which he never fully recovered.

3   The Welsh Connection

By the summer of 1803 Samuel was the apple of his father's eye and there was little doubt that his academic career would be successful. Apart from the ever-present risks of disease and accident, the greatest danger lay in Samuel's passionate nature and the traps laid for such young men by designing females.

Certainly Hannah Meyrick was alive to this possibility, for a curious document records Samuel's last conversation with her before he took an irrevocable step. It takes the form of a dialogue between a mother and her son.[1]

> Mother: My dear if you will assure me that you are not going near the Parrys; I will consent to the journey you propose.
> Son: Very well, then we are agreed.
> Mother: There are so many in this world, who lay snares for young men of any expectations ... I confess if you were going near them; I shou'd be very miserable.
> Son: There is not anything you think you can teach me, but what I know better than yourself. [added in pencil 'Wrong, what was said was "I know that very well"']
> Mother: My dear, it appears very singular; That you leave us so soon after your return; And, travel alone too ...
> Son: Tis for my pleasure, and that is enough.

Perhaps Samuel did send some deceiving letters to his parents after he left for his vacation, but that would only have served to heighten the feeling of betrayal when the appalling news arrived later in Fulham—on 3 October 1803, Samuel Meyrick had married Mary Parry by banns in the ancient church of Llanfihangel-y-Crueddyn, in the county of Cardigan.[2]

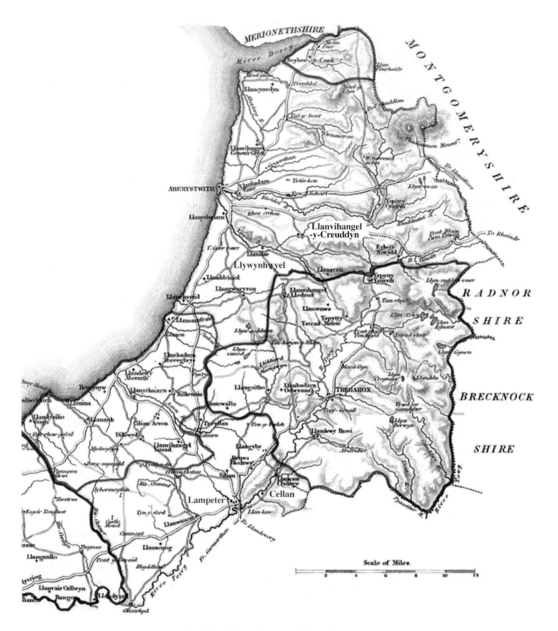

Fig. 14 Map of part of Cardiganshire

At this time, a couple planning to marry by banns had to give the parson at least seven days' notice with their names, addresses and length of residence in the parish. The banns would then be read on three successive Sundays during the regular church services in the parishes of the bride and groom, if different. Parental consent was needed if either party was under twenty-one, unless they were widowed. If the parents

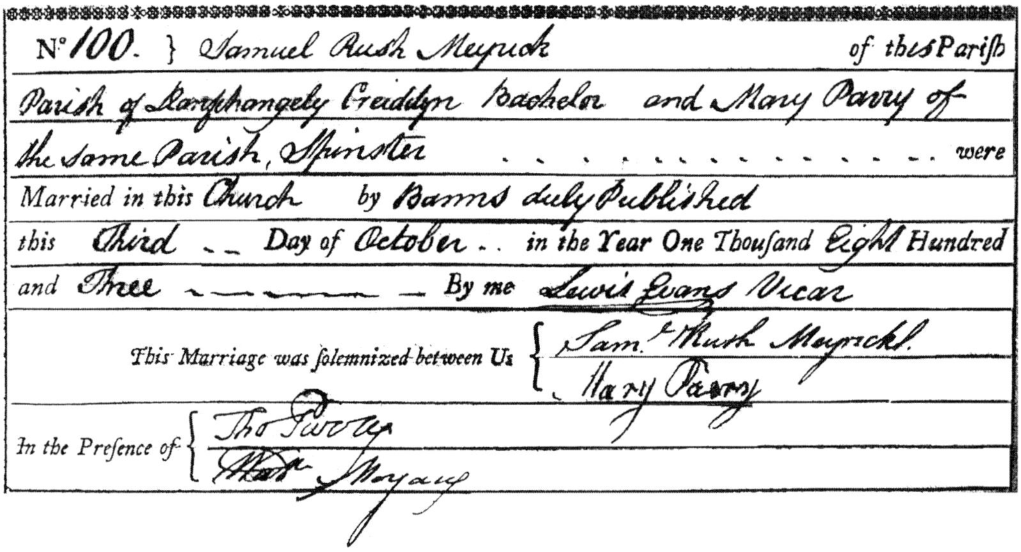
No 100. } Samuel Rush Meyrick of the Parish
Parish of Llanfihangel y Creuddyn Bachelor and Mary Parry of
the same Parish, Spinster . . . . were
Married in this Church by Banns duly Published
this Third — Day of October .. in the Year One Thousand Eight Hundred
and Three — By me Lewis Evans Vicar
This Marriage was solemnized between Us { Saml. Rush Meyrick / Mary Parry
In the Presence of { Tho Parry / Wat Morgan

Fig. 15 Samuel and Mary's marriage register entry of Llanfihangel-y-Creuddyn church

objected and the parson went ahead he would be punished by an ecclesiastical court. The banns publication would be void and the marriage null and void.[3]

Another possibility was marriage by licence, but for this the parties had to swear that they had their parents' consent if under age—and Samuel evidently did not have the stomach to do this, banns only requiring that nobody else should object to the marriage. Strictly speaking, therefore, the marriage was invalid as Samuel could not have obtained his father's consent for the reading of the banns on three successive Sundays. Mary's parents weren't at the church as far as is known, for the marriage was witnessed by her uncles, but they may have been staying in the area as otherwise Hannah Meyrick would not have made the remark about going 'near the Parrys'.

As far as the Meyricks were concerned, Mary Parry was a social nobody with not even a fortune to recommend her. Research has failed to find a single letter written by her—perhaps she found writing difficult, as witness her signature on the marriage entry. Probably she had the charming bloom of youth, and Samuel had known her for some years, as he mentions in a later letter. Mary was even younger than he, having been born in 1784 to James Parry and his wife Elizabeth, daughter of Evan Morgan of Crosswood in the parish of Llanfihangel-y-Creuddyn.[4] James Parry owned a sixty-acre farm called Llwynhywel in the parish of Rhostie, which he had inherited from his father David Parry.[5] Now in the parish of Llanilar, Llwynhywel lies to the south-east of Aberystwyth, on the road to Tregaron.

After leaving Aberystwyth, the road to Llanilar follows the lush Ystwyth valley, before striking up towards the foothills of the Cambrian mountains. The scenery becomes increasingly wild and picturesque, but the hilly land is difficult to cultivate, most farmers having to rely on dairying and sheep farming. Another source of income in the past has been lead and silver mining, Sir Gelly Meyrick having been given mineral rights here. The Picturesque attractions of the area had already drawn visitors—Devil's Bridge waterfalls were well known. There were some substantial estates and grand houses around, but the vast majority of the Welsh-speaking population lived in single-storey thatched hovels.

Fig. 16 Devil's Bridge

It wasn't long before John Meyrick was using his London contacts to try to find out more about the Parry family. Soon he had a reply via the doctor brother of a Captain Davies.[6] To his horror he found that a story he had heard about Mary's father was correct:

> It is very true that the young woman's father, who married Mr. Meyrick was tried for murder. … But his trial was under such particular circumstances, that might have happened to any man. On his return home one night, he discovered in his house two lovers (rivals) of one of his servants concealed upstairs. He had frequently warned one of them not to approach his house. A scuffle ensued. The men attacking him and he the men. They were separated. The men went home,

but one of them unfortunately died five or six days after the battle. Of course a great cry was made. The coroner's inquest found Parry not guilty … accidental death. The man very properly surrendered himself, notwithstanding the verdict of the Coroner, and was tried at Cardigan, and honourably acquitted, the surgeon proving that the blows the deceased had received could not have been the cause of his death.

… Parry's feelings were so much affected by this melancholy business that he left the country, and has since, I believe, resided in London, having been appointed to a place through the interest of Mr. Johnes, the member for Cardiganshire. I do not know that one of his brothers keeps a turnpike gate; but in all countrys, there are poor in all families. His brother Mr. Parry of Llidiade I know intimately, there is not a more honourable, better man existing. He is a magistrate, he has a very good fortune and is married to Mr. Williams of Castle Hill's sister, who has a very large fortune, and was three years ago Sheriff of Cardiganshire.

The doctor's story of the death wasn't strictly true. Morgan Morgans was 'in liquor' when he went to James Parry's house, but what happened afterwards doesn't tally with the doctor's account. Parry was so angry that he kicked and beat Morgans about the body, before strangling him with his own handkerchief (value 6d.), when Morgans fell down lifeless.[7] An inquest had been held at the house of David Davies in Llanilar on 8 March 1797, immediately after the killing, before a coroner and jury of locals when it was decided that Parry was guilty.[8] The trial was held at the Guildhall, Cardigan on 10 April 1798, and eventually Parry was found guilty of manslaughter, but seems to have escaped imprisonment.[9]

James Parry was not rich—he was a third son—but his godfathers at his baptism in 1738 were Viscount Lilburne, a distant kinsman, and Thomas Powell of Nanteos, a large estate not far from Llanilar.[10] The Parrys were thus well-connected, but by the time of Samuel's marriage only James's eldest brother, Thomas Parry of Llidiardau, could have been considered as equal in status to the Meyricks. Even then their fortunes were not comparable. Although Thomas Parry was a witness at Samuel and Mary's wedding, the couple were evidently staying with Mary's mother's family as Llidiardau is not in the parish of Llanfihangel-y-Creuddyn.

It's difficult to know whether John Meyrick was more wounded by his son's duplicity or by more worldly considerations. He must have had great ambitions for his son and a marriage into the aristocracy would have been but the first step. Instead of throwing himself in person on his father's mercy, or at least writing a simple and apologetic letter, Samuel chose to represent his case with logic and measured argument. A draft survives of a letter he sent to his father soon after his first letter had been rejected.[11]

Relying on a disposition, always more ready to forgive than to punish, I am induced notwithstanding your commands to the contrary, again to address myself to you in writing. The accusation layed, the witness examined and the trial ended, a criminal is allowed by the laws of England to speak in his own defence. I am this criminal, as I have been guilty of the worst of crimes. I have destroyed the happiness, the comfort of the best of parents. My actions need not the allpowering aid of poetry, to paint them sufficiently horrid. They of themselves exceed, perhaps, even Milton's ideas of wickedness; but when committed, their extent was not known. You have heard me condemned, now pray in justice, hear my defence. Dr. Johnson, whose words were the result of the most consummate wisdom, said 'nothing deserves more compassion than wrong conduct with good meaning, than loss or obloquy suffered by one, who as he is conscious only of good intentions, wonders why he loses that kindness, which he wishes to preserve, and not knowing his own fault, if, as may sometimes happen, nobody will tell him, goes on to offend by his endeavours to please'.

This is precisely my case. Unconscious of the villainy attending the deceit I practised to obtain my purpose, I have, while imagining that I was fulfilling the duty of a moral man, been guilty of the greatest injustice. Three years have now elapsed since I first found my attachtment [sic] to my wife, was love itself; and since that period, it has been rapidly increasing, whether present with, or absent from her. Had I seduced this girl, instead of marrying her; what glory and praise should I have had in the world. young men would have applauded me, and young women admired me. This is not my own opinion but that of Addison, whose acquaintance with the world, made him well able to judge of its' conduct. But this would never have suited my conscience, nor could my life have been a happy one afterwards. I did not act deceitfully, for the purpose of offending or hurting you. No! my intentions could not have been carried into effect without deception; but I never thought how much I was wronging you. I know, Sir, that as much as one being could love another you loved me; and continually strove to prove it in your actions; but my conduct never appeared to me in the light it now does. I have experienced all the happiness that could result from parental affection, or friendly liberality. My wants were not only supplied to their full extent but even anticipated. Upon mature reflection, I find indeed that, instead of discharging those duties, which are due to the authors of my existence, instead of making those returns which simple gratitude might claim, my actions have been such as make me unworthy [of] the name of Son. But, Sir, we are told by our Saviour himself that there shall be more joy over one repentant sinner than 99 unjust persons. I am now a repentant sinner. Point out the means of a reconciliation, give me hopes of forgiveness, and however hard the terms I will joyfully embrace them. The opinion of the world I care not for, neither its' censure.

Could I but hear that you and my mother might by any means be made happy, I should be exceeding joyful. Permit me Sir to add although unintentionally I have forfeited all claim to the epithet dutiful, to subscribe myself what I shall for ever be

Your ever loving penitent son

This overworked missive failed in its effect—there is no reason to suppose that Samuel ever saw his father again except, perhaps, as he lay dying in Peterborough House.

Samuel's intermediary in his contact with his father was his uncle William, an attorney in Red Lion Square in London. John Meyrick had asked William to write to Samuel in Cardiganshire, telling him that the only support he could expect from his father was an annuity of £100, paid quarterly, which would cease on John's death.[12] William and Samuel were obviously on terms of mutual affection—William calls him 'Sam' and he calls his uncle 'Will'—and the rift in the family was distressing to both. When Samuel replied to his uncle on 23 October, he cannot have been unaware that the letter would be shown to his father.[13] He tried yet again to justify his action:

I have married a girl descended from one of the first, and most ancient families in Cardiganshire, who have held the office of high sheriff for several centuries. The last two generations have been very numerous, the family estates have been so much divided, as to furnish very little to any of the present. But this is not the reason why I married her. No such might please the world but virtue and modesty, which she possessed in the extreem [sic] are the objects of my admiration. The chief blame seems to arise from the deception I have practised, but I am sure you will make a great distinction between marrying to deceive my father, and deceiving him in order to marry. Indeed here rests the whole subject, and if my father would receive a letter from me I would endeavour to convince him of it.

Unfortunately this sophistry failed to soften his father's heart—indeed it may have exacerbated the situation, because on 12 November 1803 John Meyrick made a new will. He had not cut off his son and his issue completely, as he had left his estate to his wife Hannah during her lifetime, and then to Samuel's legitimate children. If, after Hannah's death, Samuel's issue did not survive their minority to come into their inheritance, the estate was to be divided between the children of James's sister, Elizabeth Trotter, and his sister-in-law, Jane Devisme.[14] With particular spite, he instructed that unless Hannah wanted the use of it, the contents of his library should be sold on his death—he must have known this would particularly wound his son.

The last surviving letter is from William to Samuel, dated 4 or 11 November. After the assurance that John Meyrick does not want his son to return to London to look for employment, William pours cold water on a suggestion of Samuel's that he should go to India—'without a proper introduction the prospect of success is very forlorn, & the expence of fitting out is very great'.

Apart from the £100 a year from his father, Samuel had been left some money by his step-grandmother, Susannah Rush.[15] After numerous other bequests of money and personal possessions, she left £2,285 in 3% annuities to Philip Devisme, the eldest son of her step-daughter Jane. To Samuel she left £500 plus the proceeds from the sale of her remaining possessions or, if John Meyrick so desired, he could have the possessions at valuation and give the proceeds to his son. Samuel was allowed to have the interest from the money until the principal became his in August 1804. Assuming that the amount raised was to be equivalent to Philip Devisme's portion, this would have given him an additional £70 per annum. There is some evidence, however, that he may have taken the possessions themselves, probably as they were worth more than expected. At sometime his uncle James took pity on him and gave him an annuity, but how much this amounted to is unknown. An income of £170 is equivalent to about £7,500 today. The newly-weds probably did what any newly-weds do in such a situation—they returned to the parental home, but in this case it would have to be that of James Parry in London.

Events on the national stage again began to play a part in Samuel's life. The Peace of Amiens, which had given a temporary breathing space during the hostilities between Britain and France, had broken down and the British government had declared war on 17 May 1803. By the end of the year, the country was in a ferment, expecting invasion from Napoleon's armies in France at any moment. In 1802 and 1803 Militia Acts had been passed which provided for raising 51,500 and 25,000 men by ballot. Unfortunately, those chosen by ballot were still allowed to find substitutes, which netted the substitute a payment of £20 to £30, as opposed to the bounty paid to a regular recruit which was only £7 12s. 6d.[16] Common soldiers signed on for life, but a militiaman was supposed to serve for five years only, and could not be sent overseas.[17] Militia officers were usually amateurs of good family, who came forward to help their country in times of need.

Samuel joined up, so using his experience of drill with the Fulham Association, even if the moves and commands were likely to be completely different in another regiment. Perhaps Samuel was fired by patriotic fever or was getting in James Parry's way, for on 24 April 1804 he took a commission as an ensign in the Berkshire militia.[18] His militia pay added a little to the family finances—for the two months between 25 April and 23 June 1804 he received £14 19s. 4d. During this period he was absent with leave—the Queen's College batell books tell us he was in residence at this time, so that he could take his Bachelor of Arts (BA) examination. Hopefully he was able to visit his wife Mary on his way back to his company, as she gave birth to their son Llewellyn on 27 June.

Initially in Captain Bouverie's company, Samuel was at first stationed in the barracks at Walmer, near Deal in Kent. By early November the Berkshires were on the move, marching from Deal to Ipswich by way of Canterbury, Sittingbourne, Rochester, then crossing to Tilbury and on via Chelmsford and Colchester.[19] They were scheduled to arrive at Gravesend on Friday, 2 November, before crossing the Thames on 3 November.[20] They were part of the Southern Detachment along with the Oxford and the West Middlesex militia contingents, which were all due to pass through Chelmsford.[21]

There is no record of Samuel being absent from his company for the rest of 1804, so Mary Meyrick must be blamed for the mistake in Llewellyn's baptismal entry at St. Margaret's Westminster, when on 7 August he was entered as 'Llewellyn Mayrack' son of Sam[l] by Mary'.[22] A later affidavit in the register sets the details right—'ought to have been Llewellyn Meyrick son of Samuel Rush not Sam[l] only'—presumably after Samuel had been to inspect it. Where exactly Llewellyn was born is obscure—his entry in Foster's Oxford Alumni says 'Christchurch Surrey'. This may have been Christchurch parish in Blackfriars Road, Southwark—the sort of unfashionable location it was desirable to conceal.

From October 1804 Samuel was given the extra responsibility of making up the company's accounts, though he was absent without leave in November, but having been 'displaced by His Majesty's command' on 23 February 1805, he was promoted to Lieutenant on 27 February. He didn't enjoy the extra status for long, because he resigned on 7 May.

Samuel, Mary and Llewellyn were together again, and needed a permanent home. Samuel's name first appears on the Chelsea rate books for Midsummer 1805, when he took up a lease on 3 Sloane Terrace,[23] just a stone's throw from Sloane Square and less than three miles from Peterborough House. Lord Byron's mother had taken rooms in Sloane Terrace when he was undergoing treatment for his club foot in 1799.[24]

It's possible that Samuel returned to London at this time because John Meyrick was already ill, though from his silhouette he seems to have been a candidate for a heart attack rather than a lingering illness. Yet another curious document suggests that Samuel was smuggled into Peterborough House shortly before his father's death. A single sheet of paper[25] is headed 'Peterbro' House Nov 7th 1805' with the message: 'Come to me tomorrow: but name not your connections. H. Meyrick'.

John Meyrick died on 27 November 1805 at the early age of fifty-three.[26] Maybe the grief caused by Samuel's elopement was not directly responsible for his father's death, but it cannot have helped. A tablet on the south aisle wall in Fulham church recorded that his 'Virtues were beyond all Praise'.[27] John's brother James and his brother-in-law James Trotter did not waste any time in proving his will, which was done on 29 January 1806. As executors they took literally his instruction about selling the 'contents of my library'—probably he meant the books only to be sold, but in the event even the bookcases went, as well as the unfortunate memorial brasses. Some idea of the size of the library can be gleaned from 'A Catalogue of the elegant and valuable LIBRARY in print and manuscript of the late John Meyrick Esq. which will be sold (by order of the executors) by Messrs King and Lochée at their Great Room 38, King Street, Covent-Garden on Monday, April 21, 1806 and eleven following days (Sunday excepted) at Twelve o'clock'.[28]

There were 2,545 lots, many multi-volume sets and bundles of similar subjects. The sale fetched £3,745—about £140,000 today—but from notes in Feret's *Fulham Old and New* it seems that some items did not make a good price, and the library was probably worth more.[29] Even so, there was no question that Samuel could afford to buy very much back—though from a later catalogue of his own library[30] it is known that he attended the sale on at least one day: item 1407 was a bound manuscript by Sir John Waunrin. Called *Chroniques D'Engleterre*, it had belonged to James II, but had been bought for 6 guineas from the library of Count McCarthy in 1790, presumably by John Meyrick. Samuel had written on the flyleaf in pencil: 'This ancient French Manuscript suffered greatly by the vessel which brought it from Wales AD 1809 (whither it had been carried two years before) upsetting in the River Thames near

London Bridge & lying on her beam ends for a fortnight. I bought it at the sale of my Father's books in the year 1806, when it cost me £14. It was then bound up in yellow turkey, marbled leaves, a binding put on by Count McCarthy, who had the original one taken off. This binding being destroyed by the water, I had it bound up again. Sam¹ R Meyrick'.³¹

Samuel came across his father's copy of one of Hasted's volumes in 1813, when he bought it on behalf of the Rev. Thomas Maurice of the British Museum.³² He saw that the notes in were in his father's handwriting, and asked Maurice to bequeath it to him! John Meyrick had evidently been spending a good proportion of his income on modern books of travel and topography, but he had thirty-four volumes of Bell's *British Theatre*, early missals and books of hours. There were a lot of manuscript genealogical and heraldic treatises with emblazoned arms, which must have fired Samuel's interest as a child. He would have been familiar with the various tracts on archery, and Francis Grose's two books on *Military Antiquities* and *Treatise on Ancient Armour*—the best books available on the subject at the time. Apart from the brasses, some small British antiquities including fourteen spear heads were sold as the last lots. Finally the mahogany furniture including the doors of the Chinese style built-in book-cases were sold for £164.

John Meyrick's estate was registered for probate as 'under £25,000' according to the Death Duty records.³³ If an estate was so mentioned it meant that the value for Stamp Duty purposes lay somewhere between £20,000 and £25,000. In addition to Stamp Duty, Legacy Duty had first been introduced by William Pitt in his budget of 1796, to help pay for the war against the French. Strictly speaking a 'legacy' only concerns gifts of money or personal goods in a will, not land. Initially tax was only applied on legacies of more than £20 to persons other than the testator's wife, children, parents and grandparents, but by 1805 the tax had been extended to all except the spouse and parents, and legacies which were raised by selling land. The Death Duty registers can be very useful in working out complicated relationships in an involved will. In John Meyrick's case, as Samuel's son Llewellyn was the residuary legatee after the death of Hannah Meyrick, the final value of the legacy was not entered onto the register until 1832 when Hannah died. In the meantime the Peterborough estate had been sold, but fortunately property (or the proceeds of the sale of property not needed to pay off legacies) did not become dutiable until 1853, after Samuel's death. As it was, by 1832 John Meyrick's dutiable legacy had increased to £57,489 and Llewellyn had to pay 10% in duty.³⁴

From the evidence of the sale of the library John Meyrick's executors were carrying out their duties rigorously, and so would have made sure that Samuel did not benefit from the bequest. However, there was nothing to stop Hannah Meyrick disposing of her income as she wished, and the bequest of her father Samuel Rush was now under her control again. As instructed in his will, property had been bought with the government stocks he had left her, and in an indenture dated 6/7 February 1806 the property was made over to trustees in order that an income of £120 a year should be paid out to Hannah, Samuel and his wife.[35] However much Samuel had wounded his mother, the birth of her first grandchild must have gone a long way towards healing the breach, and the fact that she was willing to enter into a financial arrangement with him argues that she was soon won over.

One of the trustees mentioned on the indenture was Samuel William McGeorge, and it seems that this arrangement may have been connected with a business venture that he or perhaps his son had had with Samuel. In Kent's 1806 directory there is an entry for S.R. Meyrick & Co., army agents, operating from 42 Parliament Street. The business of John & James Meyrick, army agents, was in 1805 and 1806 operating from 17 Spring Gardens, not Parliament Street. Given the lead time in making up directories, it seems possible that Samuel's new venture had been started before John Meyrick's death, but in any event the *London Gazette* recorded the dissolution of the partnership on 18 March 1806, William McGeorge being liable for any debts incurred.[36]

John Meyrick's library could have been retained by Hannah had she wished to do so, but she chose to sell it immediately. It seems that she was finding the upkeep of Peterborough House too much for her, for in August 1807 her trustees joined with her, Samuel (on Llewellyn's behalf) and the residuary legatees who were his cousins, in promoting a Local and Personal Act to sell Peterborough House and invest the proceeds for her benefit.[37] The act states that Hannah has not been able to find a tenant to rent the house, and it should be lived in by someone with enough income to keep it well maintained so that it would keep its value. The house was soon sold, and afterwards had a chequered history, one notable tenant being the notorious William Beckford of Fonthill, connoisseur and sexual adventurer, who is supposed to have leased it between 1840 and 1841.[38] In later years the house became an asylum for insane ladies, before it was demolished about a century ago. The house is remembered in the Peterborough estate, a select housing area of Fulham. Hannah seems to have lived[39] at Notting Hill House for a while, but in 1817 she decided to move to Littlehampton, a seaside town to the west of Brighton in Sussex.[40] She remained there

Fig. 17   Littlehampton Harbour

for the rest of her long life, Samuel joining her for occasional holidays and every Christmas.[41]

Samuel was now without employment, and if there was already a plan that he should become a doctor of civil law (DCL) then he had to follow the prescribed road. A candidate for the DCL had to be a Master of Arts of a certain number of years standing.[42] To obtain a Master of Arts, it had been intended that the candidate should be resident in college for twelve terms, i.e. three years, and give six 'solemn' lectures as well as engaging in disputations. By the end of the eighteenth century, this requirement had been eroded to the point that many were not resident, those who were being usually those intending to take holy orders. It became merely a matter of time before an Oxford graduate could claim their Master of Arts. They had still to keep their names upon the books of the college, as Samuel did until the Easter term of 1809. Queen's College was the only college to provide formal training for those proceeding from Bachelor to Master of Arts, but this was just in the field of theology.

Samuel qualified for his Master of Arts in 1810, but also for his BCL, or Bachelor in Civil Law. From this it seems that he had been required to take an oral examination to prove his achievements in 'polite letters', and had disputed three times on civil law. By a concession a BCL was allowed to progress after a year to a DCL if they had already taken their Master of Arts, provided that they were prepared to take an oath that they intended to enter the Maritime and Ecclesiastical courts. Samuel obviously did this, and in 1811 he became entitled to write LL.D. after his name. He always held by the old style of writing the abbreviations of the Latin names of his qualifications after his name: A.B., A.M. or LL.D. He could even be the writer of an anonymous letter to the *Gentleman's Magazine* in 1817 who said he would never adopt the new style of writing 'DCL' instead of LL.D. after his name.[43]

4   The Young Antiquary

From an unusually early age Samuel had ambitions to become an author. His first venture dated from 1800, when he had just arrived at Queen's College in Oxford, but it was never printed. It was an ambitious work entitled *Oxonia Restaurata or a Chorographical, Historical, Natural, Architectural, Monumental and Heraldic Survey of the County of Oxford*. Its existence is known because the original manuscript was lot 1380 in the sale catalogue of his library, where it is described as forming volume one of an intended work.[1] Already he seems to have had the desire to instruct and inform others by publishing material that he collated from different sources. These included earlier printed works, manuscripts and physical remains in churches and other old buildings. Either through youthful enthusiasm or sublime confidence he did not seem to shrink from the large scale of the work he was proposing to undertake.

After the failure of Samuel's army agency venture in early 1806, he still had the problem of filling his time as he would not need to prepare for his civil law examinations for some years. Although there are no manuscript works dating from this year, he may have already started preparing for what was to become his first published title. He gave the reason for this excursion into print in the foreword of the work concerned—*The History and Antiquities of the County of Cardigan*. 'About five years ago I undertook the fashionable tour of South Wales … my journey being completed, I carefully read over all the publications of modern tourists, which I soon discovered did very little justice to the history of the Principality. But Cardiganshire was scarcely noticed … it was to supply this deficiency that I endeavoured to collect all the information relative to it in my power … I was recommended by a friend to make public the result of my researches'.[2]

This 'friend' was possibly the Rev. Thomas Maurice, Assistant Keeper of Manuscripts at the British Museum. They had first met in 1800 when John Meyrick had asked his young son to take Lord Cornwallis's subscription for Maurice's *History of Hindostan* to the author.[3] Samuel was already an admirer having read Maurice's *Indian Antiquities*, which his father had in his library. As Maurice was some thirty years older than Samuel, he may have been in some sense a father figure with the added virtue of a scholarly mind, and their correspondence continued for a number of years.

There are three small leather-bound manuscript notebooks in the National Library of Wales which seem almost to be intended for publication but were probably part of the process of collecting information on Welsh families. The first book[4] is amply described by its handwritten title page:

THE
BRITISH GENEOLOGIST [*sic*]
OR
A Collection of the Pedigrees and Arms
of the families inhabiting the counties
called Monmouthshire, Glamorganshire,
Caermarthenshire, Pembrokeshire
and Cardiganshire
To which is added
FRAGMENTA GENEOLOGICA
The whole compiled
From the best authorities and assistance of the
best Heralds
by
EDWARD LLWYD
Keeper of the Ashmolean
Museum in Oxford
1693.
Copied from the original and augmented from later
manuscripts, and information by Saml Rush Meyrick A.B.
of Queen's College
Oxford.
1807.

The second book is an *Heraldic Dictionary*, which Samuel writes was 'copied from another written about the latter end of the 16th, or the beginning of the 17th century:

and is an authentic heraldic compilation. The coats of arms were not added to the original'.[5] The catalogue of the sale of Sir Samuel's library dates it to 1804-7, but the title page itself says 1807. This dictionary is incomplete, some pages have only names at the top of the pages, some have coats of arms only pencilled in though others are fully drawn and coloured.

The third book[6] is dated 1807, and is entitled *Collecteana de Rebus Celticis* and is really a notebook for odd jottings. There are details of the words borrowed by the Celtic language from the Romans; the names of Welsh cantrefs; the arms and family tree of the family at Mabus and copies of poems, but most of the pages are empty.

There are two slightly later books which Samuel started in 1808. Queen's College library has a manuscript volume[7] entitled *Catalogue of the Names of the Sheriffs of North and South Wales* which Samuel started writing in 1808. His intention was to list all the details of the sheriffs from the mid sixteenth century to about 1800. In the event, some counties have no entries at all under their heading, though Cardiganshire is almost complete. The book was sold to the college by a Mr. Hipwell in 1900. The other was a translation from the Welsh of two books on the history of the early saints of Britain, *Achau Saint Ynys Prydain o Lyfr Thomas Hopcin o Langrallo. Achau a Gwelygorddau Saint Ynys Prydain o Lyfr Thomas Truman o Bant Lhwydd* which was lot 1346 in the eventual sale of Samuel's library.[8]

Research in London and Oxford was all very well, but it must have seemed that further investigations into Cardiganshire history could only take place on the spot. By October 1807 the Meyricks had rented a comfortable house at Glanfrwd, in the parish of Cellan, near Lampeter in Cardiganshire.[9] Glanfrwd lies at a crossing of the river Frwd, where there were fulling and woollen mills.[10] In his *Topographical Dictionary of Wales* Samuel Lewis says that 'The houses are wretched and the walls are made of mud five feet in height with a low thatched roof surmounted at one end by a wattle and daub chimney'. The living of the parish of Cellan had been owned by Johnes of Hafôd, yet another connection to that family.[11] Samuel gives a very full account of Hafôd, and his drawing in the *History* shows the house before the disastrous fire in March 1807, when Johnes's wonderful library perished.

Lampeter was a small market town relying on agricultural business, enlivened periodically by large cattle fairs.[12] It was supplied by dry goods from Bristol, which were taken by road after passage by sea to Aberaeron on the coast of Cardigan Bay. There was also a trade in coals from Llanelly and Newport by sea. Lampeter had had a grammar school in the earlier eighteenth century, but this seems to have fallen into decay by the time that the Rev. Eliezer Williams became vicar in July 1805. He revived the school, which went on to have a number of distinguished pupils. After 1820 Eliezer was succeeded by John Williams, son of John Williams who had been headmaster of Ystrad Meurig school, just up the valley from James Parry's home of Llwynhwyel. Sir Walter Scott's son Charles was taught at Lampeter by the younger John Williams, who was at Balliol College Oxford at the same time as Scott's son-in-law J.G. Lockhart. Scott's influence enabled Williams to be appointed as the first Rector of Edinburgh University. A Rev. Daniel who had been at Parson's Green in Fulham often taught in his place at Lampeter, but it's not known if this had any connection to the Meyricks' choice of location.

From his base at Cellan Samuel travelled all over Cardiganshire, gathering information from the families in every estate of note. He was one of the movers in trying to set up a local book society, hoping to get business for Simcoe, the bookseller in Piccadilly.[13] One desirable outcome of writing the *History* was that he could put on record his wife's antecedents. To try to estimate the demand for the *History of Cardiganshire* Samuel had issued an (undated) prospectus, showing that he had already decided on eighteen of the twenty illustrations.[14] Indeed, there proved to be a ready market for the work among those Welsh inhabitants who could expect to see their names mentioned, as well as

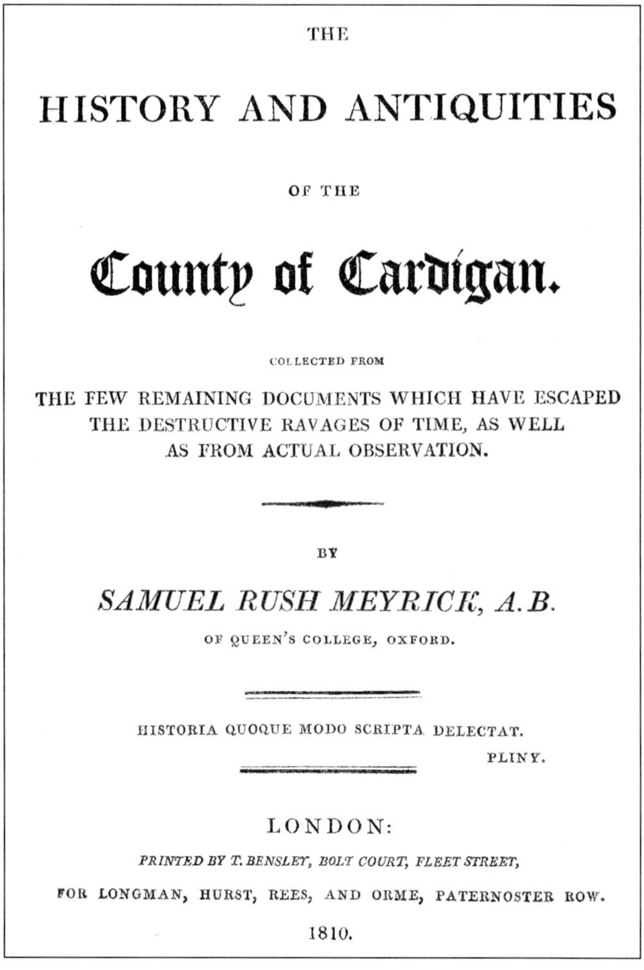

THE

HISTORY AND ANTIQUITIES

OF THE

County of Cardigan.

COLLECTED FROM

THE FEW REMAINING DOCUMENTS WHICH HAVE ESCAPED THE DESTRUCTIVE RAVAGES OF TIME, AS WELL AS FROM ACTUAL OBSERVATION.

BY

SAMUEL RUSH MEYRICK, A.B.

OF QUEEN'S COLLEGE, OXFORD.

HISTORIA QUOQUE MODO SCRIPTA DELECTAT.
PLINY.

LONDON:
PRINTED BY T. BENSLEY, BOLT COURT, FLEET STREET,
FOR LONGMAN, HURST, REES, AND ORME, PATERNOSTER ROW.
1810.

Fig. 18 The title page of the *History of Cardiganshire*

Fig. 19   Hafôd—the home of Thomas Johnes

friends and family, residents of Fulham and Chelsea and acquaintances from Oxford. More illustrious subscribers included Sir Richard Colt Hoare of Stourhead and the Bishop of St. David's in Wales.

The *History of Cardiganshire* is valuable for describing archaeological features which have now disappeared, though regrettably this was sometimes due to Samuel himself. At that time the value of context was unknown, and there was a long tradition of removing choice items from their original sites for private enjoyment or for their own protection. Samuel had a number of cist graves opened in Cellan parish, in one of which he found an urn with cremated bones.[15] He acquired a piece of the medieval painted tiles with which he conjectured the church at Cellan had been floored. He also relieved the church at Tregaron of two Roman pillar memorials with the remains of early inscriptions, which were later set in the wall of the chapel at Goodrich Court.[16] Fortunately they were given by the last owner of the Court to the National Museum of Wales, where they are safely preserved. The *History* is enlivened by a number of etchings taken from Samuel's original drawings, one of which was later castigated as being so 'ludicrously inaccurate' that it must have been drawn from memory.[17]

Initially Samuel had hoped to have the book printed at Thomas Johnes' press at Hafôd and publish it himself, but the delay that this would have caused led him to change his mind, and it was published by Longman, Rees, Hurst and Orme.[18] The Longman family had gone into publishing in 1724, and at this time Thomas Norton Longman was a partner. He was known for his liberality, and the firm gave regular receptions and dinner parties for their writers, among whom were Wordsworth, Southey and Walter Scott. Samuel had suffered from considerable difficulties in

Fig. 20   The arms of Lloyd of Allt yr Odyn as illustrated in the *History of Cardiganshire*

proof reading, as he apologises in the Introduction for any mistakes caused by the fact that he was '200 miles away' from his London printer. The book was published in 1808, but an additional paragraph about the fire at Hafôd was not added until the 1810 reprint. Longman's commission book shows that by the end of 1809 they had printed an initial run of two hundred and fifty copies of the *History* to satisfy the original one hundred and ninety copies required by subscribers. This had been followed quickly by another print run of identical length, but the early promise did not last, and two hundred and five copies were left on their hands by the middle of 1812.[19] Longman had been selling the copies at £3 3s. each, and they retained three copies when they finally settled the account on 26 August 1812—the date of Samuel's 29th birthday. The venture was not a financial success—the initial costs paid by Samuel amounted to £1,100, but receipt of the subscriptions lagged behind. One reason was that Samuel's bookseller, Williams of the Strand, who collected the subscriptions, had taken umbrage at his decision to use Longman as the publisher and held on to the money for as long as possible.[20]

It's worthwhile to consider for a moment the confidence and nerve of a young man who publishes a major county history when he is only twenty-five. Most such were written by local antiquarians who had made substantial collections of documentary material before they embarked on projects which lasted many years, and often were never finished. According to one authority, Samuel used an account of Lampeter, written by the Rev. Eliezer Williams for Carlisle's *Topographical Dictionary of Wales* in 1808, in his *History of Cardiganshire* without 'owning up to the fact'.[21]

Soon after returning to Sloane Terrace in the autumn of 1809, Samuel was occupied with another literary venture. Had this been successful, his subsequent reputation might have been established in the theatre. He had been inspired by the history of the last princes of Wales, and this had 'suggested itself as a subject for the Drama, and although highly unqualified for such an undertaking, the trash which of late years has been applauded on the stage emboldened me to proceed'.[22] Having already asked a friend for his critique on the play—and presumably having had no response—he approached the Rev. Maurice to see if he would read it and offer suggestions. Maurice quickly replied that he had no time, but Samuel sent him a synopsis of the play in any event.[23]

The play was called *Llewellyn – an Historic Play in Five Acts*, of which a copy fortunately survives in the National Library of Wales.[24] The plot, as described to Maurice, was as follows: 'The prince of Wales while celebrating at a banquet … is suddenly informed of the capture of Eleanor de Montfort, his intended spouse, who was on her passage from France to Wales. This determines him again to prepare for war. His successes induce Edward 1st to take the field, who aware of the advantages accruing from such a measure, detaches the Welsh chieftains from their allegiance …'. There was an underplot with a love story between a Welsh girl called Angharad and Mountjoy, a soldier, but 'I do not know how to finish the plot. Sometimes I think ultimately to make Ednyfed [Llewellyn's lord steward] kill Mountjoy, and Angharad to die with grief. But perhaps this would be too much like Tom Thumb and all Murder!!! Perhaps as a contrast these under actors should be more merry!'.[25] The manuscript is unfinished, so the ending was never resolved.

Here is a sample of the opening scene, set in Llewellyn's hall at Aberfraw:

Llewellyn: Now shall the sparkling mead, from high in the glittering Hirlas
                 Fill, horn bearers, fill full bumpers for us all.
                 The walls of Aberfraw shall far resound our gladd'ning shouts of triumph

> For Cambria's sons have gained a splendid victory.
> This my brave countrymen is the sure result of genuine valour.
> And far as the sea extends, the fame of Britannia's sons is known.
> The battle o'er it is the chiefest wish to loose oppression's bonds
> And if there's one that hath complaint to make,
> Now let him come, and speak his inmost soul most freely.

The text is copiously annotated with footnotes explaining the historical terms — for example, a 'hirlas' is noted as a long blue drinking horn. The play seems never to have gone any further, and its fate is shared by *Syr Owain, a POEM in VI CANTOS*, also in the National Library of Wales.[26] The verses on page seventy of the manuscript give a taste of the epic:

> Yet these were not the whole who came
> To have a share in Strongbow's fame.
> From Castell Nedd came Richard Grenville
> With his sworn friend Syr Payne Turberville
> Who could more safely Coelty's land
> Leave, since he possess'd Asar's hand.
> For this acknowledg'd Coelty's Lord
> Strengthen'd his title by the sword.
> William de Londres sent his son
> Who often valiant deeds had done
> For he could not quit Cydweli
> Nor sooth, could Reginald Sili.
> De Remi had his life been spar'd
> Would doubtless Strongbow's perils shar'd
> But now immur'd within the womb
> Of mother earth; on altar tomb
> His sculptur'd effigy reclines
> And round the edge we read these lines
> **Sire Roger de Remi gist isci**
> **Deu de son Alme eit Merci**

Another manuscript work which dates from what could be called the 'early Welsh' period of Samuel's life is a book in Hereford Library.[27] It is entitled:

CAMBRIAN

ECCENTRICITIES

containing

A BRIEF SKETCH

of the

Antient customs, Legends, and Superstitions

OF THE

Welch,

Together with an account

of their

Weddings and Burials.

Pensa, che questo di mai non raggiorna.

Dante.

This is another considerable body of work of well over two hundred pages. It starts with an explanation of the custom of wearing the 'leak' on 1 March, and goes on to describe and explain many Welsh customs and traditions. For example, Samuel tells of the importance of pipers at weddings, and writes down the music for one air called *[Erd]Digan y Pibydd coch* or 'the red piper's song'.[28]

Samuel's most time-consuming work of this period was started in 1810, and continued almost until his legal duties at Doctor's Commons began on 13 April 1812. In a letter, written in March 1812, he tells the Rev. Maurice that he has got through the greatest part of a 'history of the inhabitants of the British Isles from the earliest accounts to the year 703'.[29] When it was finished he was proposing to sell it to a bookseller, but yet again it did not make the shelves.

This work, the *Antient History of the Britons*, fills three substantial volumes preserved in the National Library of Wales.[30] In all there are '1,600 pages closely written',[31] and as it must have been transcribed from a rough copy the work involved was considerable. The first volume covers the history from the first people in the British Isles until the arrival of Julius Caesar; the second until the departure of the Romans; the third until the reign of Cadwaladr in 703. Each volume has the same structure of historical topics: civil and military; political; religious; commercial; scientific and literary; and lastly physical. Although the publishing project was abandoned the material came in very useful for his later printed works.

Fig. 22   Music from *Cambrian Eccentricities*

In the summer of 1812 Samuel's increased income encouraged him to take a lease on a new house very near to his old one in Sloane Terrace, this time in the more salubrious location of Upper Cadogan Place. At the front the house looked towards Cadogan Place Gardens, where Mr. Salisbury laid out his Botanic Garden on the Linnaean system. One of Salisbury's aims was to prevent accidental poisoning, and he gave lectures in the garden during the season on the identification and classification of plants.[32] Categorisation by style and form was a subject very dear to Samuel's heart and of utmost importance in his armour studies, and it's interesting that he should have an example so close to his home. At the back of the houses in Upper Cadogan Place the gardens ran down to a small brook, and onto fairly open ground.[33] It was a salubrious spot, and No. 20 was to be the Meyrick family home for the next eighteen years.

It was probably during this time that Samuel drew up an inventory of his possessions, perhaps for insurance purposes. It is contained in a small notebook entitled a *Catalogue of the Paintings, Prints, Plate, Linen, Furniture &c of Samuel Rush Meyrick* in the library of Queen's College, which was written by him sometime after 1806, as he has one of the engravings of Nelson's funeral.[34] The list is notable for the number of top quality artworks in his ownership, perhaps inherited from his step-grandmother, Susannah Rush, or which may have been given to him by his mother. One of the most important works was an early Benjamin West, the *Introduction of Helen to Paris*, which

Fig. 23   20 Upper Cadogan Place

was painted in 1767, soon after the painter came to England from America. Besides a number of family miniatures, there were religious pictures by Burnell and Cuyp; landscapes by Wynants and Ruysdael; sea pieces by Brooking and Gaspar van der Boss and a number of prints and engravings.

The Meyricks lived in reasonable style, judging by the list of furniture and soft furnishings. The drawing room, which was decorated in the Egyptian style, must have been striking. The windows were hung with cotton curtains in a leopard-skin pattern, with Egyptian borders. They were lined in orange, and hung from bronze and gold cornices with eagle supporters. There were a dozen handsome satinwood drawing room chairs, inlaid with black, with stuffed cushions and leopard-skin cotton soft furnishings, with Egyptian borders, supplemented by a matching pair of reclining couches. To hold Samuel's books there were two handsome mahogany bookcases, eight feet in length, and a mahogany desk on mahogany feet with brass castors.

The dining room was equally bold: a pair of scarlet French curtains with black Etruscan borders and black pelmet were complemented by a green baize cloth with a red Etruscan border for covering the dining table. This was a handsome set of mahogany dining tables, consisting of two centre and two end tables, each with claw feet. In all the Meyricks could seat twelve people, on four mahogany inlaid Grecian chairs with horse hair seats and eight more Grecian chairs inlaid with ebony, which had red morocco seats with Etruscan borders, two with arms. A mahogany sideboard with lion's head handles and a mahogany cellaret in shape like a sarcophagus completed the dining suite.

It's possible that the Meyricks bought their sets of furniture to complement their new house, or indeed that it was needed to replace items they had taken to Wales, and which was destroyed in the shipwreck which damaged Samuel's books. The book by Waunrin was not the only casualty—Samuel had to replace his copies of the *Gentleman's Magazine* by bartering a copy of his *History* with John Nichols, its editor.[35] The fact that the ship had brought the books from Wales is an interesting illustration of the busy coastal trade of the time.

Samuel was now almost ready to start his legal career, and the operation of the civil courts of the time requires some explanation. Most doctors of civil law practised as 'advocates' in the ecclesiastical or admiralty courts. This job was equivalent to a barrister or counsel in the common law courts, but the advocates also had other sources of income from probate work and marriage licences. At the time that Samuel became a civil lawyer, the southern part of England, Wales and the Channel Islands were under the ecclesiastical jurisdiction of the province of Canterbury. Over hundreds of years, a number of different ecclesiastical courts had evolved to cover the areas of jurisdiction of bishops and archbishops.

Every bishopric—and there were twenty-three in the Canterbury province—had a 'consistory court', as did the archbishop as he was also a bishop in his own diocese. Each province had a probate court for dealing with wills and administrations of people dying intestate, known as the Prerogative or Testamentary court. Wills had to be proved in the Prerogative Court of Canterbury (PCC) rather than consistory courts if the value of the estate was above a certain amount, or if the testator had property in more than one diocese. There was also a certain *cachet* in having your will proved in the PCC, even if it wasn't strictly necessary. Another important court was the general appeal court of Canterbury province, where those dissatisfied with the verdicts of lower ecclesiastical courts could bring their cases—this was called the Court of the Arches.[36]

The Admiralty Courts were quite a different proposition, as they sat to determine cases arising outside the national jurisdiction of any country—that is, on the high seas. Admiralty law had its roots in Roman law, and this was the speciality of civil lawyers. In order to be able to practise in the various church and admiralty courts, an advocate had first to be admitted as advocate of the Court of the Arches, by rescript of the Archbishop of Canterbury.[37] When Samuel qualified, the various London civil courts no longer met in diverse locations, but sat at Doctors' Commons. This name was first used about 1496 to describe a kind of 'college' or gathering of similar professional men, who would meet and dine together. For the price of an annual subscription, even those

Fig. 24   The Doctors' Commons at the time they were demolished in the 1860s

who weren't civil lawyers but who had ecclesiastical connections were assured of a
friendly place to go when in London. Initially all advocates in the ecclesiastical courts
had to be in holy orders, but by the early nineteenth century this had completely
reversed, and the clergy could not practise.

As time went by, the name 'Doctors' Commons' was applied to the Prerogative
Court of Canterbury, and even to the location of the various courts. After the original
buildings were destroyed in the Great Fire of London, a new establishment was built
in the original location in Knightrider Street, south of St. Paul's Cathedral in the City
of London. All the ecclesiastical courts and the admiralty court sat in the new courtroom, and new sets of chambers were built to house advocates and their families. In
addition to the Court or Common Hall, there was a dining room and a library, and
outside a large garden.[38]

The court business was transacted during the usual law terms of Michaelmas,
Hilary, Easter and Trinity. A number of the doctors lived with their families in one of
nineteen sets of chambers. Each had a front door which led directly off a courtyard
into what was a three-storey house with attics and cellars, unlike most chambers which
lead from a communal stairway.[39] There were not enough chambers to accommodate

all the advocates, and, as membership of the Commons continued in theory until death as long as the advocate paid their dues, there was probably a waiting list. The advocates' sleep may have been disturbed by a watchman who cried the time every half an hour during the hours of darkness. On entering chambers the same system applied as at Oxford, the newcomer paying a 'third' of the agreed value of the fixtures, fittings or furniture they took over from the previous tenant.

When they were admitted, an advocate had to pay a fee of £20 as well as paying an annual fee of 6s. 8d. for their membership of Doctors' Commons. In addition there were charges for wine and food—'commons'—because the advocates were expected to eat in the communal dining room; it's possible to follow their attendance by the records in the fees books. An advocate had necessarily to come from a wealthy background, as they did not usually start earning before they were thirty. Apart from the requirements for their doctorate, they had a year of 'silence' after being admitted before they could practise. On 3 July 1811, the Archbishop of Canterbury authorised Sir John Nicholl to admit Samuel as an advocate in the Court of the Arches. On the next day, Samuel signed his admission oath:

> *Ego Samuel Rush Meyrick collegii Reg: Oxon: admissus fui in commensalium Dominorum Advocatorum de Arcubus Londini, et solvi riginiti libras introitu juxta decretum prodictum.*

The progress of an advocate through the years can be followed in the Law List, which shows all the members of Doctors' Commons in their order of seniority. In 1812 there were twenty-nine, when Dr. 'Merrick' brought up the rear. Samuel was now one of a distinguished company, though he does not seem to have formed long-term close friendships with any of his colleagues. Sir William Scott, later Lord Stowell, was a judge in the High Court of Admiralty whose decisions still impact on today's maritime law. He obviously made a deep impression on Samuel, as Stowell's portrait was to be one of the three on the wall of his private room 'when I go to the country'.[40] Another advocate only a few years older than Samuel was Stephen Lushington, who argued for reform of the ecclesiastical court system, as well as being active in the agitation for the abolition of slavery, toleration of Jews and parliamentary reform.

When Samuel became an advocate the days of Doctors' Commons were already numbered. After a series of Acts in the 1850s which separated the Court of Probate and the Court for Divorce and Matrimonial Causes from ecclesiastical jurisdiction, they and the High Court of Admiralty were brought together into one Division in 1873 and their jurisdiction was transferred to the High Court.[41] The Doctors' Commons building was sold in 1865 and demolished.[42]

It's often said in biographical sources that Samuel 'made a fortune' practising as a civil lawyer 'for many years'. The amount that he did earn is impossible to calculate, but it seems unlikely to be very substantial as he did not rise high in the profession. He practised for less than twelve years, starting in the Michaelmas term of 1812 and 'declaring his intention of quitting the Profession & his chambers' in February 1824.[43] According to the dues he owed, which are noted in the Fees book, his attendance was very regular between 1812 and 1816, but in 1817 and 1818 there are major absences.[44] These must relate to Mary Meyrick's final illness and death.

Apart from the 'regards from Mrs. M'. in many of Samuel's letters, no more is learnt about their marriage and life together. Mary is buried in the graveyard of Chelsea Old church, her tombstone having been rescued by the Meyrick Society in 1947 and placed against the wall.[45] Even then, the stone was very eroded but the inscription reads:

Underneath
Are deposited the remains of
MARY
the Wife of
SAMUEL RUSH MEYRICK LLD
of Upper Cadogan Place
in this Parish
who with a pious resignation
yielded up her soul to Heaven
on Thursday 4 June 1818
aged 34
Ah! MARIA
Matrona Optima

Samuel and Mary had been married for less than fifteen years. There's no evidence whether the marriage was happy, for no letters have been found where Samuel's feelings on the subject are expressed. The fact that he did not marry again, even though he was only in his mid thirties when Mary died, argues less for a life-long dedication to Mary's memory than for a preference for the freedom to follow his own pursuits.

In fact, within days of Mary's death Samuel moved out of his chambers at No. 17 in the Commons and became embroiled in heated exchanges with the new occupant, Dr. Addams, about the amount that the latter should pay him in 'thirds', as he had spent £35 on fittings including a new seat for the water closet.[46] Addams preferred the Commons' own surveyor's valuation, and had the blinds and carpets left at Samuel's new chambers in Bell Yard. This was named after the Bell Inn where Charles Dickens later wrote part of *David Copperfield*, which describes the court sessions at Doctors' Commons.

Samuel viewed his professional duties as drudgery from the beginning, as evidence a letter written from the Commons in July 1813 when he calls it 'this vile place'.[47] One of his characteristics, remarked on by his friends and evidenced in his letters, is a very rigid system of timekeeping. In 1823 he described to a friend his daily schedule while at the Commons: 'I rise at 7, breakfast at 8, start from home at 9 and walking four miles reach chambers at 10. Here I am professionally engaged till 4. I reach home (if I have no where to call, a very rare occurrence) at 5 dine between that and six and have only the evening to receive friends, pay visits or what generally occupies me ... Nor have I more leisure on Sundays; what portion I can spare on that day from religious duties being given to explaining and exhibiting my son's armoury'.[48]

The start of Samuel's career as an advocate had coincided with the political unrest caused by the Luddites, and he had written to the Home Secretary, Lord Sidmouth, suggesting a means of intelligence gathering.[49] He proposed dividing the country into logical regions, then compiling a book with pages for each region giving statistical, geographical and military information, including the names of people of influence, and the numbers of political activists. When an emergency did occur, police could be readily rushed to the area. This interesting letter did not signal a desire for the political stage, as the years 1812 to 1824 witnessed his commitment to two of his most important publications. The first was a joint venture with a friend called Charles Hamilton Smith, and was to establish Samuel on the national stage—and to some extent to eclipse Smith's own amazing career.

5   The Master Works

Charles Hamilton Smith was an extraordinarily talented man of Flemish descent—his family name was Smet—and he had been born in East Flanders in 1776, seven years before Samuel.[1] Having been sent to school in England, he then studied at the military academies of Mechelen and Leuven, now in Belgium but at that time in a province of Austria. He joined the British forces as a volunteer, and by 1797 was a brigade-major in the 60th regiment in the West Indies, where he stayed for ten years.

On his return from the West Indies he spent some time in Coventry recruiting for the army, but also had two spells of active duty fighting in the Low Countries. The preface to his 1814 work on costume is dated from 'his majesty's ship *Horatio*, in the Ram-pot, on the coast of Zeeland, 6 Dec 1813'. From an early age he was a keen artist and scientist, being particularly interested in natural history. In 1800 he conducted controlled experiments on behalf of the army into the best colour for military uniforms, using coloured targets of red, green and grey.[2] There was no doubt that grey was the best at minimising casualties, but the British army did not take his results into account for many years. His talents in observation and organisation were utilised by the army in intelligence gathering in the Ardennes, and in formulating a plan for the defence of Canada in 1816. He retired on half-pay from the army in 1820, and was given the brevet rank of lieutenant-colonel in 1830. For the rest of his life he lived in Plymouth, and for the forty years of his retirement devoted himself to his researches and his art.

His earliest publications were on military subjects: firstly a translation of a history of the Seven Year's War in 1808, followed by a translation of the *Secret Strategical Instructions of Frederick II* in 1811. He published a small account of Napoleon's retreat from Moscow in French, illustrated with maps, in 1813. He also wrote the military part of Coxe's *Life of the Duke of Marlborough*; in 1842 Samuel bought from Smith a copy which Archdeacon Coxe himself had given to Smith, containing Smith's notes and maps.[3] Smith also wrote an article on War for the *Encyclopaedia Britannica*.

From 1812 onwards Smith started to take advantage of the higher standard of illustrations by publishing *The Costumes of the Army of the British Empire*. These were lively pictures of the uniforms of various regiments according to the last regulations of 1812, published by Colnaghi. They were issued as sets of four prints progressively between March 1812 and June

Fig. 25   Charles Hamilton Smith

1815, until the collection numbered sixty, though Colnaghi may have had the complete set to hand by 1812. The horses are particularly well drawn, foreshadowing Smith's later books on mammals. The drawings supplied by Smith were aquatinted by J.C. Stadler, one of the most experienced and well-known artists in this field.[4]

The forty years from 1790 was the golden age of coloured aquatint illustrations. Because of the different stages in the process of bringing the artist's original to the finished page there were several opportunities for either improving or marring the final production. The production of an aquatint starts with a copper plate being evenly coated with powdered resin. The plate is then heated, leaving a fine film of melted resin which gives a 'granulation' to the finished picture. Using the original drawing or watercolour, the outline and the shading to indicate folds of drapery or shadows were transferred to the plate, probably in reverse using a mirror. This was done either by the artist himself or by one of many skilled engravers.

At this stage a pedestrian original could be 'improved' in the hands of a skilled engraver, as the plate would then be etched with acid or 'strong water' a number of times, progressively protecting areas with varnish until only the strongest lines were left. A top artist such as Rowlandson would have used a proof copy of the print at this stage to show which light colour washes could be produced as part of the printing process, and which would have to be added later by hand. An absentee artist was in the hands of the engraver, and then of the colourist who added the final paint to the picture after it was printed. Although the final colours used should follow the artist's original, a colourist sometimes altered a non-critical component such as a horse from roan to grey, and a heavy-handed use of the paint could wreck the final work. The most sumptuous works could be gilded or burnished. Some works were also sold uncoloured for purchasers to colour to their taste. Books at this time were often issued in a series of parts, and a subscriber would expect to have these bound into one or more volumes to his own library design.

Smith's first book on ancient costumes was published in 1814, again by Colnaghi. For *The Ancient Costume of Great Britain and Ireland from the Seventh to the Sixteenth Century*, Smith had drawn all the illustrations and had also written the text to accompany each plate. In the preface he wrote on board the *Horatio* in December 1813, he says that 'the Collection of Ancient Costumes … is selected from an immense mass of materials in the possession of the Author'. The views expressed in the preface might almost be Samuel speaking: 'truth of costume was little regarded by Painters or Actors'. Smith's other remarks are interesting: 'the materials from which the costumes are compiled are Monumental Effigies, Brass Plates, Paintings on Glass, Seals and ancient Illuminations' and 'it was the intention of the Author to have … given more precise notions of the introduction, alterations, and improvements of ancient armour'. Smith was thwarted in this intention by his military duty, but even so there are a number of plates with figures in armour, and it cannot be denied that it must have influenced Samuel's later works.

Books of costume at this period are sometimes criticised for using imagination rather than scholarship to provide the styles and colours of dress. Given that no fabric remains had been discovered at that date, Smith's approach of using contemporary accounts, documents and effigies which were often painted was the best that could be done. The authorities are religiously documented, and where imagination has been used to 'supply a deficiency' or paint a background it is noted. Samuel is mentioned several times—for example as supplying a drawing of a Cambrian prince from a manuscript belonging to Sir John Sebright, and for supplying a drawing and particulars of the recumbent effigy of Sir Rhys ab Thomas from Carmarthen church. This Smith converted into a standing drawing, as he did with many of his other plates. The text accompanying each plate gives historical anecdotes of the people depicted, who are usually royalty or nobility. The plates themselves are very lively and colourful, sometimes of an outside scene but more often of one or two figures in the dress of the period. Smith took care always to quote his authorities, even going so far as to scrape paint from an effigy to determine the original colour of a costume.

Smith's collections of sketches and notes represent a herculean body of work. Even without the fifty volumes of drawings and notes lost when the Plymouth Athenaeum was bombed in the Second World War, there are copious collections at the Society of Antiquaries, the Victoria and Albert Museum and the Linnaean Society. Given that many of his references are to early manuscript collections then in the British Museum, it is unlikely that he could find time to do his research when he was so rarely in London before 1813, and many of his drawings must have been copied out of other publications.

As for Samuel himself, he had probably judged the mood of the wealthier book-buying public correctly when he complained to the Rev. Maurice in 1813 '… as I find people will not read nowadays, I must endeavour to please by the pencil and etching needle'.[5] In this letter is the first intimation that he proposes to venture into the world of illustrated costume books. He enclosed a prospectus for a work which would have pictures of the ancient Romans, part two to contain an etching of 'M.T. Cicero from his statue in the Ducal Palace of St. Mark in Venice coloured on the authorities of Cicero and Horace. He is represented as in a Roman study at Puteoli'. This prospectus 'must be without a name to prevent the slander inseperable [sic] from this branch of the profession'. He says that he has already selected his proposed illustrations but nothing seems to have come of the venture. This may have been because he came across a similar work published in 1810 by Thomas Baxter, later to become a renowned ceramic artist. In the sale of Samuel's library in 1871, lot 1383 was a bundle of ninety-three drawings of Egyptian and Roman costumes. Instead he started to collaborate with Smith, a collaboration which ripened into a lifelong friendship.

In 1814 a prospectus was issued for another book: *The Costume of the Original Inhabitants of the British Islands and the adjacent coasts of the Baltic … from the Earliest Periods to the Sixth Century by Samuel Rush Meyrick and Charles Hamilton Smith.*[6] It was published on 1 June 1815. Although all the illustrations were again drawn by Smith, the first author's name on the title page is that of 'SAMUEL RUSH MEYRICK, L.L.D. and F.S.A'., followed by that of Smith. In his preface, Smith says that 'Dr. Meyrick, in three large quarto manuscript volumes, has collected, in the manner of Henry's History of Great Britain, whatever relates to the inhabitants of the Britannic Isles, from their first arrival till the termination in the year 703 of the British sovereignty in England; and it is from this elaborate work that the principal matter contained in the following pages has been extracted'. It would seem that although Samuel's *History of the Britons* was never published verbatim, at least some of his research was used in the body of this book.

These two volumes would appear to make a natural set, and logically one might expect that the volume dealing with the period up to 703 would have been issued first, the reverse of what actually happened. Perhaps there were problems with proof-reading—Samuel seems to have been fairly slow at this and prone to revision, for the amount of text is substantially greater than in the volume that deals with the period post 703, and draws liberally on Welsh sources as well as classical authors. There are numerous instances where information was used which had been gathered during Samuel's sojourn in Cellan. These range from prehistoric encampments in Cardiganshire to the fabric of current Welsh costume which were compared with bark materials from the Pacific, presumably that in the Meyrick collection. Smith does say that the subject of ancient (Celtic) burial rites is too extensive to introduce in the book: 'in Dr Meyrick's MS ... it occupies nearly 40 quarto pages'. The text accompanying the plate of Boadicea (see plate 7) gives a sample of the scholarly nature of the text:

Of Boadicea or Aregwedd *Voeddug*, i.e. the victorious, as she was styled by her countrymen, of which epithet the Romans latinized a name for her, ancient authors have been studious to preserve a particular description. Comparing therefore the accounts of Strabo with those of Dion Cassius, and by carefully examining the dresses of the Celtic females on the columns of Trajan and Antonine, the basso-relievos found in this country, and the coins of Carausius, there is little difficulty in delineating the costume of this princess. Accordingly this plate depicts her as a full-grown handsome woman, but of a stern countenance with long yellow hair flowing over her shoulders. She wears the Pais much longer than what is worn by the men, hence that word is now confined to designate the petticoat. It is woven chequerwise of many colours, which, according to Strabo and Pliny, were purple, light and dark red, violet and blue. Over this is the shorter garment, open on the bosom, and with short sleeves exposing the arms, termed Gwn, the Guanacum of Varro, which reached as far as the knee, also of interwoven colours. On her shoulders was thrown her cloak, fastened by a fibula, and from her neck depended a golden torque. Bracelets ornamented her arms and wrists, and rings her fingers. This was her usual habit, says Dion.

Fig. 26 Frontispiece of *Costume of Original Inhabitants*

John Dowding, a book-seller of Newgate Street, bought the rights in both the books of costume. He issued 'improved' editions of the first in 1817, and of the second (Samuel's) in 1821. The improvements are hard to find, and the plates are unaltered from the earlier editions. Both books have recently been re-issued as a single volume in a more modern format.[7]

During this period Samuel was also busy formulating the future of his only child, Llewellyn. Samuel had made plans for him from very early on, and Llewellyn seems to have been both easily managed and intelligent enough for the arrangements to succeed. His life plan was laid out in a letter[8] Samuel wrote to the Rev. Maurice in January 1815, when Llewellyn was only ten:

> With regard to my boy of whom you were speaking to me the other day, my intention certainly is, notwithstanding he has been so amply provided for by my father, so to plan his education as shall qualify him for a probable seat in Parliament, and for the more certain admission to our Bar … Having great regard for Alma Mater, I would certainly prefer sending my son to Oxford, and although myself of Queen's College, I would much rather he should be at Christ Church in order to follow up that other object of his education, by keeping the best society.
>
> The scheme of education I have, after mature consideration, planned for my son is this. I sent him in the first instance to the Revd. Mr. Pearson's where as you know he has been associated with the sons of the first people in the country, and well grounded in Greek and Latin grammar. Thence to the Revd.

Mr. Ruddock's where at the expence of £150 a year he will acquire in addition to Latin Greek French and the Sciences, *les meilleurs formes*, in my opinion, a very essential part of the education of a young man destined to move in the first circles. It is while at this school that I should wish him to enter at the University, and as he would not have to reside till three years after he might I should think avoid the expence of entering as Gentleman Commoner, as he could on commencing residence put on a civilian's gown, but in this I should be guided by the Head of the College. Two years before he goes to reside at Oxford I shall send him to Eton, where he will have the opportunity of renewing those acquaintances he formed at this first school; and which he may afterwards cement at the University. When he has resided three years at Oxford I purpose sending him to Göttingen for a year. There they teach Civil Law better than any where, and his acquaintance with the professors will introduce him to all the German courts. By the by he might take his Bachelor of Law's degree before he left Oxford. When the year at Göttingen has expired he will be 21, and consequently entitled to his fortune; but after having embibed so much German *pesanteur*, I design him to visit St. Petersburgh, and to lighten it with the *gaiete de coeur* of the French. You see by this I would send him to Paris last, and I do so for this reason, to prevent the effects of that *persiflage* he will there necessarily learn, that ridiculing contempt of every thing that is not French. On his return to England I should presume he would be completely qualified for the great Council of the nation, and he might also occupy his time in studying law. At five and twenty he would take his Doctor's degree, and at six and twenty hold a brief.

Such, with divine permission, would be his course of studies, and though too many examples have occurred for me to rest sure that his inclinations will not run counter, particularly when subjected to the temptations of the world, yet I think you will agree with me that whatever path in life he may choose, such an education will not be found without it's value. Thank God! at present with a quickness of apprehension, a perseverance in acquiring knowledge, and an amiable disposition, he seems by his declarations to encourage me in the hope of attaining the objects I have in view, and in the furtherance of which I trouble you with this long letter..You may trace another object ... to prevent my son's independent fortune becoming his ruin.

Llewellyn had inherited items from Peterborough House which Hannah Meyrick presumably did not want, and he had the *objets* which Samuel had acquired for him during the years of his minority. A catalogue of his collection, made about the year 1815 when he was eleven, was written in a thick exercise book issued to the governors of the Chelsea & Brompton dispensary in Sloane Square in September 1814.[9]

THE MEYRICKIAN MUSEUM OR COLLECTION OF CURIOSITIES SHALLES, MINERALS, FOSSILS PETREFACTIONS COINS, AND ANTIQUITIES OF LLEWELLYN MEYRICK

The first 150 items are from islands around the Pacific, and include cloth and matting as well as idols and war implements, one of which was brought back by Captain Cook; the sailors on the various Cook expeditions had had a profitable sideline selling things they had acquired in the South Seas. A number of pieces in the collection were presented by Col. Robson, who may be the Francis Robson who was governor of St. Helena, the homeward port of call of the Cook expeditions. There were also spears, bows and arrows, shields and tattooing instruments, and a number of scimitars and daggers from the orient. Many of these items continued in the Meyrick collection until it was dispersed. Other armour included the three iron helmets of different forms from Fulham church, which had iron spikes on top and visors; a barbed dagger; swords worn by a Knight of the Bath at his institution; various spurs and bits of seventeenth century armour and a suit of armour of the time of James I, decorated with rosettes.

Antiquities included the fragment of a tombstone of Mael from Caernarvonshire; another from Tregaron similarly ornamented with a cross; various carvings from St. Alban's Abbey; an ancient spear head; an ivory carving which was perhaps a chair-back;[10] a pedestal for crucifix in ivory presented by a Mr. Swabey and a cross and crosiers. The solemn tone of the collection was enlivened by a model coracle, a stuffed parrot, various fossils and shells and a 'boiled white of egg presenting a curious appearance when kept'.

Samuel's father John had been elected as a fellow of the Society of Antiquaries in 1786, and his uncle James in 1787. Samuel himself must have been pleased to have been elected at the age of twenty-six, on 17 May 1810, after having presented the Society with a copy of his *History of Cardiganshire* in the previous December.[11] He was recommended by John Nichols the publisher to whom he had sent a review copy of the work, and also by Francis Douce the antiquary and Henry Ellis.

Fig. 27   A Society of Antiquaries meeting by Cruikshank

At the time that Samuel joined the Society of Antiquaries the public view of the institution and of antiquaries in general was not a flattering one. They were seen to be snobbish, dull and rapacious in their hunt for specimens. Their meetings were often ill-attended—just as Samuel was about to be elected in the spring of 1810, Francis Douce wrote to his friend Kerrich: 'I think this Society is fast going to the D---, when there is a contested election the room is brim-full; at other times a desert, 800 members, and not a paper in the Secretary's hands to read at the next meeting!'.[12] These were then held in Somerset House, in a room next to the Royal Society's meeting rooms. The fellows sat in tiered benches on either side of a long table on which specimens could be displayed, the officers presiding facing them from a raised table at the head of the room. The fellows were drawn from the wealthier members of society, but as well as royalty, noblemen and gentlemen of independent means there were clergymen, professional artists, politicians and a few scientists. It was, in effect, a select club for those with an interest in antiquities, where the best people in London could be met with—if they turned up. Many members did attend the annual dinners held on St. George's Day.

Although there was a growing interest in the systematic excavation, recording and publishing of antiquities and ancient architecture, the society's journal, *Archaeologia*, was too often full of historical transcripts and publications of texts. The other publications of the Society such as *Vetusta Monumenta* were sumptuously (and expensively) illustrated, and were probably the reason why many artists and architects joined.[13] Samuel was not backward in providing papers to be read, one in 1811 on Roman

Antiquities discovered in Bognor being so long that it had to be spread over three meetings.[14] On 29 February 1816 he brought along 'an ancient crosier, lately purchased by him in France'. He might well have met Edward Blore at the meeting on 9 May that year, when the latter was a guest of Mr. Radcliffe.

Samuel was elected to the council of the Antiquaries twice, for the years 1822 to 1823 and 1828 to 1829. He must have been happy to see Llewellyn elected as a fellow

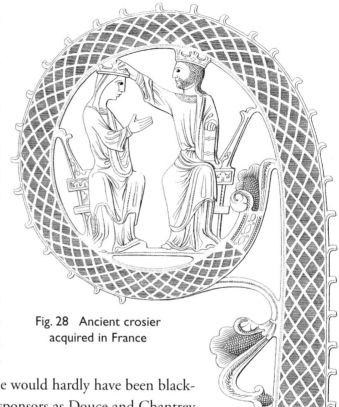

Fig. 28 Ancient crosier acquired in France

on 14 April 1825, though he would hardly have been black-balled with such illustrious sponsors as Douce and Chantrey the sculptor. The late 1820s were troubled years for the Society. Although individual members fought many battles for the preservation of ancient buildings under threat, the society as a body seems to have been characterised by inertia. The Resident Secretary, Nicholas Carlisle, was a man of whom it was said that he did nothing for the Society without being paid for it, although he had a reasonable salary and living quarters.[15] The library contained many valuable books but was hardly noticed by him.

Matters came to a head in 1827 when Nicholas Harris Nicolas began to turn his attention to the Society's affairs. Nicolas was a precocious and energetic antiquary who had been a fellow since 1824 when he was twenty-five. In 1827 he was already preparing one of his great works, *The Siege of Carlaverock*, a translation of a poem written on this siege which took place in 1300. The book also describes the arms of the earls, barons and knights who were present; Samuel is quoted extensively in the notes and was obviously consulted by Nicolas. Nicolas had already attacked the Society in the *Retrospective Review*[16] for selecting personal friends of the chief officers for the council, for the frivolous nature of its publications and for the manner in which it was conducted. Having been unsuccessful in persuading the council to allow him to examine the Society's books, Nicolas mounted an all-out attack in the *Westminster Review* of October 1829, when he described the Annual Meeting of 1828 in vituperative terms. This was the background to Samuel's year on the council. No wonder that Nicolas was so scathing about Samuel's ancestry in his review of Samuel's piece in *Archaeologia* on Gelly Meyrick. Even Thomas Fosbroke in distant Herefordshire became embroiled in that incident when Samuel asked him to insert a reprimand to Nicolas's jibe in his review of *Archaeologia* for the *Gentleman's Magazine*.[17] Probably Samuel was relieved that his name was not put forward for the council for the next year, but in any case Herefordshire was beginning to occupy his thoughts.

His departure was noticed in other quarters—below is a sample of a satire on the meetings of the Antiquaries, published in the *Intelligencer* of 31 October 1830:[18]

> SCENE, an upstairs room in Somerset House. The Antiquaries Society assembled in full fig. At the upper end of a long table a President's chair, vacant, in front of which Mr. Martin, the Librarian, is occupied in placing a large cocked hat on a cushion.[19]

Jun. Sec.   'Sir – Gentlemen – ere we proceed
Farther, permit me to read
My worthy colleague's minutes, treating
Of what was said and done last Meeting.

      .....

Presented - first, a Bow and Arrow,
Supposed the same with which the Sparrow
Cock Robin's bosom did transfix:
(See Mother Goose, Vol. 1 page 6)
Discovered underneath a Hay-rick
In Herefordshire – by Dr. Mayrick.
      (Hear! Hear!)
Much like another in the Dwelling
Of Dr. Meyrick's Son, Llewellyn.
Read – the accompanying essay,
Some Forty folios as I guess, a
Brief Statement, Luminous and Clear,
Of how 'twas found, and when, and where,

With arguments of greatest nicety
In favour of its Authenticity.

.....

Presented, by the Junior Sec.,
(Myself again) a Royal wreck,
An antique Thimble, that with which
In Seventeen hundred forty-six,
Flora Macdonald drove her Stitches,
While mending Prince Charles Edward's Breeches
When, from Culloden forced to fly,
He tore them in the Isle of Sky.

.....

(The tray is brought in – a simultaneous rush at the Muffins. Mr. Martin is scalded by a Cup of Coffee upset on his Inexpressibles, and, in the confusion, our Reporter quitted the Room.)

It seems from this that Samuel already had a public reputation for wordiness—the 'forty folios' is probably a dig at his paper of the same length on the *History of Hand Fire-Arms* which was read to the Society on 22 February 1827, and later published. Happily he was too young to be the original 'Dr. Dryasdust' addressed by Walter Scott in his introduction to *Ivanhoe* which was published in 1819.

The survival of Samuel's letters is very much a hit-and-miss affair, though antiquarians such as the Rev. Thomas Maurice kept their correspondence as a matter of course. Perhaps as a result of his growing status as an author, increasing numbers survive after 1820. From this one-sided correspondence, and from Samuel's own published works it is possible to give a truer picture of his relationships than from later writers who claim that so-and-so was 'a friend' of his. Fortunately, long series of letters survive from Samuel to two of his four intimates. Even though there are suspicious gaps at critical junctures of his life, and we may be sure that some censorship has taken place, without these letters the picture of his character and personal life would be superficial indeed. For his part, Samuel says that he has kept all those 'from eminent persons … [such as] Sir Walter Scott'[20] which he intended to have bound, but their whereabouts are a mystery. One early letter from Scott to Samuel became detached from Samuel's collection and survives, probably because it had been used as rough paper for practising French translation.[21]

The main group of Samuel's correspondents are antiquarian acquaintances, some very close, but in general not party to the more intimate details of his life. The volume of antiquarian correspondence at this time is truly astonishing, and a well known authority on a given subject could expect to have to answer a barrage of questions from all over the country. Most of these methodical gentlemen kept their incoming letters, and sometimes out-letter books as well. The Rev. Thomas Maurice, Keeper of Antiquities at the British Museum has already been mentioned as an early mentor and father figure. Membership of the Society of Antiquaries had brought Samuel into contact with another of the doyens of the antiquarian establishment—Francis Douce. This relationship was to pay early dividends in Samuel's master work on armour, culminating in a much more spectacular coup on Douce's death.

They probably first met at the Society of Antiquaries when Douce had seconded his application, and in 1815 Samuel wrote to him to ask for more information about the paper on the seal of Wilton Abbey which Douce had published in *Archaeologia*.[22] By 1820, when Samuel began to pursue him in earnest, Douce was sixty-three, twenty-six years Samuel's senior. Douce's early life had been made miserable by the lack of affection of his father, and all his life he resented his elder brother whom he believed had turned his father against him. Regardless of this, his smaller inheritance was sufficient for him to indulge a life-long love of books and antiquities, and in 1807 he was appointed Keeper in the Department of Manuscripts at the British Museum, though he resigned in 1811 because of a series of imagined affronts to his dignity.[23]

Although highly respected for his scholarship, Douce's personal grievances seemed to have infected his whole attitude to life. He was doggedly old-fashioned—he still affected a

Fig. 29   Francis Douce

wig, and saw no need to follow fashion. He kept a series of notebooks, now in the Bodleian Library, which he stipulated must not be opened until 1900. This was just as well, because those in which he recorded his true thoughts on some of his friends would have distressed them. One notebook called 'Modern Absurdities' castigates modern manners because 'a set of silly and affected dandies of both sexes feel quite shocked & horrified ... to see anyone eat his food with the end of a knife or a steel fork instead of a silver trident ... [and] would rather drink hot coffee from a cup than use a saucer designed for the purpose'.[24] In common with others of the time, he found puerile puns funny and noted them down: 'Cicero declines to Ciceras – "kick her arse"', and 'among the most unfortunate marriages was Miss Laycock to Mr. Badcock'.[25]

In spite of these personal oddities, Douce's friendship once gained was warm, and he was on the best of terms with two generations of men distinguished in the 'study of antiquity either in literature or art'.[26] Apart from a genuine respect for his learning, Samuel knew that his library was one of the finest private collections in London, as Douce had been buying old manuscripts for years and was often given items by his friends. Douce's library was to be Samuel's private British Museum, with the benefit of access to a vast fund of knowledge in its owner. Douce himself published very little— his major works were *Illustrations of Shakespeare* in 1807, and a copiously annotated edition of Holbein's *Dance of Death* in 1833.

Douce's interest was primarily in the documents' content—he was an authority on medieval English and French romances and he often bought transcriptions where the original was unavailable. The numerous Books of Hours and psalters in his collection testify to his interest in their beautiful illuminations.[27] Added to that he was an avid collector of woodcuts and engravings, and his value to Samuel becomes clear. Very often the illustrations showed armour and weapons contemporary with the date of the manuscript, even if it was about historical events.

In 1823 Douce's friend the sculptor Joseph Nollekens died, and after much acrimonious wrangling he inherited a fortune of £50,000.[28] Ironically, now that he had all the riches he could have ever desired, the turmoil of the litigation had destroyed his pleasure in it. However, it enabled him during his last years to acquire some of his finest manuscripts, and also many of the beautiful ivories and antiquities which are to figure later in the story. There can be no doubt that the relationship between Douce and Samuel developed over the years into a genuine friendship, despite the difference in their ages. Indeed, a portrait of Douce was specially commissioned by Samuel to hang in his bedroom, so that 'I see your resemblance first thing in the morning and last thing at night'.[29] There are hints in the letters that their conversations often ranged over personal as well as antiquarian matters.

While Mary Meyrick was alive it would not have been appropriate for Samuel to spend much time visiting any bachelor friends in their private dwellings. With her death the position changed completely, as when Llewellyn was at Oxford Samuel could please himself in his time away from the Commons. He was, in effect, a bachelor as were three of his closest friends: Francis Martin, Thomas King and Abraham Kirkmann. Martin was one of the heralds at the College of Arms, somewhat older than Samuel and had a rather ribald character—at least from the evidence of remarks about him in Samuel's letters. He was born in 1767, the third but eldest surviving son of Francis Martin, Secretary to the Bank of England, and died unmarried in his chambers at the College of Arms on 3 Jun 1848 aged eighty-one.[30] He had been appointed to the post of Bluemantle at the College of Arms in 1797, was Windsor Herald from 1819, Norroy King of Arms from 1839 and Clarencieux King of Arms from 1846 until his death.

During the early 1820s Martin had the unenviable task of persuading Samuel that the evidence he was presenting on his pedigree for the scrutiny of the heralds was still incomplete.[31] When Samuel moved to Goodrich, Martin acted as a collecting point for the books and other items that Samuel had purchased from dealers' catalogues. He would then pack them up in boxes and despatch them—though he did sometimes keep the books overlong to read them himself. He may have commissioned a portrait of Samuel for his chambers, as in October 1839 Samuel wrote to another friend that 'I have not yet commenced reading the books as the young artist, Mr. Quentin, is here painting for Mr. Martin'.[32] As this was just after Samuel had been very seriously ill Martin may have wished to take the opportunity while it was still possible. If there is such a portrait, it has not been found.

Through his friendship with Martin, Samuel became firm friends with another herald at the College of Arms. Thomas William King was nearly twenty years younger than Samuel, and was the son of Thomas King of Great Yarmouth, being born there in 1802. An industrious and capable officer of arms, he was appointed Rouge Dragon Poursuivant in 1833, and York Herald in 1848. He first visited Goodrich in 1837, and his collection of letters from Samuel start at around the same time. In spite of their difference in ages, the two men had a warm regard for each other, and King was very distressed at Samuel's death.

When King retired from the College of Arms he sold his manuscripts to them for £300 including his notebooks and his many letters from Samuel. The collection comprises twenty-four volumes of 'Heraldic Miscellanies', which include much material of Herefordshire interest. For example, King and his fellow guests at Goodrich would often visit local churches and transcribe the information from the monumental inscriptions. He kept diaries of his summer visits to Goodrich from 1837 until 1847, detailing the rates he paid for coach travel as well as the excursions he made to local beauty spots. Just one

Fig. 30   Thomas William King

letter from King to Samuel has come to light—preserved in the Earl of Essex's own copy of Silver's *Paradoxes of Defence* of 1599, which Samuel owned and which was sold with his library in 1871. King had given Samuel the explanation of the quartering of Essex's arms, which are painted in the book.

Samuel's third bachelor friend was Abraham Kirkmann, an attorney of Lincoln's Inn, whom he may have met through Francis Martin. Samuel always spelt his name as 'Kirkmann', though the family came from Alsace and was originally called 'Kirckman', the firm of Jacob Kirckman holding royal appointments as harpsichord makers from 1710 to 1792.[33] Kirkmann was born in 1796 at St. Giles, Camberwell in London, though his family also had a house at Blackwell Hall near Chesham in Buckinghamshire. Kirkmann's father was a solicitor, and his son also chose the legal profession, entering Gray's Inn in 1831 and being called to the Bar in 1836. Kirkmann was already a keen antiquary in 1824, when he visited Goodrich Castle in the early spring and made sketches for Samuel, and they remained firm friends until Samuel's death. In 1847 James Young painted a portrait of him, which is labelled 'Goodrich Court in agro Herei'.[34] Kirkmann had connections with Crickhowell in Breconshire, and in later years bought a gothic house not far from there near Llangorse lake, called the Noyadd (Neuadd). He died in London in 1866, but although he was buried in Kennington a memorial tablet was raised to him in the parish church at Llangorse, calling him a 'profound antiquarian'. In his will he left the residue of his estate to the village to provide for a well and a pump, with the balance to the village school.

These three gentlemen formed the inner circle of Samuel's friends. They were not averse to a bit of fun on occasions, and although their summer holidays in Goodrich were jolly affairs by profession they belonged to the soberer classes. Not so another very good friend of Samuel's—the playwright and later herald James Robinson Planché. Much the same age as Kirkmann, Planché came from a totally different background. His father was a watchmaker of Hugenot extraction, and he was articled to a bookseller when only fourteen. His taste turned to the stage, and after a time acting as an amateur in various private theatres he became successful writing burlesques, melodramas and operas. In 1820 he had a triumph with a play he had translated from the French called *The Vampire or the Bride of the Isles*, when he made use of a recently invented trap in the stage floor, christened the 'Vampire trap'. His first opera was based on Thomas Love Peacock's *Maid Marian*, and was produced in 1820 at Covent Garden.

In 1823 Charles Kemble was planning to revive Shakespeare's *King John* at the

Fig. 31   James Robinson Planché

Drury Lane theatre, and Planché convinced him that it would be to his advantage to have the actors clad in historically exact costumes. As part of his research, Planché became acquainted with Samuel, who also introduced him to Francis Douce.[35] This was the beginning of Planché's long and happy association with Samuel, which continued after the latter's death, as Planché arranged and wrote the catalogues for exhibitions of the Meyrick collection. At the same time as writing and producing innumerable works for the stage, Planché published widely respected

Fig. 32   Thomas Pettigrew

works on costume often using as illustrations pieces from the Meyrick collection. He did not hesitate to acknowledge his debt to Samuel, indeed he became so knowledgeable on the subject of armour that he wrote a catalogue for the sale of the collection of one of Samuel's friends, Bernard Brocas, in 1834. Samuel often used him as his agent in the London salerooms. After Samuel's death he became a thorn in the side of the authorities at the Tower of London, until they finally allowed him to complete Samuel's work in 1869. In 1854 he was appointed to the College of Heralds as Rouge Croix Poursuivant, and he was promoted to Somerset Herald in 1866.[36]

We would know very little about one intimate aspect of Samuel's life were it not for his friendship with a medical man, Thomas Joseph Pettigrew. Pettigrew's father had been a naval surgeon on the *Victory* long before Nelson's time, but he became a parish doctor in London where Pettigrew was born in 1791. The young man had a precocious talent for medicine, and when still in his mid twenties was appointed as surgeon of the dispensary for the treatment of diseases of children near Doctors' Commons and secretary of the Royal Humane Society, where he became acquainted with the Duke of Kent and later vaccinated the young Princess Victoria against smallpox.[37] Although he was an excellent physician, he may have been helped to some of his posts by the fact that he was a prominent freemason. After the death of the Duke of Kent he became physician to Augustus Frederick, the Duke of Sussex, another of the sons of George III, and like himself a mason—as was Samuel's uncle James Meyrick who was Provincial Grand Master of Surrey from 1795 until his death in 1818.[38]

Fig. 33   The Duke of Sussex

Pettigrew became not only the Duke of Sussex's physician but also his librarian, and in that capacity he published a two volume catalogue of the duke's library, a presentation copy of which the duke gave to Samuel. Although he published a number of books on medical subjects, in later life he became progressively more interested in antiquities, particularly in Egyptian mummies and the subject of embalming. He was a leading figure in the British Archaeological Association from its foundation, and published a number of papers. Samuel was happy to accept an invitation to stand as a godfather to his daughter in 1831.[39]

It was probably through Pettigrew that Samuel became acquainted with the duke, although Douce knew him as well. Like many of his brothers, Augustus had made a morganatic marriage. He was the most reformist of the royal dukes, often at odds with his father George III and his eldest brother, and Samuel became one of the duke's most fervent supporters. He first started cultivating the duke in earnest in 1826, when he made drawings of armour and loaned pieces from his collection to him, and then gave him his mother's own copy of his work on armour.[40] Llewellyn was made an equerry to the duke in 1830, but his duties do not seem to have been onerous. The duke died in 1843, after some years of ill-health and loss of eyesight.

6   An Acknowledged Expert

More than a hundred and fifty years after his death, the name of Meyrick is still a powerful talisman in the world of armour. The account of Samuel's early life has made it clear that the collecting interests of his father must have had a powerful influence on his subsequent career. What is not so easy to determine is whether his head only was involved in his relationship with the vanished world of knights and armour, or whether he felt its romance all his life? He certainly had a passionate nature—his rigid schedules for his everyday affairs hint at a need to control himself, as well as those around him. Later in his life there are incidents which point to his tendency to lose his hold on his emotions suddenly and explosively. Given this, it's not surprising that his infrequent spending sprees happened throughout his life at times of especial stress—'retail therapy', in other words.

For a number of years after John Meyrick died, the family finances cannot have allowed for much expenditure beyond the necessities of life. Samuel was notoriously mean with money, his habits of economy perhaps stemming from his father's careful upbringing as much as from his earlier straitened circumstances. Under the terms of John Meyrick's will his widow Hannah was entitled to the annual interest on his estate during her lifetime—the equivalent of £50,000 today. It's probable that some of this sum found its way into Samuel's pocket, but on condition that it was used for Llewellyn's benefit. It was fortunate, therefore, that Llewellyn seems to have acquired an interest in armour unusually early in life. Samuel is always meticulous in referring to 'my son's collection' in his correspondence.

Samuel's interest in armour had perforce taken a back seat during his years of research in Wales, but was invigorated on his return to London and the collaboration with Smith on the works on costume. His friend Planché was to describe how he had gathered information about the period of different styles of armour—he 'appropriated certain drawers to certain centuries and threw into each, as he made or acquired them, the notes, antiquities, engravings, drawings, tracings etc. which appeared to appertain to such certain periods. Having thus in the course of many years collected an immense mass of material, he sat down patiently to examine and compare the dated and undoubted evidences with those supposed to belong to the same era. ... Everything that did not tally with the general features of the age to which it had been assigned was ejected from that compartment, and if genuine, speedily found its place in another. Shrewd, cautious, indefatigable, warped by no theory, misled by no assertion, he toiled on in the pursuit of TRUTH'.[1]

The house in Upper Cadogan Place soon started to resemble a rambling antique shop. Robert Curzon, later Lord Zouche, visited the house when a schoolboy at Charterhouse when he had 'just begun to collect armour' and was 'passionately devoted to the pursuit'.[2] Writing in 1868, Curzon said 'the house was full of armour, from top to bottom, his [Samuel's] own bedroom & the stair case, was crammed with arms. On washing my hands in the bedroom, I opened the wardrobe to look for a towel, but there was nothing but a bronze Greek helmet, and other such antient clothing'.[3] The collection was founded on the antiquities collected by John Meyrick at Peterborough House, but by 1820 a number of beautiful pieces of armour had been added which were the basis of its fame.

Even before the age of the practical use of armour in battle had passed, pieces which were reputed to have a connection with a historical personage were exhibited in the appropriate castle, family home or public building. These displays, often on a large scale, were not distinguished by the accuracy of the attribution of their age or owner-ship. Many suits of armour and their accoutrements had not been designed for use in battle or tournament in any case, but as an expression of wealth and taste for use in more peaceful parades. These were works of art which could stand comparison with any others from the world of sculpture. In continental Europe, there were many fine pieces still in the city armouries or those of important families who had perhaps fallen on hard times.

Mary's death, and possibly the removal of her restraining hand on the family finances, was followed by a major coup. Domenic Colnaghi was the son of Paul Colnaghi, an Italian-born printseller of 14 Pall Mall. The Colnaghis had published the early Charles Hamilton Smith works on uniforms and costume, and Samuel would have known them well from this period. In the years 1816 and 1817 Domenic

Colnaghi set off around Europe, where the power vacuum following Napoleon's fall gave rise to opportunities for the purchase of art and antiquities at bargain prices. He came back loaded with arms and armour. There was no better person to help him to make a catalogue of his collection than Dr. Meyrick, and a copy of this document is held at the Wallace Collection.[4]

The Colnaghis were in some financial difficulties at this time, and they decided to raise money by selling their armour collection. Their affairs must have been pressing as Samuel managed to acquire his pieces at cost, according to notes attached to a copy of his catalogue-cum-scrapbook.[5] Robert Curzon claimed that Colnaghi's price was £2000—something less than £100,000 today.[6] Somehow Samuel raised the money—perhaps Hannah Meyrick was persuaded to make an advance on Llewellyn's inheritance—and at one stroke the Meyrick collection entered a different league.

The complete catalogue of the collection as it stood while in Colnaghi's hands shows that there were some twenty-three suits, plus a child's suit and two small model suits. There were fourteen shields or targets, including one depicting the signs of the Zodiac and episodes in the life of the Emperor Charles V, which is now in the Wallace collection.[7] There were cross bows; more than fifty swords and daggers; as many different firearms; a large number of powder flasks and all kinds of battle weapons such as axes and halberds. It is not possible from the short descriptions in the Colnaghi catalogue to correlate them all with Meyrick collection pieces, but many can be identified in the Wallace Collection.[8]

The other early major source for the finer pieces in the collection was Thomas Gwennap, whose armour was displayed in the Oplotheca (an anglicisation of the Greek word *hoplothêkê*, or armoury) at 20 Lower Brook Street, and later at the Gothic Hall in Opera Colonnade, Pall Mall.

Gwennap had obtained some of his armour from William Bullock, who had an exhibition called Bullock's Museum at the Egyptian Hall, Piccadilly. Between 1815 and 1816 Bullock made £35,000 by showing many Napoleonic relics that he had bought in Paris after Napoleon's fall. The armour Bullock purchased had been looted by Bonaparte's troops from continental armouries on their progress around Europe, but the collection was sold by auction in 1819.[9] Gwennap presented Francis Douce with a print of the Oplotheca in September 1816, and a perpetual ticket of admission.[10] The catalogue for the exhibition was written by Gwennap and Dr. Meyrick.

The public could also see armour in the grand historical and classical paintings of the period, but failing any taste for culture and the money to view it, there were always the historical plays and entertainments performed at the many London theatres. That, of course, was one great problem that Samuel set out to address. The theatre producers of the early nineteenth century had no idea of historical correctness, and would clothe their actors as their fancy or the limitations of their wardrobe dictated. It's ironic that many theatre productions now follow their example, but in order to make some artistic point.

The same attitude was true of artists—their primary consideration was a well-composed picture. Planché relates how Sir David Wilkie deliberately ignored his advice in his work *Knox preaching to his Congregation*, choosing to depict men in armour of the time of the Civil War so that they could be concealed but their faces still be seen.[11] Wilkie did this in full knowledge of the anachronism, but he was an exception. Planché also relates how the publication of Samuel's book on armour led Abraham Cooper, whose speciality was painting horses, to consult Samuel when he was painting *The Battle of Bosworth Field*. This shows Richard III on his horse *White Surrey* near the end of the day. Samuel explained that Richard's horse would have been covered with housings of silk, embroidered with the arms of France and England. "'Oh!" exclaimed Cooper in consternation, "that will never do! My principal object is to paint *White Surrey*, and if he is to be muffled up in that manner there will be nothing to be seen of him but his hoofs'". Fortunately Samuel suggested that if the painting depicted the last stages of the battle the housings would be almost in tatters, and they would show as much of the horse as necessary. In fact, it made for a much more dramatic composition.

Before Samuel started on his systematic study of the chronological development of arms and armour, there had been few published works on the subject, although there had been illustrations in books on antiquities and costume. Samuel comments on an earlier work in the preface of his book 'there is a treatise on antient Armour by Captain Grose, occupying half a volume of his work *Military Antiquities*, and founded on Père Daniel's *Milice Francoise*. These are referred to as textbooks, because they are the only works of the kind extant. Much praise is due to Captain Grose for this collection, … but here is no critical arrangement, no correct illustration to be found throughout the work. A mass of crude materials is presented to the reader, accompanied with incorrect and absurd traditions, and with some representations of military usages which could only be taken from the imagination of the author'. He does admit that Grose's illustrations were correct in their delineation of the arms and armour.

The display of the armour in the Tower of London, which should have been free of the solecisms perpetrated in the name of art, was just as inaccurate. The Tower was already a great tourist attraction in the eighteenth and early nineteenth centuries, the visitors keen to see the Crown Jewels, the menagerie and the Line of Kings. This was a series of effigies of English monarchs from the time of William the Conqueror, supposedly clad in their own armour, and mounted on wooden horses.[12] The Tower had functioned as an armoury for many years, first recorded impressions starting in the late sixteenth century. There is an inventory of 1660 which mentions that sets of armour are mounted 'on horse statues', which had probably come from the palace of Greenwich a few years earlier. As each king died it became the tradition to have a new horse carved, and a wooden effigy of the king made to carry the armour. The horses and effigies were carved by well-known sculptors such as Gibbons and Nost.

Unfortunately by Samuel's time the horses were held up by props of wood on each side, and the dummies looked like 'a quantity of dislocated limbs'.[13] The worst sin to Samuel was not the presentation, but the fact that the armour was anachronistic—for example, William the Conqueror was dressed in a late sixteenth-century Greenwich armour. Any particular suit was not necessarily complete, pieces which may have been of different date being added to make a whole. Another room in the Tower was called the Spanish Armoury, as many of the weapons it contained were supposed to have been captured as part of the rout of the Armada. Although it is possible that some of the weapons did find their way into the Tower as the result of the capture of Spanish ships, others could have been part of the booty from the looting of Cadiz, part of which had been appropriated by Sir Gelly Meyrick. Some of the exhibits were not Spanish at all, but a hot-potch of objects around which the Yeomen Warders had woven fanciful stories which helped them to earn tips from visitors.

This was the situation which Samuel sought to correct by the publication of his first book on arms and armour: *A Critical Inquiry into Antient Armour as it existed in Europe but particularly in England from the Norman Conquest to the reign of King Charles II.* There was never any question but that the work must be fully illustrated. Having been associated with Charles Hamilton Smith on the well-received *Costume*, it would have seemed to Samuel that a coloured book would sell very well. The composition of the work must have occupied the period between the appearance of the *Costume* in 1815, and his first mention of it in a letter to Douce dated October 1820: 'I have written, and parted with, to a bookseller who is to be at all the expence and get all the profits a work on antient armour from the conquest to the time of Charles 2d. and I have completed as far as Charles 1st. As I want only subjects for a plate of Oliver Cromwell's period do you think you can assist with some curious figures in point of

Fig. 34 The frontispiece of *Critical Inquiry into Antient Armour*

armour? You will guess by this that the work is arranged in the reigns of the English monarchs'.[14]

He goes into more detail about the book in the preface to one of his later works when he says that it 'originated from a wish expressed on the part of an eminent dealer in curiosities and objects of virtu to have a few drawings with explanatory notices of Ancient Armour, in return for two or three specimens which he possessed. The materials grew to an unexpected size, but as portions of the manuscript were delivered to him from time to time, I had hoped the whole would have been returned to me for reperusal, previous before being sent to press. The owner, however, had committed himself, sold one half of his copy-right, and distributed parts of the remainder among solicitors as securities for his debts. Three years elapsed ere I saw it again.'[15]

Relations between Samuel and his first publisher, called Forster, were very strained as witness Samuel's complaint to Douce that 'the etchings are such vile imitations, or rather departures from my drawings as to compel me to have my name erased from each plate. ... You may form an idea of the style of the plates when I tell you that the side eye of a horse is represented by the full eye of a man!!! and [a ma]n's fingers resemble a plate of sausages!'.[16] He continued 'for writing the work, lending 80 drawings (that have been *miser'ly* etched) and correcting the proofs I have received armour to the amount of about £150, and am to have six copies ...'. It seems from the same letter that Samuel had offered the book to the Colnaghis in 1819, who also failed to

Plate 1 Portrait of Sir Samuel by H.P. Briggs, 1826,
by kind permission of Torre Abbey Historic House & Gallery, Torquay & the Meyrick family

Plate 2 New Peterborough House, © Guildhall Library, Corporation of London

Plate 3 Fulham Volunteer, from Rowlandson's *Loyal Volunteers of London & Environs*, 1798, by kind permission of the President and Fellows of Trinity College, Oxford

Plate 4 Doctor of Laws, Oxford, from W.H. Pyne, *Costume of Britain*, 1808

Plate 5 Courtroom of Doctors' Commons showing the advocates in session, 1808,
© Guildhall Library, Corporation of London

Plate 6 British fishing and husbandry, Pl. V from Meyrick & Smith's *The Costume of the Original Inhabitants of the British Islands and the adjacent coasts of the Baltic ... from the Earliest Periods to the Sixth Century*

Plate 7 Boadicea, Queen of the Iceni ,Pl. XII from Meyrick & Smith's
The Costume of the Original Inhabitants of the British Islands and the adjacent coasts of the Baltic …
from the Earliest Periods to the Sixth Century

Plate 8 Watercolour of a soldier on horseback by Charles Hamilton Smith,
© Victoria & Albert Museum (CT89871 D.375 - 1890)

Plate 9 Bullock's Museum, typical of the eclectic private collections of the time,
© Guildhall Library, Corporation of London

Plate 10 Portrait of William Henry Meyrick, Samuel's half cousin,
by kind permission of Torre Abbey Historic House & Gallery, Torquay & the Meyrick family

Plate 11 Portrait of Abraham Kirkmann, one of Samuel's closest friends,
by kind permission of Christopher Parker of Browsholme Hall

Plate 12 Sir Theobald de Verdun, unpublished plate for *Critical Inquiry*,
© Victoria & Albert Museum (CT89868 8964.K)

capitalize on three later bankruptcies of the various publishers to acquire the work. In the prospectus Samuel sent to Douce subscribers were invited at the price of £18— about £1,000 today. The work was to be published in three volumes imperial quarto, with nine hundred pages of letter press, and was dedicated by permission to 'His Most Excellent Majesty'. There would be seventy 'appropriate' coloured plates and emblazoned drawings, ten 'outlines' and twenty-four coloured initial letters. Subscriptions would close on the appearance of the work in April 1822. In the event, another two years were to elapse before publication.

Some intimation of the difficulties in bringing the book to market can be glimpsed from a letter Samuel wrote to the *Gentleman's Magazine* in January, 1823:

> In my letter relative to the remarks made by your Reviewer on some papers of mine in the *Archaeologia*, which you were so obliging as to insert in the last volume p309, I mentioned that a work on Armour was forthcoming, with 80 plates and 27 vignettes, which I hoped would give him more satisfaction than they did me. This expression I am aware might convey to the mind of the reader, that I was dissatisfied with the manner in which the aquatinted etchings had been done, and I candidly own that that was the case. Since then the work has changed owners, and the present proprietor, at a considerable loss and great expence, cancelled all the objectionable plates, and replaced them by others done by a very superior artist. You will oblige me by the insertion of this, as I think such an avowal from me due to the generous sacrifice Mr. Jennings has thus made to my feelings. I have now, therefore, no hesitation in saying, that the work will be brought out in an accurate and splendid style, and such as I hope will induce the public to remunerate the publisher for this laudable determination.[17]

Although the 'most objectionable' plates had been replaced, Samuel was still not really happy with the illustrations. Fortunately some of his original water colours for the book survive, as well as drawings that were not included in the published version.[18] In 1826 he gave his mother's own copy of the *Critical Inquiry into Antient Armour* to Pettigrew to give to the Duke of Sussex, begging Pettigrew not to induce the duke to look at the 'vile gingerbread engravings'.[19] A measure of sympathy must lie with the final publisher, Robert Jennings, for the drawings loaned by Samuel had to be etched, printed and then coloured and gilded, a considerable preliminary investment. The letters to Douce give the lie to a theory[20] that the illustrations were in fact provided by Charles Hamilton Smith, but Samuel did acknowledge the loan of Smith's memoranda and drawings in the preface. Only a few of the mounted figures show Smith's characteristic liveliness, others are often wooden and awkward, whilst just a handful of the later illustrations show armour from the Meyrick collection. In spite of Samuel's fulminations against the quality of the etching, the same plates seem to have been used again in the second edition of 1842.

The work occupies three large volumes, with a considerable preface and introduction and a large glossary. Samuel also adds details of the display in the Tower of London and some notes on famous collections outside the country. Despite the restriction in the title to European armour after the Norman conquest, the introduction goes into some details on the history of the subject outside Europe, and there are line illustrations of Roman and Asiatic armour. The main body of the work being organised by the reigns of different monarchs, it was not always easy for him to marry this with the developments in styles of armour which did not necessarily align themselves accordingly. It is a work of its time—after the analysis of many objects including living things by stylistic classification, but before the wholesale adoption of Darwinism. Samuel does occasionally relate adaptation of armour to external stimuli, as when breastplates were thickened to protect against firearms, and he points out the influence of contemporary clothing on armour. In general, the *Critical Inquiry* is a chronicle of arms and armour used through the ages, but considerably enlivened by extracts from contemporary documents and stories of warfare.

The heavy work of correcting the proofs occupied Samuel through 1821 and into 1822. It was now that his friendship with Douce proved invaluable, for even though Douce's health was poor he was dragged willy-nilly into the process. In spite of Douce's considerable input, Samuel did not present him with a copy of the work, as the six free copies were already spoken for and Samuel probably considered Douce could well afford to buy himself a copy. Douce's help is acknowledged very handsomely, however. Eventually the work appeared and to almost universal acclaim. One of the most favourable reviews was from Thomas Fosbroke, later to be Samuel's neighbour across the Wye in Goodrich.[21]

Some of Samuel's original artwork for another publication still exists in the Victoria & Albert Museum.[22] There are a number of drawings in various states of preparation from pencil sketch through to fully coloured painting, which seem to have been prepared to illustrate the monarchs of each reign. Even Mary and Elizabeth are accommodated by having their attendants clad in armour. The paper used for the *Critical Inquiry* watercolours is quite different from that used for these drawings, and neither can be dated by watermarks. The pencil sketch of Henry VI in this 'monarchs' set is virtually identical with that realised in full colour in the *Critical Inquiry*. Without documentary proof it is not possible to say which came first.

Well before the *Critical Inquiry* was published, the Meyrick collection of armour was beginning to attract attention. Llewellyn had a visitors' book dated 1820 which survived in the library of Goodrich Court until it was sold in 1946—it was described as containing signatures of George Cruikshank and George IV.[23] Cruikshank may well have gone to see the collection as he was still a young man while it was in London, and he did engrave a picture of the King's Champion in armour in 1821. A visit from George IV would surely have been recorded in Samuel's letters.

One of the most famous people to see the collection was Sir Walter Scott, but although Samuel was pleased to call Sir Walter his friend, perhaps it should be termed a mutually beneficial acquaintanceship. Having met briefly[24] in London in March 1821, their interest in armour led to Scott visiting the Meyrick collection before he returned shortly afterwards to Scotland.[25] Having seen the quality of the material, Scott was happy to trust Samuel's judgement, and asked him to start acquiring arms and armour at the London sale rooms. Probably Samuel was unaware of Scott's ever-present financial difficulties, but Scott had noted the prices he was prepared to pay at the Gwennap sale in April 1821. As most of the items went for twice his marked price Scott was thwarted, but at least he was able to convert an old pike he'd bought into a lance by copying one in the Meyrick collection.[26]

By hard bargaining Samuel eventually managed on Scott's behalf to reduce the price of a couple of two-handed swords from 10 guineas each to £12 10s., one with a plain and one with an 'undulated' blade.[27] In gratitude Scott gave him an item for his collection,[28] unnamed, but possibly some seventeenth century thumb-screws, as Samuel had asked for information about these in his previous letter.[29] However, at the end of 1821 Samuel's enthusiasm overstepped the mark, and Scott was obviously not pleased that he had spent £18 on a very large two-handed sword, an executioner's sword and two maces, even though they were good value.[30] Grudgingly sending a

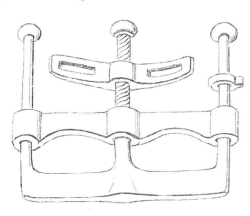

Fig. 35   Thumbkin given to Samuel by Sir Walter Scott

cheque, Scott at least bought a shield recommended by Samuel, and they were all packed up and sent up to Scotland by steamer, by far the easiest method of delivery.[31]

Scott had bought a farm, called Carley Hole, on the banks of the Tweed in 1811, which he renamed Abbotsford, and proceeded to upgrade it into a fine Gothic residence. This happened in two phases, in 1817 and 1822, when the remains of the old farmhouse were demolished. Edward Blore had supplied Scott with plans for the changes to the original house in 1816, but in the event William Atkinson's designs were used instead. The second stage of building in 1822 went on for most of the year, and it was while this major work was in progress that Samuel and Llewellyn made a trip to Scotland during the summer months. They certainly visited Scott at his house in Edinburgh, 39 Castle Street, and thanked him for his hospitality on their return to London.[32] Scott probably wished the Meyricks had chosen another time to visit him, as he had already had to take time out from his supervision at Abbotsford to take charge of the arrangements for the royal visit in late August. He donated an Andrea Ferrara sword to the Meyrick armoury.[33] The quality of the Meyrick collection was broadcast to the wider world when Sir Walter mentioned it in *Peveril of the Peak*, which was written shortly after he visited Cadogan Place. Apropos silk armour, which was supposed to be proof against any steel he says that 'neither the horse-armoury in the Tower, nor Gwennap's Gothic Hall, no, nor Dr. Meyrick's invaluable collection of ancient arms, has preserved any specimen'. It seems therefore unkind (if true) of Samuel to write openly to a fellow antiquarian: 'Sir Walter is by no means a critical antiquary and therefore the danger of reading his works. Though I know him intimately I have never read any but his poems'.[34]

After this short period of exchanges, there are no more letters to Scott preserved until one dated December 1824 which makes it clear that Samuel hasn't written for months.[35] Scott had urged him to write a catalogue raisonnée of the armour collection in 1821, a suggestion which was not to come to fruition until the publication of his second (and last) major work on armour, *Engraved Illustrations of Antient Arms and Armour*, in 1830. As no visitors' books were kept for Abbotsford until 1832, one cannot be certain that Samuel never went there, but he never mentions it. His name does not appear in the subscription to the Abbotsford preservation fund, started after Scott's death in 1832, but by this time he was hard put to find money for Goodrich Court itself.

7   A Search for Home

One consequence of the death of Mary Meyrick in 1818 was that Samuel could devote his hours away from Doctors' Commons to his researches, as Llewellyn was away at Oxford during term-time. When the summer vacation came around he was perfectly prepared to put his books aside and set out with his son on a jaunt. Their trip to Scotland in 1822 has already been mentioned, and fortunately the journals of their travels have survived for 1821[1] and 1823.

In 1821 Samuel and Llewellyn harnessed the mare to their gig, and set out from Upper Cadogan Place on Saturday, 14 July. Llewellyn's journal is rather impressive for a boy barely seventeen, as he records in some detail the monuments and architectural details in the churches they visited. The faithful mare bore them for twelve days through the Midlands to Shrewsbury. Exploring the church at Coleshill near Birmingham, Samuel discovered a helmet which he was at pains to bring to the notice of Edward Blore on his return.[2] This must have been the 'Coleshill helm' which re-surfaced in 1932 when it was exhibited at the Society of Antiquaries.[3]

On their way to Shrewsbury they explored the caves and cascades at Hawkestone Park, a woodland fantasy garden created in the previous century, and kept their entrance tickets as a souvenir.[4] Llewellyn must have enjoyed their excursion from Chester to Liverpool, hitching a ride on a straw boat crossing the Mersey, and passing the prison hulks on the way. The mare, having been left in Chester to recover, then trotted on through North Wales, via Wrexham, Ruabon, Corwen and along the Conwy vale to Llanwrst. Samuel was to make a valuable contact on this leg of his journey, when he met with the Rev. George Cunliffe, vicar of Wrexham. Rev. Cunliffe's father was Sir Foster Cunliffe of Acton Park near Wrexham, the first president of the Royal British Bowmen, an upper-class archery society that had been revived at the time of Samuel's visit. Rev. Cunliffe gave Samuel an entrée to an entirely new circle of Welsh scholars because he was an acquaintance of Angharad Lloyd (Llwyd), a rare female in the antiquarian world, and from his introduction grew a correspondence which lasted many fruitful years.

Miss Llwyd was the daughter of John Lloyd, the scholarly rector of Caerwys in Flintshire, North Wales.[5] He taught her Welsh and Latin, and had many literary friends who mourned his death in 1793, when she was only thirteen. Undaunted, and unhampered by a husband, the rest of her life was dedicated to historical research. Her many correspondents were unfortunate if they did not meet her and fall under the spell of her wicked sense of humour.[6] She wrote prize-winning essays on Welsh historical subjects, edited and published a new edition of *The History of the Gwydir Family* in 1827, but her chief work was *The History of the Island of Mona* published in 1833.

Fig. 36 The Coleshill helm

All her other publishing plans came to nought, but her extensive collections are now held in the National Library of Wales.

Samuel's letters to her start in 1821, and their correspondence carries on until the 1840s.[7] She must have been a sympathetic listener, because Samuel tells her of his search for a suitable Welsh home and his struggle to prove his descent from Sir Gelly Meyrick. Unfortunately the copious notes she sent him have been lost. His only criticism was that 'she is one of those who by copying prevents knowledge being lost but I don't think she uses that discrimination that has a tendency to increase it'.[8] In fact, it's from a letter to Angharad Llwyd that we first learn of Samuel's true desires that 'though not born in the principality I feel that it is Welsh blood that flows in my veins, and continually urges me to eat, drink, live and speak within the precincts of my darling Cymry'.[9]

The highlight of the trip in 1821 must have been the great castles of Conwy and Caernarfon, brooding over their estuaries. Samuel's unpublished historic play, *Llewellyn*, is based on the life of Llewellyn ap Gruffydd, the last true-born Prince of Wales, after whose death Edward I built the menacing chain of castles around North

Wales. Edward II, the first English Prince of Wales, was born and proclaimed at Caernarfon. If Llewellyn Meyrick was indeed named after Llewellyn ap Gruffydd, it must have been an emotional moment when at last they stood on the walls of Caernarfon Castle. It's not too fanciful to see this as the confirmation of the idea of a castle as the appropriate setting for the Meyrick armour collection.

Hopefully the travellers managed to glimpse the summit of Snowdon through the driving rain as they passed by on the way to Beddgelert. Now was the time, had Samuel so wished, to push south and introduce Llewellyn to his mother's ancestral home near Aberystwyth. Instead they started for home early on 13 August, passing through Bishop's Castle, Montgomery and Kidderminster. On the 18th they visited Ragley Hall in Hertford, and on the morning of the 21st they departed on their separate ways from Banbury, Llewellyn to return home via Stowe and Samuel to Oxford to vote in the forthcoming parliamentary election for the M.P. for the university. Samuel's vote for Sir John Nicholl, one of the most respected civil lawyers, was not enough to secure him the seat against the 'bibliomaniac' Richard Heber.[10]

By April 1822 embryonic plans had firmed up enough for Samuel to tell Miss Llwyd that 'if in another year's time we can get Llanstefan Castle … that ruin shall again receive its roofs, and become one of the Cambrian attractions. If foiled in this, then I must look for another ancient fortress and if still unsuccessful for some residence in a well-wooded part of Wales'.[11] He says that he does not wish to live in 'an old castle, being not so romantic as that', which in view of his earlier remarks probably means that he does not wish to *live* in medieval style—a fact not always appreciated by later commentators. It was his clear intention to set up the armour collection to be an attraction to the district. Already he was dreaming of the time he could give up the drudgery of being a lawyer and have the 'delightful luxury' of being an inhabitant of Wales.[12] It was to be six long years before the foundation of his dream house was laid.

By the autumn of 1822 Llanstefan Castle had fallen through, and Llewellyn's— or Samuel's—fancy had lighted upon Carew Castle, near Tenby,[13] though as Mr. Carew seemed recalcitrant Lamphey Court nearby was another possibility. The Meyricks' requirements were not great—enough land for four pleasure horses and three cows, a vegetable garden, opportunities for Llewellyn to hunt and shoot, and the sea nearby.[14] The expedition to North Wales had shown him the difficulties of travel in that remote and hilly country. Cardiganshire, so desirably inaccessible when he was eloping, now seemed inconveniently far from civilisation. Expediency triumphed over a desire for a seaside location in Wales—and Herefordshire became his target. As he said,

Fig. 37   Llewellyn's drawing of Carew Castle (© The Board of the Trustees of the Armouries)

'Herefordshire and Sussex are now the most distressed counties in England, being purely agricultural, and estates are selling at a third of their war prices'.[15] Samuel was able to rationalise his decision to live in Herefordshire with the fact that parts of the county were still Welshries at the time of the Norman conquest. Welsh interpreters were on hand for Hereford Assizes, and the western part of the county still had numerous Welsh speakers in the 1800s.[16] The Welshry of Archenfield was an ancient land division which included Goodrich and its impressive castle.

During the Easter vacation of 1823 Samuel and Llewellyn boarded the coach for Herefordshire. Within ten days Samuel was in London again, having travelled back overnight. 'We have seen the very thing to suit us, so exactly that it seems to have been made on purpose. This is Goodrich Castle [near Ross] on the Wye'.[17] There was the slight drawback that the castle was not up for sale, being owned by the Griffin family, lords of the manor of Goodrich. Neither indeed was the Flanesford Priory farm adjoining the castle, which would make a neat estate of the whole; the priory ruins could only add to the antiquarian attraction and Samuel set an attorney to negotiate on his behalf.

Ross-on-Wye was already well-known as a starting point of the Wye Tour, a favourite resort of lovers of the picturesque. The view across the river meadows to the Royal Hotel and St. Mary's church is still beautiful, even if it is best obtained from a bland new bridge carrying the A40 across the Wye. The old bridge nearby was built in 1600, to replace the treacherous crossing still guarded by Wilton Castle. The Wye Tour came into being as the result of a well-connected rector of Ross, John Egerton. A hospitable man, his guests were treated to trips down the river, and by 1760 boats were

Fig. 38   Wilton Bridge, by Waudby

being hired out for this purpose.[18] Where tourists came, guide books were not far behind, and by 1770 William Gilpin and Thomas Grey had made the Tour and published their observations. Below Ross, the Wye at first meanders through rolling farmland and orchards. Within a few miles the hills begin to close in, until at Pencraig the first headland towers above the river. It's not easy today to recreate the awesome sensations the tourists felt as they approached Goodrich. Only from river level do the rocky crags loom menacingly above, but nowadays they are concealed by vegetation. The scene was set for the first picturesque view of the Wye Tour—Goodrich Castle.

The castle dominates the ancient river crossing below, seeming to grow from the very rock from which it was made. Two roughly contemporary views of the castle show it from picturesque and prosaic viewpoints. The picturesque Bonnor exaggerates the wildness and elevation—the heights of the Forest of Dean loom menacingly ahead and the small ferry house lies tucked under the trees. By contrast, the prosaic Ireland is more accurate, and also shows the ancient chain ferry in operation.[19] A more reliable draughtsman was Joshua Cristall, who fell in love with Goodrich when he sketched the castle in 1803[20] in the company of Cornelius Varley.[21] This was twenty years before Cristall came to live there. Another pair of visitors in 1803 were Joseph Farington and

John Hoppner. All lovers of the picturesque were agreed that the battered ruins were satisfyingly ivy-clad.

Visitors intent on inspecting the castle could land at Goodrich ferry, or downstream at Flanesford and walk uphill past the old priory buildings used to house farm implements and animals. The castle had been owned by the Griffin family since the manor of Goodrich had been purchased by Admiral Griffin from the Duke of Kent in 1755. It had come into the duke's family by marriage having descended from the Talbots, Earls of Shrewsbury, but it was largely uninhabited by the time of the Civil War. After a Royalist garrison was besieged and finally defeated in 1645 the castle was slighted.

From the outset, it was Samuel's intention that the armour collection should form an additional attraction to the Wye Tour, indeed at Goodrich it would be the 'first object' in the tour.[22] The location had a number of advantages, apart from the obvious scenic attraction: it was within an overnight coach journey of London, allowing friends and students of armour easy access, and in contrast to the remote Pembrokeshire locations, hundreds of tourists (of the better class) visited the area every year.

Having visited Goodrich Castle the tourists had various options. They could re-embark at Flanesford, and make the seven mile trip by river to the foot of Symond's Yat. This had the advantage of passing under Coldwell Rocks and the Yat Rock, great

Fig. 39 Flanesford Priory, by Bonnor

92

overhanging slabs of limestone which looked to crash down on the onlookers at any moment. A less time-consuming option was to walk a bare mile to the ferry across the Wye at Huntsham. Perhaps they would visit St. Giles' church in Goodrich to see the tomb of Thomas Swift, grandfather of Jonathan Swift. The steep climb to the top of the Yat Rock was rewarded by a panorama over the great flank of Coppet Hill towards Goodrich, still the most popular view of the tour. To the west lay the majestic bulk of the Doward, ravaged by industry since prehistoric times. The full sight-seeing trip to Monmouth took a whole day, and many pushed on afterwards to Chepstow. The lower Wye valley was more industrialised, but this merely intensified the piquant contrast with such icons of the picturesque as Tintern Abbey.

Visitors with limited time could walk from Ross and cross the Wye under Goodrich Castle, then return to their hotel in Ross along the country lanes. There's every reason to suppose that Samuel and Llewellyn did just that. In a letter to Joseph Skelton the engraver written in 1824, Samuel says 'when you visit the castle walk through Ross church-yard not forgetting to enter a field on your right where you will have what is called "the view from Ross church-yard". In the church are some fine monuments. Then walk on to the ferry and while waiting for the boat recollect that you stand on the spot where Henry 4th first received intelligence of the birth of his renowned son'.[23]

Fig. 40   Coldwell rocks with gondolas

Admiral Griffin's son George had left a widow and three daughters, one of whom ultimately inherited the manor and castle of Goodrich. The Griffins employed a custodian who lived at the gate to the castle lane, and would show visitors around the ruins for a few pence. It's difficult to imagine the Goodrich Castle of 1823 in the sanitised ruin of today. Self-seeded trees grew in the piles of rubble choking the roofless buildings. The well had been superseded by a lead conduit leading from springs on the next headland, which was easily cut during the Civil War siege. Whatever the purists may say, the vision of a Goodrich Castle restored to its former glory has certain attractions. This dream no doubt kept Samuel's hopes alive during the long and ultimately fruitless negotiations.

Sir Walter Scott obviously had certain anxieties should the purchase go ahead, but he was reassured: '… you need not dread demolition, for unless I could make it fit to live in without the slightest alteration, even cutting an additional window, I would forbear and build my residence within view. If therefore I succeed in making such a purchase it will be with perfectly antiquarian motives'.[24] Given the dilapidated state of the castle, this promise was not unduly restrictive, but there is every reason to suppose that the fanciful excesses of the subsequent Goodrich Court would have been curbed. There is a certain irony in the fact that had Samuel fulfilled his ambition, his vision of the medieval castle would still exist today.

It seems that there was a profitable side-line excavating in the rubble around the castle and selling what was found to local antiquarians or to the tourists.[25] Samuel was given 'the seal of Walter Marshal who died in the castle in 1245'[26] by his attorney Hooper[27] which had been found on the barbican by a boy in 1803. Abraham Kirkmann presented him with the 'font of the chapel' in the castle,[28] which he must have acquired on his sketching trip there in 1823 or 1824. The font is not mentioned in early descriptions of the castle, and it may have been a piscina, as the building accounts for the Court do mention a stonemason who carved a font.

The negotiations for the purchase of Goodrich Castle were not allowed to vary the plans Samuel had made for the summer of 1823. He had told the Rev. Maurice in 1815 that he intended that Llewellyn should spend a year studying civil law at Göttingen,[29] and not even Mary's death had changed his plans for his son. He wrote to Angharad Llwyd in 1822 that 'next summer, as I mentioned, our journey will be to Germany, through Brussels to Nuremburg, Vienna, Dresden, Berlin and Göttingen, where leaving my son I shall return by the low countries'.[30] One of the motives behind the trip must surely have been to admire the many armouries which were still in place in their ancestral castles, and perhaps get some ideas about how their own collection should be laid out.

Both Samuel and Llewellyn kept journals of their German expedition, though Llewellyn's peters out towards the end.[31] This was the last major expedition that they would make in each other's company and they certainly needed stamina—they stayed more than a single night in few places. The itinerary for their tour may have been suggested by Thomas Dibdin's *A Bibliographical Antiquarian and Picturesque Tour in France and Germany.* This had been first published in 1818, and although Samuel had the 1829 edition in his library, he had already quoted from an earlier version in the *Critical Inquiry into Antient Armour.* He probably used Douce's copy of the 1821 edition, which is now in the Bodleian library.

Fig. 41   Drawing from Samuel's journal of a curtain in their hotel at Bruges

The journals are amusing mixtures of the traditional comments by English travellers abroad, along with notes on the antiquities seen enlivened with little sketches, most notably by Samuel. These were not necessarily of antiquarian interest: horse harness, women's hair styles and dresses and ways of arranging curtains were all included. Having landed at Ostend on 3 July, they stayed at the English hotel kept by Nicholson before driving on to Bruges—'a very clean town'—where they visited the cathedral and a picture gallery—Ghent and Brussels. The identical sketches of an ancient cannon at Ghent conjures up a picture of them sitting side by side with their notebooks and pencils. Llewellyn's version is rather more accomplished, and it may have been this which was used to illustrate Thomas Fosbroke's *Encyclopaedia of Antiquities.*[32] The route must have been chosen with the object of making a visit to the battlefield

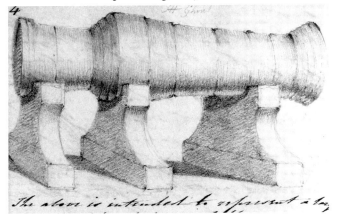

Fig. 42   Drawing from Llewellyn's journal of a cannon at Ghent

Fig. 43 Drawing from Samuel's journal of a gateway at Frankfurt

of Waterloo. Samuel remarked that the situation of Liège greatly resembled that of Rouen. From Liège they passed on to Aachen, where Samuel bought some thirteenth-century enamelled candlesticks,[33] Cologne, Bonn and Coblenz.

Near Ingleheim they stayed at the village of St. Goar which was 'most enchantingly situated on the edge of the river, but the hotel is very uncomfortable from the indifference of the master and his people'. From Mayence they came to Frankfurt, and spent some time perambulating the city walls and walking along the serpentine paths in the shrubbery. They had a whole day at Nuremburg, where Samuel saw a tapestry which he later drew, probably from a book, coloured and gave to Douce.[34] He also made a drawing there of a relief depicting St. George killing the dragon, printed in the *Gentleman's Magazine* in October 1823. After Regensburg they took a boat down the Danube for Vienna. This was a chance to rest and enjoy the beauty of the river, and they stopped at the towns of Passau and Linz on the way.

The visit to Vienna was one of the highlights of the tour, and they stayed for two complete days. The little Belvedere palace in Vienna held a collection of armour which had previously been in the castle of Ambras near Innsbruch. Samuel had been longing to see it ever since he had seen Douce's copy of *Armamentarium Heroicum Ambrosianum*. This book dated from 1601, and was a description of the armour displayed at Ambras which had been set up some half a century before. It was fully illustrated, and showed that each suit of armour was assigned to some historic personage. Of course, Samuel had already made a list of these suits with their correct attribution.[35]

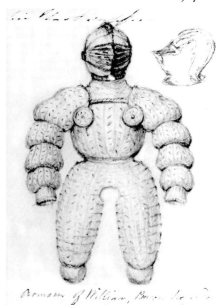

Fig. 44 Drawing from Llewellyn's journal of armour at the little Belvedere palace in Vienna

This did not dampen his enthusiasm to see them in Vienna, and he was hoping for great things after reading Dibdin's account of the little Belvedere. 'The sides of the first room were quite embossed with suspended shields, cuirasses and breast-plates. The floor was almost filled by champions on horseback, yet poizing the spear, or holding it in the rest; yet almost shaking their angry plumes, and pricking the fiery sides of their coursers. There rode Maximilian, and there halted Charles his son. Different suits of armour belonging to the same character are studiously shown you by the guide: some of these are the foot, and some the horse armour, some were worn in fight, yet giving evidence of the mark of the bullet and battle axe; others were the holiday suits of armour, with which the knights marched in procession, or tilted at the tournament'.[36] He was rather less happy when he had actually seen the display: 'this florid account is calculated to produce disappointment, my own observations allow me to write in a more matter-of-fact manner'.[37]

Samuel and Llewellyn were fortunate enough to be shown the original drawings by Hans Burgmeyer of the Triumph of Maximilian I, by Mr. Lechner at the Library of Vienna in Josef Platz. Their opinion on Vienna itself was not so favourable—the streets were narrow and the shops paltry, the poor lived in dirt and slavery, the English were imposed on as fair game and the hotelier had tried to detain them at the Hotel de Londres. Samuel was impressed that when they bought milk the woman seller and her daughter kissed his hand 'as was the custom'.

They set off from Vienna on 29 July and reached Prague on 2 August. Although they liked Bohemia there were more

Fig. 45 Maximilian, by Burgmeyer

97

Fig. 46 Drawing from Samuel's journal of the St. George fountain in Prague

animadversions on the general dirtiness and cheating nature of the inhabitants. Samuel found time in Prague to sketch the St. George fountain. They stayed at Toplitz for two nights, and also at Dresden where Samuel was most impressed with 'probably the finest armour collection in the world, if considered as works of art. ... The jousting armour is most splendidly set up [and] the splendour of the horse trappings mostly of the year 1630 is astonishing'.[38] Now they were hurrying along, through Meissen, Wurtzen, Leipzig and Merseburg. They seem to have stayed in Göttingen for one day, and there was no more talk of a legal career for Llewellyn. Perhaps his health was already giving cause for concern—within a year Samuel was telling his friend Kirkmann that Llewellyn would be unable to go grouse-shooting, although he would have liked it above all things because 'the delicate state of his health prevents his undergoing the ... necessary fatigue'.[39] The other reason may be that, having looked around the university at Göttingen and admired the library and buildings, Samuel was not impressed with the life there: 'The practice of smoaking [sic], gaming, drinking and duelling prevalent among the students is a disgrace to the University'. They reached Hanover on 17 August where they saw a few suits of armour at the Arsenal, and Samuel noted an ancient iron cannon from 1635, nearly twenty feet long, which was loaded from the side. Their homeward leg led them through Minden and Münster, until they arrived at Rotterdam where they took ship for England on 27 August 1823. The travellers had not lost the opportunity to make the rounds of the dealers on their travels, for Llewellyn gave Douce a Roman quadrans which he bought in Germany.[40]

On their return to England, they found that the Goodrich Castle business was not going well. The Griffin family seems to have taken a dislike to Samuel, and the feeling was certainly mutual. For somewhat obscure reasons they kept raising his hopes, and then dashing them down. In early 1824 he refers to the sisters as 'the three petticoats', and then tells his friend Kirkmann that he has lost all hope of success 'conveyed to him in a most petulant, ill-bred letter from their mother'.[41] His hopes were raised again in August 1824 when he met an agent of the Griffins and offered them £1,500 for the castle and the lordship of the manor. He warned Joseph Skelton, the engraver, not to divulge his intentions to anybody Skelton might meet on his proposed sketching trip to Goodrich.[42]

The months went by, and he was still hopeful of success when he returned from a visit to the Meyricks of Bush, in Pembrokeshire, in June 1825.[43] He asked Kirkmann to find out whether there was any property for sale contiguous to the castle, as he hoped this might facilitate his purchase of the castle itself, at the same time requesting Kirkmann to keep his identity secret.[44] Eventually, however, it seemed as if the dream of Goodrich receded with every passing month, and in any case the events in the next two years pushed Goodrich to the back of his mind.

Sir Walter Scott had suggested to Samuel that a catalogue of the entire Meyrick collection was needed, illustrated with engravings to show the finer details of the armour. Samuel had a great respect for the work of Joseph Skelton, a talented engraver who lived in Oxford. Skelton had already published *Oxonia Antiqua Restaurata*, a part work which consisted of engravings of old Oxford buildings already demolished, from pictures by many well-known artists. In 1824 he started to issue another part work, *Engraved Illustrations of the Principal Antiquities of Oxfordshire*, from the original drawings by Mackenzie. What makes this interesting is that Samuel's *Oxonia Restaurata or a Chorographical, Historical, Natural, Architectural, Monumental and Heraldic Survey of the County of Oxford* from 1800 had drawings of church windows and other architectural details. It's not surprising that Samuel gave Skelton helpful information about the descriptive and historical notes which accompanied the plates.

Skelton seems to have been a somewhat pessimistic fellow, as he was always depressed at the start of any publishing venture. Samuel went to a considerable degree of trouble to try to find subscribers for the Oxfordshire work, writing a laudatory review which John Nichols published in the *Gentleman's Magazine* in September 1824.[45] He also drafted Skelton's application for membership of the Society of Antiquaries, and was his third sponsor.[46] Their collaboration on the Oxfordshire book led to Samuel's next major publishing venture, for Skelton agreed to engrave and publish a catalogue of the Meyrick collection, using Samuel's drawings of the pieces.

The project was already far advanced by January 1826, when Samuel sent a prospectus of the work to Douce, asking that he should let it lie on his table—so that his visitors would see it.[47] The work was called *Engraved Specimens of Ancient Arms and Armour from the justly admired Collection of Llewellyn Meyrick Esq. LL. B. and F.S.A.*[48] Only later was the title changed with the addition of *at Goodrich Court*. It was to be issued in twenty-five parts, costing 9s. 6d. each or about £20 today. Each part would have six plates, and would appear as nearly as possible every two months. In spite of the fact that this seems not quite such good value as the *Critical Inquiry* which was only twice the price, there were already seventy-four subscribers. These included the king, the King of Bavaria and the Duke of Sussex, as well as Frances Martin and James Planché, there were the artists James Ward and Richard Westmacott, Thomas Willement the stained glass artist, Robinson the architect, Porrett and Singleton from the Tower of London and Sir Richard Colt Hoare.

Skelton's pessimism extended to this book as well, and it was useless for Samuel to point out that prospective purchasers had to see some of the issues before they would readily put their name down for more. As Samuel told Douce, three hundred and eighty people had bought Jennings' expensive book—the *Critical Inquiry*—and five hundred people had visited the armoury itself.[49] He had to resort again to John Nichols at the *Gentleman's Magazine*, asking him to publish his review of the work, as he could not himself ask for subscribers.[50] Nichols published the letter, which could have been thought in some quarters to be far too blatant a puff for the work.[51] Samuel suggested that the work would complement the *Critical Inquiry*, being much more detailed particularly with regards to arms. He pointed out that on the walls of the upcoming exhibition of art at Somerset House there would be at least six pictures whose artists had used the Meyrick collection. Having suggested the project in the first place, Sir Walter Scott could not have been surprised to get a prospectus as well.[52]

The new work was not written to the same chronological scheme as the *Critical Inquiry*, but organised by different categories of arms and armour. As the first section was about suits, the whole work had already to be sketched out in some detail. The first part to be published consisted of descriptions and illustrations from different sections of the whole work. This was Samuel's plan, no doubt to prevent people from buying just the sections they were interested in. He wrote to Skelton[53] in early January 1826:

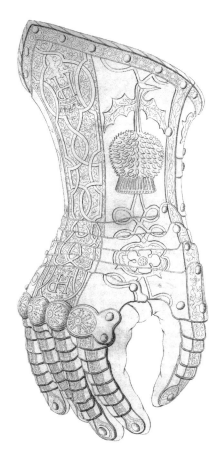

Fig. 47 Gauntlet of Henry, Prince of Wales, Plate LXXVIII in *Engraved Specimens*

Now for the armour. No. 1 will contain:

Plate XXII Fluted armour
Plate XLI Cuirassier's ditto
Plate LXXVIII Gauntlet of Henry Prince of Wales
Plate CII Sword eng[raved] by A Durer
Plate CXXII Various pistols
Plate CXXXIV Turkish armour

From this letter it appears that Joseph's brother William was also involved in the engraving, and the pages were being printed by Schulze in London. In the event the parts do seem to have come out about every two months, as Samuel occasionally mentions them as he sends them to Douce. Douce must have expressed doubt that Samuel was indeed the artist, as in January 1828 Samuel sent him his drawings for part eleven, which was issued that March. Among the later plates to be printed must have been the title page as this is where 'Goodrich Court' is mentioned as the location of the Llewellyn Meyrick collection. Samuel included his drawings of rooms not yet built, complete with his arrangement of the arms and armour therein. When these came to be arranged, they were exactly as he had foreseen. He also included at least one item which he did not own until some time later, a pair of sollerets of the time of Henry VII.[54]

From the illustrations it is apparent that Sir Samuel had added a very important Herefordshire item to the collection. Sir Richard Pembridge's tilting helm had hung over his effigy in Hereford Cathedral since soon after his death in 1375. The tomb, with the helm and Sir Richard's shield hanging above it, had been engraved in Gough's *Sepulchral Monuments* before the major collapse of the cathedral on Easter Monday 1786. The magnificent west tower had fallen, along with part of the nave, and the railings around the tomb and the shield were destroyed.[55] The west front was re-built,

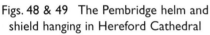

Figs. 48 & 49 The Pembridge helm and
shield hanging in Hereford Cathedral

minus tower, at the end of a shortened nave.[56] The helm from above Sir Richard's effigy
had attracted Samuel's interest, and the Act Book for the meeting of the Chapter at the
cathedral on 25 June 1828 records that: 'Dr. Meyricke having applied to the Chapter
for the old helmet formerly upon the monument of Sir Richard Pembridge Knight his
request was granted'.[57]

The helm is a rare early example with a solid provenance, and it is now in the
National Museum of Scotland, as the result of its acquisition by Sir Noel Paton who
said 'my covetous eye had been fixed on it for many years before the breaking up of the
Goodrich Court collection in 1872 ... and in April that year I bought it from Colonel
Meyrick'.[58] Paton was supposed to have promised to have given the Dean and Chapter
the opportunity of buying back the helm, but this has never come to pass. Paton also
bought the Battle Abbey sword given by Lord Gage to Samuel, and a number of other
Meyrick pieces. Incidentally, it was through Samuel's good relationship with the Dean
and Chapter of the cathedral at this time that Edward Blore was asked, on Samuel's recommendation, to design and estimate costs for new pinnacles for the tower of the cathedral
in November 1830.[59] Blore's design is in the Victoria and Albert Museum.[60]

The last number of the *Engraved Specimens* was issued towards the end of 1830,
when Samuel was foiled in his attempt to get Thomas Fosbroke to review the work by

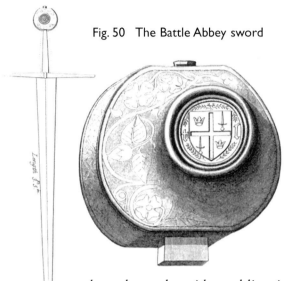

Fig. 50   The Battle Abbey sword

the fact that Samuel's copy was as yet unbound, and Fosbroke was unwilling to answer for its safety.[61] Instead, Samuel wrote his own review, and enclosed it for John Nichols to print in the *Gentleman's Magazine*.

The other project which occupied Samuel at this time was the fulfilment of a long-held ambition. Although by the early 1820s Samuel was already very well known in antiquarian circles, his name was brought to the wider public with his re-arrangement of the armour at the Tower in 1826. The anachronistic displays of this armour have been described earlier, and by November 1821 Samuel had made his sentiments known when he wrote a ten page letter to the Duke of Wellington in the latter's capacity as Master General of the Ordnance.[62] The document was entitled 'Of the present state of the antient Armour in the Tower of London, with proposals for its amendment'. His opening paragraph pulls no punches:

My Lord Duke,
As the present state of the antient armour at the Tower of London has become so notorious as to be the subject of ridicule to the malicious; and as it's [*sic*] defective state is, with disappointment, invariably perceived on recurring to it for originals whenever a revival of any obsolete mode of offence and defence has been under consideration; it is evident that it requires revision. An interval of peace seems best adapted to rescue that fine collection from it's [*sic*] present degraded appearance, to render it useful as authorities for the purposes of the Government, the historian and the artist, and to afford the public an instructive and pleasing gratification in contemplating the skill and ingenuity of remote periods.

After some remarks about the origin of the collection, he goes on to say:

No one, I assume, could object to pay the two preparatory shillings, as four rooms are open to inspection, but a similar sum demanded again after seeing the sight is sorely felt by persons in general, and loudly exclaimed against by foreigners as a national disgrace. It is true that this second demand is not enforced as a legal right, but it is accompanied by so much abuse and such threat in case of demur, that individuals are glad to withdraw themselves at any rate from the terror which such language in such a place occasions.

The obligatory two shillings was quite enough to deter the *hoi polloi*, being about £5 today.

He commented unfavourably on the darkness and small size of the rooms in which the armour was displayed, and recommended throwing the rooms into one. He makes a very modern suggestion with regard to the lighting:

should this project be approved of, the effect would be considerably heightened by leaving an anteroom for the checktaker in a comparative state of darkness, as may be observed in the contrast between the entrance saloon and the adjoining hall of audience at the palace of St. Cloud.

Not only were the rooms dark, there was a

disagreeable and offensive smell arising from the use of oil. Indeed if this with the sand and scouring paper are persevered in, what little they have left of the engraving on the armour will be wholly obliterated.

His suggestion as to the Line of Kings was perhaps too radical, as he proposed that only those kings for which the Tower actually had contemporary armour should be portrayed, starting with Henry VIII, and finishing with Charles II. The female monarchs did not wear armour—paintings that show Elizabeth I at Tilbury so clad are inaccurate. For those reigns Samuel suggested showing contemporary armour such as that of Robert Dudley, Earl of Essex. He also put forward the idea of displaying the armour of Henry, Prince of Wales at various ages as historically curious; Henry was the son of James I who died before his father. The horses and carved faces were given a due appreciation, but the dummies that the armour was displayed on were so anatomically improbable as to give the onlooker 'involuntary sensations of horror' rather than delight. Samuel suggested that if the apartment was altered as he suggested then it should be styled to match the fortress by 'giving the doors and windows a Gothic appearance'. His suggestion of a gothic-style building was eventually taken up when the new Horse Armoury was built against the White Tower, the building work being finished in 1826.

His whole aim in making his suggestions was to give the display an educational value and usefulness for artists and students. To this end he recommended that the Greek and Roman armour in the British Museum should be shown in a glass case at the beginning of the display, and that there should be two versions of a new and correct catalogue printed, one with engraved illustrations and one without.

His final offer could have appealed to a government always careful of its money:

> Now my Lord Duke, should His Majesty be pleased to nominate me Master of his Armouries, I would gladly superintend the amelioration of that at the Tower, that at Windsor Castle, and that at Woolwich, and should my efforts fortunately meet with the approbation of so good a judge in matters of taste as His Majesty, my humble talents should be at his disposal in order to form at Carlton House, or any other palace, an antient & modern and an Asiatic armoury, the materials for which though dispersed are in His Majesty's possession. In making this application, I disclaim either for myself or any other person, place, pension or emolument in any shape not wishing to ask for more than a mere name in order to have an ostensible designation, and if in requesting this, I interfere with the title of anyone else, I would rather some other appellation were bestowed on me.

It only remained for him to go into some detail on his ancestry and his qualifications for the job. As a postscript he gave a list of the monarchs presented in the Line of Kings, and a correct description of the armour each was wearing, which was reprinted with some differences in the *Critical Inquiry*.

Although the authorities at the Tower replied to the letter,[63] and Samuel seemed hopeful that something might come of his approach, nothing happened immediately. The publication of the *Critical Inquiry* in 1824 and the subsequent regard in which Samuel's expertise was held may have had something to do with the Tower authorities' approaches to him in 1825. They were considering buying new armour for their collection, and their Mr. Porrett was sent to look at Samuel's collection on 2 April, and afterwards went to look at the armour for sale with Samuel.[64] This was the first of several occasions when they accepted Samuel's advice on purchases.

Finally, on 23 June 1826 the Office of Ordnance at the Tower wrote to the Duke of Wellington to say that the building in the armoury was available and almost fitted, so would he like them to take up Dr. Meyrick's offer of 'gratuitous assistance'? The duke having no objection, a letter was sent to Samuel to ask him to start his re-arrange-ment, but unfortunately he was away in Herefordshire and did not get the message until 1 August. He immediately assured them of the honour he felt had been conferred on him. The *Gentleman's Magazine* reported that he had been asked to make the arrangement in the new Horse Armoury building and that 'a number of curious and beautiful cannons ... have been for some days past hauled into the room'.[65] Samuel rushed off a letter to the editor, explaining that he had made offers of help in the past, but the suggested alterations to the armoury had been considered too expensive at the time. His only input into the design of the new building had been the colour of the interior, some glass cases and a skylight.[66]

At the end of his work he wrote a report to the Tower authorities.[67] They had impressed on him the need for economy, and in the total of thirty days that he spent on the project he was very often the one up a ladder hammering in nails, or cutting out patterns. He told them somewhat bitterly: 'I trust it will be found that I have not put the Board to one half the expense that has been lavished on what is termed the Spanish Armoury. I would willingly avoid details as too trifling, but to select one amidst many instances, under my directions a wig was made for James the second not for six guineas as demanded, but for less than six shillings'.

Although he managed to revise the Line of Kings into a chronological sequence, the many duplicate items had to be accommodated and so he had to design wall-mounted displays for them. The dummies which had given such horrible sensations were re-built with thighs of wickerwork, and it had been no mean task to arrange twenty-two mounted and ten standing figures in different attitudes. The horses now stood up on their own without being propped up with splints. Given that there were no very early suits to display, he was disappointed that he had not been allowed to install painted blinds for the windows showing armour for each English monarch in turn. By 19 March 1827 the work was finished, and he commended the helpers from the Principal Storekeeper's department: Mr. Joseph Jackson, Brown the journeyman carpenter and De Hayes the under armourer.[68]

Samuel didn't keep it a secret that the re-arrangement hadn't gone quite as he had hoped, for his pride was at stake. In March 1827 he wrote publicly that the work would have been finished earlier but for 'the obstacles that the Clerk of the Works and his partisans have, through a petty jealousy, contrived to throw in my way'.[69] The new building had been erected 'without any knowledge of how effect is produced', though he had managed to substitute some of Willement's painted glass for the 'childish and

Fig. 51   The Line of Kings at the Tower after Samuel's re-arrangement

tasteless *ornaments* of two out of the four semi-circular windows'. Samuel wanted to put it on record that he had nothing to do with what is called the Spanish Armoury—described as a 'cradle of falsehood'—nor with 'the contemptible puppet show of Queen Elizabeth'. His strictures about the Spanish Armoury paid off—it was subsequently re-organised and its name changed to the Asiatic Armoury, just as he had wished.[70]

That the relationship with some of the people at the Tower was soured can be judged from a little incident concerning the painter Benjamin Haydon, who was known for his use of armour in historical paintings. Haydon had happened to mention to Samuel when he was visiting the Meyrick collection that he had some pieces from the Tower. Samuel went to Haydon's studio to look at them, and forthwith told the Tower authorities where they were and that they should be back in the Tower with the suits from which they had been removed. They were returned, but Samuel nursed a grievance for some time that the Tower did not seem properly grateful for his action.[71]

It only remained for Samuel to make a suggestion that may have been unpalatable: 'the tradition in the Tower is that when the mechanic who had put up the guns in the small armoury had finished his undertaking he was honoured by the presence of King William and Queen Mary who dined in the midst of them. I own it would be to me matter of the highest gratification, if the Master General and the Honble. Board would ascertain whether His Majesty [George IV] would please to inspect what I have done before it is open to the public, and I would make a point of being in attendance to give every information required'.[72] He later complained to Pettigrew that although his labours had been appreciated, 'had this been expressed at the time by the gift of a sword, dagger or any trifling piece of armour, or indeed in any way beyond their mere letter of office it would have been gratifying to me'.[73]

When the summons from the Tower had arrived in August 1826, Samuel had been in Herefordshire with Llewellyn, and he had left his son at Malvern.[74] Maybe the waters at Malvern Wells were necessary to improve Llewellyn's already fragile health, because he took a lease on a cottage from Lord Somers of Eastnor Castle. Called Brand Lodge, it still exists and lies near the crest of the busy pass between Herefordshire and Worcestershire where walkers set off for the British Camp iron age fort. In 1827 the house was quiet, and 'on the most beautiful spot to be found on this earth', having the advantage of the wind coming from the Cambrian mountains.[75] The house at Malvern drew some interesting visitors. In October 1827 Francis Martin was there, having returned from conferring the Garter on the Emperor of Russia, and also Thomas Lister Parker with the young artist John Chessell Buckler.[76] Lister Parker and Buckler, who Samuel later dismisses as 'Lister Parker's travelling draughtsman'[77] had been with Sir Richard Harris at Stourhead. Buckler took advantage of the opportunity to paint watercolours of Goodrich Castle, now in Hereford Museum.[78]

Eventually Samuel seems to have abandoned his battle with the ladies of Goodrich Manor. The fields on the next headland upstream had as fair a view as the castle, and it seems that matters were well under way for their acquisition when Llewellyn made several entries in his notebook in the winter of 1827.[79] Having sketched the prospective site from the opposite side of the Wye, he also mapped the fields and made a rough plan of the area the building would occupy, noting from where he had sketched a view of Goodrich Castle. At this time his name for the building was Archenfield Court. In March 1828, the news became public when Samuel wrote to Douce that he had bought the land adjoining Goodrich Castle. Ever optimistic, he would 'build instantly a dwelling in the style of Edward 2nd under the superintendence of the first Gothic architect of the age, my friend Edwd Blore'.[80] He

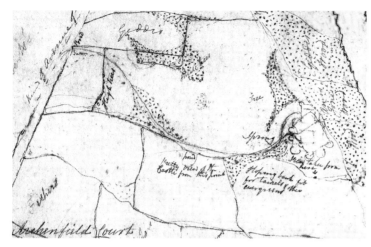

Fig. 52   Site of Goodrich Court drawn by Llewellyn in 1827
(© The Board of the Trustees of the Armouries)

told Douce that he had since decided to call his castle Goodrich Court.

Within two months of announcing his purchase to Douce, the following item appeared in the May issue of the *Gentleman's Magazine*. 'We are happy to announce that the armour at Windsor, previous to its arrangement in the King's and Queen's guard chambers, is to undergo a revision. His Majesty was pleased to command Dr. Meyrick's attendance on this day, for the purpose of inspecting it; and, after honoring him with a long private audience, directed him to undertake its superintendence'.[81] There was no intention of any chronological or instructive arrangement at Windsor—the effect was to be purely decorative. The task was not nearly as onerous physically as that at the Tower, for Samuel was concerned with the design rather than the mounting. At intervals he would go to Windsor for a day or two, or even three weeks in the June of 1830.[82] He had advised Sir William Knighton some years before that the armour at Malta which Lord Petersham had described to him should be acquired for Windsor because 'it is by no means duly appreciated by the natives of that island'.[83]

Fortunately the project does not seem to have been interrupted unduly by the death of George IV on 26 June 1830—though this happened when Samuel would have been at Windsor, surprisingly he doesn't record the fact. Armour from Malta had arrived at Carlton House before March 1831, when Samuel asks Pettigrew to mention it to the Duke of Sussex, and also the 'armour for Windsor now at the Ordnance Depot in Tooley Street'.

The final results of Samuel's arrangements in the guard chamber at Windsor were described in *The Analyst* in 1835.[85] The chamber was a grand room, seventy-five feet in length, from which doors opened into the great St. George's Hall which lay at right angles. On the wall on either side of the fireplace were corbels supporting splendid suits of armour from the late sixteenth and early seventeenth centuries. They included the suit made for Henry, Prince of Wales, brother to Charles I. On either side of the great window at the end were niches: one contained a suit of armour which had belonged to the Duke of Brunswick, the king's ancestor who lived in the earlier sixteenth century. Samuel had caused this to be brought from Carlton House. The other niche contained the suit of Lord Howard of Effingham, who had commanded the English fleet at the time of the Armada.

Two ornamental trophies, or groupings of arms and armour faced each other across the room, and Samuel had a wall-hung glass display case made for an exquisitely embossed 'rondache' or small circular shield.[86] The pièce de resistance was an arrangement above the fireplace, where it could be seen when the door to St. George's Hall was open. George IV, when shown Samuel's design, was moved to say 'now we shall have something worth looking at', though unfortunately it was not completed until early July 1831, the year after George's death. Appropriately, the decoration was a depiction in arms and armour of St. George killing the Dragon. The saint was represented by a richly engraved and gilded suit of armour belonging to a youth, placed so as to appear that he was striding over one wing of the dragon and thrusting his lance into its mouth. Behind the suit an arrangement of ramrods on a gilt ground signified the saint's 'glory', like the sun's rays. The scales of the dragon were made of sword blades turned blue, and the beast seemed to be rising from a jungle of rushes made of swords.

In June 1831 Samuel told Pettigrew that 'the armour has been sent to Windsor Castle and I intend to be there on Thursday for a few days when I hope I may have the good fortune to see the King and obtain his approbation for what I have done'.[87] Samuel may have been nervous that William IV would not approve the alterations his brother had set in motion. By 6 July, when Samuel wrote to Pettigrew again he had 'arrived at Windsor Castle last Thursday, unfortunately the King had left it. ... I should feel greatly indebted to H.R. Highness if he would condescend to acquaint his Majesty that I am at the castle superintending the arrangement of the armour, and hope to have it complete for his inspection on his arrival on Saturday. My reward would be his approbation should he think me intitled to it as that of the public has been for what I did at the Tower. ... What I have done for Windsor has been by no means so troublesome and difficult, so that the approval of the Royal Family would exceed its merits'.[88] By 10 July he could tell Pettigrew that 'I have had the gratification of seeing His Majesty today in the Guard Room and the delight of hearing what I have done most highly praised by him in every particular'.[89] Samuel's reward would come in due course.

8   Building the Court

The work at Windsor, though gratifying, was a distraction from Samuel's consuming interest from early 1828, which was the building of his dream house in Goodrich. However discreet the approaches to the various Goodrich landowners had been, there's no doubt that Samuel paid over the odds for the land he had acquired. The core of the estate was an ancient farmhouse called Giddis, which together with its fields cost him £6,200.[1] Additional purchases and exchanges brought the acreage up to 200 over the next few years.[2] Goodrich Castle and Goodrich Court were both built on headlands rising steeply above the valley of the Wye. In a small valley in between them runs the ancient road down to the Goodrich 'Boat' across the river, and it's believed that this crossing dates to prehistoric times.

By the time that Samuel informed his friends of his purchase in the spring of 1828, his architect Edward Blore had already spent considerable time in preparing plans, as Samuel offered to show them to Douce and James Markland. Indeed, the sketches in Llewellyn's notebook were made in the winter of 1827, and indicate a many-towered building. Probably Llewellyn and Samuel already had a clear idea of what they wanted, and looked to Blore to turn the ideas into architectural drawings. The drawings that Blore had prepared for Samuel still exist,[3] and are remarkable in that unlike many artists' impressions the architectural details were fairly faithfully reproduced. Samuel lost no time in having the plans shown to the Duke of Sussex, who 'graciously allowed the principal tower to be called Sussex Tower in his honour'.[4]

The exterior of the Court would look like an Edwardian castle from the more distant viewpoints, the stables and domestic offices being accommodated out of sight behind. The site chosen was on the edge of the headland, overlooking the length of the Wye from Ross until it disappears beyond Goodrich Castle. On the south lay the valley

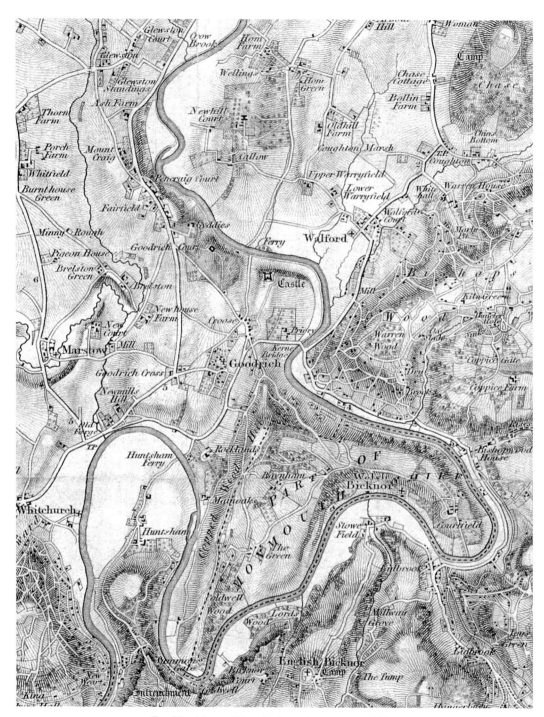

Fig. 53   Map of Goodrich and environs *c.*1835

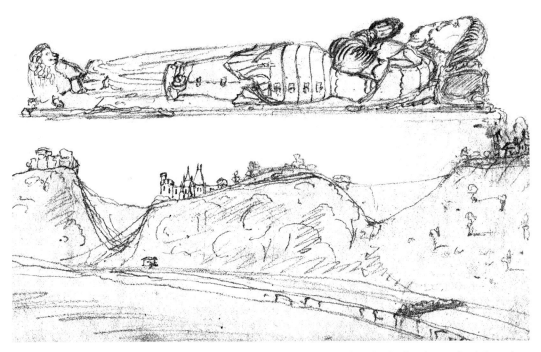

Fig. 54   A page from Llewellyn's sketchbook, 1827, showing Goodrich Castle on the left and
Goodrich Court in the middle (© The Board of the Trustees of the Armouries)

with the road down to the ferry, on the north another valley leading down to the river. The only drawback was the proximity of the public road into Goodrich from the nearby Ross-Monmouth highway. This was easily resolved by moving the road some way to the west, Samuel owning the land on all sides. He applied for permission at the Quarter Sessions in 1829, and no written objections having been received, the work was completed in 1830.[5] The new road cuts straight over the top of a hill, much more inconvenient for horse traffic than the old road which followed the contours.

Well before this stroke of *force majeure*, the parishioners of Goodrich must have been agog with the news of Samuel's intentions. The first sod was cut on St. George's Day, 23 April, 1828, by Llewellyn in the presence of Samuel and Francis Martin. This was in fact a good six months before the deeds of the sale of the Giddis estate were signed, when Francis Martin acted as trustee for the lands.

One of the local antiquarians, already well known to any reader of the *Gentleman's Magazine*, was Thomas Dudley Fosbroke, the incumbent of Walford which lay directly across the river from Goodrich Court. From his church he had a prime view of Goodrich Castle set upon its headland, and in due course also of the construction of Goodrich Court. He quoted extensively from Samuel's books on costume and armour

Fig. 55   Giddis

in his *Encyclopaedia of Antiquities*, and Samuel drew a plate for the work illustrating different types of armour. He is often quoted as being a 'friend' of Samuel, but it can't be denied that whatever his outward demeanour to Samuel, his letters reveal him to be often embittered and bad-tempered.[6] His chief problem was that he was usually short of money, although he worked hard writing reviews for the *Gentleman's Magazine*. A number of his surviving letters are to its editor, John Bowyer Nichols.

From him we learn that by August 1828 the local people were calling Goodrich Court the 'New Castle', and that Blore had already visited him in Walford. Whoever came with Blore on that occasion met with Fosbroke's disapproval as they 'wilfully disregard veracity and endeavour to intimidate by defamation, unprovoked and unfounded, and, of course, are dangerous'.[7] He later makes his view upon the construction clear in a letter to his son: 'Meyrick's castle is going on - very like something on the Rhine - a stumpy wooden spire is placed upon a fine tower, machicolated, & four corner spires - I hope the next lightning storm, will knock down the whole five *thingamies*'.[8] Although Fosbroke's wish wasn't granted, the building works were hampered by the wettest four years for a long time—in 1829 it rained heavily every day from the beginning of July until mid August, and in 1830 the Wye flooded in June.[9]

Given that Blore was based in London, his first necessity was to appoint a Clerk of Works whom he could trust to manage the building programme in his absence. Initially he seems to have been unlucky in this respect, as Samuel has no good words for the man

Plate 13 Sir John Cheyney, Pl. LVIII from *Critical Inquiry*, 1824

Plate 14 Henry VI, Pl. XLII from *Critical Inquiry*, 1824

Plate 15 Two suits of black armour, one with cross of St. George,
Pl. LXIII from *Critical Inquiry*, 1824

Plate 16 Embossed armour & buckler, Pl. LXXI from *Critical Inquiry*, 1824
(now in the Wallace Collection)

Plate 17 Queen Mary, from unpublished Monarchs series,
© Victoria & Albert Museum (CT89869 7921.12)

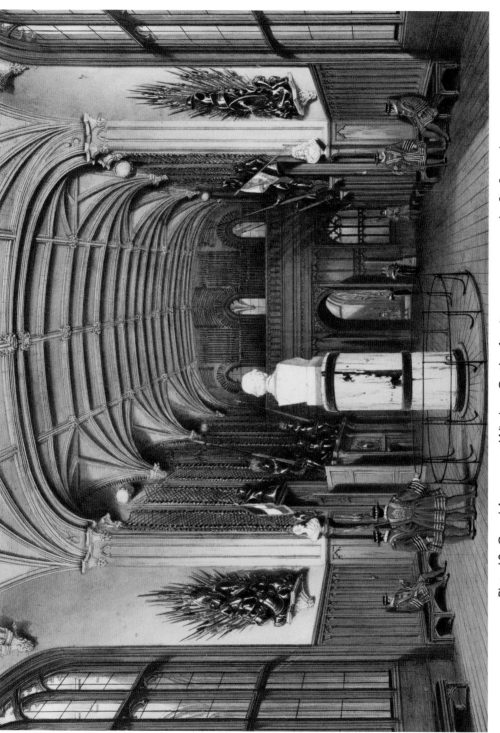

Plate 18 Grand Armoury at Windsor Castle after its re-arrangement by Sir Samuel
from Joseph Nash's *Views of the interior & exterior of Windsor Castle*, 1848, © Bodleian Library

Plate 19 Drawing by Edward Blore of south aspect of Goodrich Court,
© RIBA Library Drawings Collection

Plate 20 Drawing by Edward Blore of courtyard of Goodrich Court,
© RIBA Library Drawings Collection

Plate 21 Willement design for stained glass
depicting Meyrick ap Llewellyn
for the staircase at Goodrich Court,
© British Library (BL Add 34871 p6 (20))

Plate 22 Willement design for stained glass
depicting St. Barbara & St. George
for the chapel at Goodrich Court
© British Library (BL Add 34871 p2 (8))

Fig. 56   Goodrich Castle and Walford church seen from the site of Goodrich Court, 1827
(© The Board of the Trustees of the Armouries)

charged with this office for the first few months. He complained to Douce later that he had lost £1,500 because of this man's incompetence.[10] Work on Goodrich Court seems to have stopped entirely at one stage, as a letter from Goodrich explains: 'Dr. Meyrick's new building is to go on, Monday next, after a cessation since Xmas last.'[11]

Fig. 57   Edward Blore

Matters improved with the appointment of a new Clerk of Works, William Heiton, in April 1829. Heiton's competence and hard work must have earned Samuel's respect, as he named one of the towers at Goodrich Court the Heiton tower—though it was the one containing the laundry. At one stage Heiton even paid the workmen out of his own pocket when their money had not arrived; the difficulties and stresses of the job surely contributed to his early death in June 1833. Samuel was his executor, and the housekeeper at the Court, Mary Coward, his residuary legatee.

From the beginning, Heiton kept meticulous books detailing payments to workmen and suppliers, and noting progress in the building

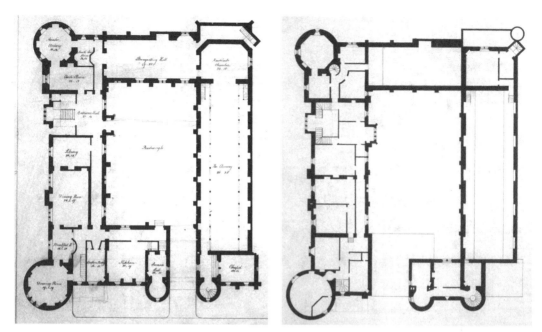

Figs. 58 & 59   Ground (left) and First Floor plans of Goodrich Court prepared by Edward Blore,
© RIBA Library Drawings Collection

work. Of these, two survive in the Royal Armouries library and two in Cambridge University library.[12] Unfortunately there are no entries for Goodrich in the two client books which exist at Cambridge, which give summary details of invoices sent to clients.[13] When Heiton took over, he made an inventory of the work which had taken place between July 1828 and January 1829, and the equipment on site.[14] There was a fully equipped smith's shop, a store with all manner of workmen's tools, and an assortment of trucks and scaffolding. There were about twelve stone cutters or masons, eight labourers, nine quarrymen and sundry others working on the construction. The Day Book in the Royal Armouries Library gives their names and their rates of pay, hours worked each week, pay due and their signatures (or X's) as they received it.[15] It also gives details of all the building materials received.

Another Royal Armouries book was, in effect, a report to Blore or his office of the workmen employed and the progress made during each week's work.[16] Given that one of the Cambridge books covers much the same ground as this book, it seems likely that the books themselves made journeys to and fro to Blore's office, a distinct possibility given ample evidence of the efficiency of the mail service at this time. Probably Heiton kept another rough book as well. Using all the sources it would be possible to build up a complete record of all the workmen who took part in the building of Goodrich Court, and many of the suppliers of goods and services.

The quarrymen were at first directly employed because the stone for the Court was obtained from the hillside below the site of the building. The local red sandstone, while generally easy to work, does not stand up well to the weather. Goodrich Castle provides a good example of this, as most of the building is constructed from the rock excavated from the dry moat. The keep, which is the oldest part of the castle, is made from Forest of Dean stone and is far less eroded. Heiton delegated the quarrying to a contractor, who charged by the tramload, and a little tramway was set up to pull the stone up the steep hillside, with a gin at the top. The tram plates for the track were bought from Bishopswood, where the Lydbrook tramway ended. The quarrying continued until the middle of 1830, after which the variable quality of the stone was perpetually causing problems. There are later entries for Forest of Dean and Painswick stone in the accounts.

When Heiton took over, a good start had already been made on the part of the building nearest to the river and furthest from the access road. The large tower was well above ground level, and the entrance porch ready for its keystone. Some of the work was not up to standard, but could be made to serve. Where the quarry stone was hard through exposure to the air, a mason could only dress nine inches of window jamb in a day, or seven feet of ashlar. The numbers of men working increased rapidly: at the start of 1830 there were twenty-one men on the payroll, but this rose to sixty-three by May, when thirty-four men were employed on the keep tower and the banqueting hall alone, plus three joiners. Obviously, as the shell of the building was completed the masons were progressively replaced by joiners and carpenters.

Fig. 60   A drawing for the Banqueting Hall by Edward Blore
© RIBA Library Drawings Collection

Heiton's typical expenditure on wages and basic materials in 1830 was between £60 and £90 per week, with wages varying from 1s. 6d. for a labourer to £1-0-5d. for a turner. Heiton himself earned £2-10-0d. a week. Major expenditure such as that for lead were accounted for separately. The tramloads of stone from the quarry arrived inexorably—sometimes over a hundred a week.

Workmen must have been drafted in from some considerable area around, and one Welsh labourer, Henry Faithfull, who started in the bitterly cold December of 1829 was to remain with Samuel as a general servant for many years; his daughter was left an annuity of £50 in Samuel's will. Although Blore had made a number of drawings to enable the work to get underway, there is frequent mention of the receipt at Goodrich of packets of drawings sent down to Heiton, and in the book continual requests by Heiton for detailed drawings to be sent so that delay could be avoided in the construction. Certainly Blore's surviving architectural drawings in the Victoria & Albert Museum are hardly detailed enough for Heiton's needs.[17] After every visit of Samuel or Llewellyn to the site, Heiton passed on to Blore their instructions:

> Dr. Meyrick … is very anxious that the flying buttress should be introduced to the chapel.
> Dr. Meyrick wishes 10 niches or recesses upon each side of the Armoury.
> Dr. Meyrick wishes flues introduced into the 2 turrets and the other made into a belfry
>   and the roof of the staircase raised into a cone roof.
> Dr. Meyrick wants a drawbridge next to the staircase window.

As well as the building itself, Blore designed a number of fittings such as display cases, but also pieces of furniture. In December 1830 Samuel himself added the instruction 'Dr. Meyrick will be obliged to Mr. Blore to send the design for the pianoforte for the Drawing Room at the same time that he sends that for the eagle in the chapel'.[18] The drawings for the designs made their way to Goodrich by Pickford's van to Gloucester, thence by the *Regulator* coach to the Pencraig turnpike. They were accompanied by 'the windows'—possibly the stained glass that was painted by Thomas Willement for the entrance hall. The descriptions of progress are exhaustive, and a week by week model of the building would be easy to build up, but tedious to read. However, certain features are of particular interest.

There is no natural spring right at the site of the Court, but a fault-line in the sandstone rocks means that Goodrich has a line of springs and wells running from west of the church through the village to the headland on which the Court was built. The nearest spring had been used by the inhabitants of the castle after their well had dried up, and the lead pipe connecting the two had been cut during the siege in the Civil War. The flow from the spring must have been quite reliable, because Heiton used it to drive a 'force pump' or hydraulic ram which sent water to a reservoir on the top of the keep tower, which supplied the building. Heiton also talks of the 'conduit' being 12 feet deep, and holding 3,000 gallons. During excavations the lead pipe which had supplied the castle was found. The site of the spring was covered by a small well house, which still survives.

As well as the spring water, a large cistern was cut in the rocks under the inner stable yard, to take the rainwater run-off from the roofs of the Court. This could hold twenty thousand gallons.[19] The reservoir and the cistern supplied all the house needs until another plant was built some years later to extract water from the Wye. The ruins of this later building survive just upstream of the Goodrich Court headland. The Court was built with a number of water-closets, Samuel having one attached to his room. Channels for the effluent ran down to cellar level, but where they discharged is a mystery.

One of the famous rooms in the Court was the library, which was known as the Breda room because the carved oak ceiling and frieze were supposed to have come from the Council Chamber of Breda, in the Netherlands. The ceiling was reputedly carved in the early 1500s by Italian craftsmen.

The ceiling was constructed of square panels mounted in a supporting grid which was carved with two sets of symbols: the burning brand (more correctly 'ragged staff fired') of the Meyrick arms, and fleurs de lis. Quite clearly, this supporting grid was made by Samuel's workmen. At each intersection of the grid was a domed carving of acanthus leaves, supporting a pendant. In each of the square panels was set a diamond-shaped

Fig. 61   The Well House

119

panel containing further carvings of acanthus, supporting larger pendants. In the four triangles created between each square panel and its diamond-shaped insert was placed a cherub's head.

What's quite clear from Heiton's accounts is that in April 1831 carpenters Lewis and Powell were carving 'ornaments for the library ceiling'. It seems that some new pendants at least

Fig. 62 Breda Room showing the ceiling pendants

were carved for the central panels, and one is visible in a surviving photograph.[20] A throwaway remark by Fosbroke in an undated letter[21] to Nicholls in early 1831 raises the suspicion that yet more of the ceiling may not have been from Breda: 'Mr. Rhodes, the eminent cow-keeper of Gray's Inn Lane has bought an estate in Monmouthshire and is building a mansion. He has bought a lot of old wainscotting from a house at Hereford and Dr. Meyrick, I believe, has purchased a cieling [*sic*] of the same'. Some of the cherubs in the central panels look as if they have been cut down to fit. Certainly the only 'old carved oak ceiling' Heiton mentions as being installed is that in the library, but carpentry did continue long after he left. As the tradition of the Breda ceiling is mentioned in the

Fig. 63 Panelling in the Breda Room and the relocated fireplace from Sir Gelly's bedchamber shortly before demolition

Fig. 64   Close-up of one of the ceiling panels in the Breda Room
(taken when it was later dismantled)

guidebooks written during Samuel's lifetime by Fosbroke and Charles Nash[22] there must be some truth in it, but Nash does say it was 'restored wherever defective'. It seems possible that only the frieze and the pendants came from Breda, the cherubs from the Hereford house, and the rest was made during construction.

Samuel wished to raise flags on the entrance towers, and drink the health of the king on 12 August 1829, when 30 shillings was set aside for drink for the men. At the same time he probably celebrated the fact that the foundations of the Armoury had just been laid, though it would be another year before the roof would be fitted. The Armoury was designed to house the most spectacular part of the Meyrick armour collection and was an enormous room some 88 feet long, and 23 feet wide. The original design of the roof was not to Samuel's taste, as Heiton reported to Blore in February 1831 that 'Dr. Meyrick doesn't like the exterior appearance of the lights [windows] in the armoury, he suggests buttresses with finials upon each corner'. The redesign of the Armoury roof may have had other consequences; Samuel complained to Douce in October 1833 that 'it is a great nuisance that Blore did not make the roof of the Armoury water-tight before he gave it up to me. The rain comes in, in every part and I am forced, to prevent the armour being completely spoilt, to move it into the banqueting hall'.[23]

The natural lighting in the Armoury came from great skylights overhead, and a round window in the east wall. A gallery ran along three sides of the room, designed for the cabinets which held choice specimens of arms and armour. Underneath, the supports for the gallery divided the room into bays, and set along the back walls were display niches. It wasn't until the beginning of October 1831, shortly before Samuel summoned Blore for his final tour of inspection, that work on the shell of the Armoury was finished. Though the Armoury was floored by April 1832, the carving of the oak gallery rail meant another three months work for two carpenters.[24]

The Armoury was tucked away out of sight in the middle of the Court, between the Wye front and the stables, but the Sussex tower is featured on many paintings and engravings. This isn't surprising considering the exotic nature of its roof. The tower was built largely according to Blore's original design, almost certainly inspired by the buildings seen by the Meyricks on their trip in Germany, for it bears a strong resemblance to a sketch in Samuel's notebook of the entrance gate at Frankfurt. But for some reason Blore's elegantly proportioned central cone was shortened, to no longer soar above the surrounding pinnacles, perhaps due to a problem with the corbels supporting the machiolations. Heiton reported that these were cut from huge stones which went right through the tower wall, and it's quite possible that the weight of the roof had to be reduced in compensation. Samuel certainly caused slate to be used instead of lead on the roof, but this may have been because of cost rather than weight. Fosbroke's 'thingamies', or at least the smaller turrets, were used to sport flags on such occasions as the Duke of Sussex's birthday. Whether from practical or artistic considerations, the Sussex tower had lost all its pointed roofs by 1869, as witnessed in the engravings in the Court's sale particulars of this date.[25]

Although the Court was not to be fully habitable until well into 1831, Samuel had determined to pack up the armour and leave London permanently by July 1830. This may have been from financial necessity—he could not afford to keep the house in Upper Cadogan Place for his own use,[26] though he still owned the lease when he made his last will in 1848.[27] He told Pettigrew that if he visited Goodrich he would find he 'had taken up quarters in a carpenter's shop in the midst of a stonemason's yard'.[28] The Pettigrews themselves were prevented from visiting by the expected birth of their daughter, Samuel's god-daughter. However, friends such as Francis Martin the herald, Henry Peyronnet Briggs the artist and Planché the dramatist were prepared to suffer the inconveniences in the summer of 1830. Briggs and Planché happily set about drawing the beautiful surroundings. It was their practice once the armour had been arranged to sketch outside in the mornings, and then spend the afternoons drawing in the Armoury.[29]

By January 1831, most exterior building was complete. Only part of the stables, the wall and bridge of the moat and part of the garden wall remained to do. Inside it was a different story, in spite of the fact that there were a hundred workmen on the site.[30] Samuel and Llewellyn were obliged to use one of the bedrooms as a sitting room,

Fig. 65   The Armoury as engraved by Joseph Skelton in 1830

but it must have been a problem that some walls were still running with damp as late as November.[31] At the beginning of October 1831 Samuel wrote to Blore that he expected the work to be finished in three weeks, and that Blore should be there 'to see that all was right'. From Heiton's accounts, his building costs to this date were £11,852-3-1d.[32] To this would be added items such as Blore's fees, but the total seems remarkably small. Heiton had made an estimate a year earlier of the cost to completion, which included items such as oak for the Armoury at £300, painting at £300 and plumbing & glazing at £800. Nevertheless, Samuel had been forced to mortgage Giddis and the surrounding land in order to cover the cost: in April 1831 he had borrowed £2,500, and in October a further £1,500.[33] It was not repaid until 1835, probably after Hannah Meyrick's affairs in Littlehampton had been settled.[34]

In early November 1831 Samuel was at last able to tell Douce: 'I have discharged all my people except four joiners, two masons, the blacksmith and three labourers, but it will be some time yet before I get rid of the painters and plasterers. I have finished the garden wall which cost me three hundred pounds'.[35] The building of the Court was not without accident, but for this Samuel could not be blamed: on 28 May 1831 the workmen were given cider to toast the king's official birthday, when a pipelayer must have imbibed rather too freely. Against all advice he made a firework from an iron pipe, and blew himself to pieces with it.[36]

Llewellyn took a special responsibility for the pleasure gardens, and he was concerned to give them an appearance of maturity. To this end he used the system devised by Sir Henry Steuart[37] for moving mature trees, similar to that in use today. Steuart of Allanton, Lanarkshire had published his influential book *The Planter's Guide* in 1828, in which he advocated transplantation of mature trees to improve the landscape surrounding new mansions. Some trees Llewellyn moved 'two miles or more and has placed a couple of yews near the building, which being thirty feet high give the place completely the air of antiquity'.[38] During the winter and spring of 1832 many more trees were planted, though a good number were inexplicably vandalised in an overnight attack in March.[39]

By April 1832 the garden terraces were being levelled and sown with grass seed.[40] In keeping with the quasi-medieval nature of the Court, the south-east front of the building looked 'over a large grass flat called the tilt ground'.[41] Samuel wrote to Douce in February 1833: 'The terraces which extend on three sides of the building with their level grass-flats and gravel walks, always dry, contribute greatly to health. We have an easy zig-zag walk cut in the wood down to the river and another to the quarry that

Fig. 66   The gardens around Goodrich Court (as shown in the sale catalogue of 1884)

afford ample shade in summer time'.[42] The planting continued for some years, as Thomas King wrote to a friend Richard Cotton in January 1835: 'my friend Llewellyn Meyrick has had a very favourable November for transplanting - he has moved some very large hollies and placed them on his terrace walks - they are quite thriving - & those he transplanted last November twelvemonth are so flourishing that they have made many new shoots and are profusely covered with red berries'.[43] He also acquired from his attorney, Hooper, a window from the demolished chapel at Glewstone, eventually setting it up in his garden.[44]

The most evocative building belonging to Goodrich Court which still exists is the great Monmouth gateway, known to all who pass along the main Ross-Monmouth road. Some commentators believe it is based on the Marschiertors in Aachen, which Samuel would have seen on his trip to Germany[45] but the name is suggestive, and it is just as likely that it was based partially on the Monnow bridge in Monmouth. An entrance to the Court itself with the same shape as the Monmouth gateway seems to have been considered initially, according to Llewellyn's sketch in his notebook, but was replaced by two smaller round towers. The gatehouse was not in fact completed until the end of 1837—presumably before then there were only gates or some lesser structure.[46] The rear of the gatehouse, which is only accessible from a private road, is decorated with the 'burning brand' from the arms of Sir Gelly Meyrick.

Before the Court was even finished, and before the first visitors' book was ready for signature, the curious started to arrive. Some of the earliest were the Rolls family from the Hendre near Monmouth. They had visited the Meyrick collection in London in May 1829, and were obviously curious about its new home, as they called to see the work in August the same year.[47] They also came when the Court was finished, and they must have been impressed by Willement's stained glass on the staircase, in the banqueting hall and the chapel as he was commissioned in 1834 by John Rolls to paint heraldic compartments in the staircase window at the Hendre.[48]

The Court was now established as a major attraction of the Wye Tour. To all Samuel's friends and well-wishers, it must have seemed that the 1830s heralded for him a golden age. Although regretting that he should be removed from their antiquarian circles in London, it couldn't be denied that lack of display space for the collection had been a problem. The house in Cadogan Place was stacked with arms and armour, encroaching on staircases and bedrooms alike. There were constant interruptions from visitors to the collection, and increasing noise and distur-bance from a crowded metrop-olis. Now the armour could be displayed in a dignified setting, according to his instructive principles. The peaceful and healthy location must surely result in ever more scholarly works. Instead, the next ten years are marked by his fortunes see-sawing between public triumph and private misfortune.

Fig. 67 The Monmouth Gate showing (in frame) Sir Gelly Meyrick's device of three burning brands on the face that fronts the estate

126

9 Triumph and Tragedy

At long last Samuel had joined the ranks of the landed gentry, and with Llewellyn as heir there was every expectation that the Meyricks were established at Goodrich for generations to come. As a distinguished newcomer to the district, it wasn't long before Samuel was solicited for various public offices. He had been appointed magistrate by the beginning of 1831,[1] was a deputy lieutenant of the county, and was already complaining of the time this consumed. His support was eagerly sought by the opposing candidates in the parliamentary election for the county of Hereford, which took place in the early summer of 1831. The Tory candidate was given short shrift— he 'answered an application from Sir John Cotterell for his vote for the county with a refusal and hope the opposers of the Reform Bill will everywhere meet with the same'.[2] Poor Sir John was not to know that the Meyrick heart was beating with reforming zeal.

The Meyrick family had been associated closely with the great Whig dynasty of Fox through the connection with John Calcraft. However, the very nature of their business as army agents meant that they had to be careful not to offend either end of the political spectrum—often the colonels of regiments would be the younger sons of aristocratic families. Samuel's contact with the liberal Stephen Lushington at Doctors' Commons has already been mentioned, but his political philosophy is most clearly stated in a later letter,[3] when he is discussing his presentation of historical events: 'Depend on it, the act of an ancestor would never have any weight with me. He took his own course, I do mine, and it is to look into the principle upon which all governments ought to be founded, viz: to procure the greatest benefit, if possible, for all, if not, for the greatest portion of the people. You will when you have read my lectures to the close of the reign of James 2d: see that I have flogged all parties, and then I expect at your hands an acknowledgement that I have been quite impartial. My cousin the

Colonel, and Lady Laura are Tories, my cousin John Trotter M.P. for West Surry [*sic*] an ultra Tory. I was a liberal before I knew that my uncle the General was the same'.

In 1831 the whole country was in a ferment over the question of reform of the electoral system. Samuel threw his weight behind the local Reform candidates, Sir Robert Price and Kedgwin Hoskins. Polling day was Saturday 7 May, when the Reform supporters accompanied Price and Hoskins into the city, as described in the *Hereford Journal* of 11 May:

> At 9.00 Mr. Hoskins was at the Red Hill, Sir R. Price at White Cross … before 10.00 the procession entered the city in the following order:
>
> A Band of Music
> The city Flags
> Upwards of 600 freeholders on horse back in fours, having ten Equerries
> The Crown flag, borne by a horseman
> The Deputation Carriage with gentlemen who prevailed on Mr. Hoskins to
> come forward, with banner
> Grand-standard 'Hoskins the Champion of Reform' born by two freeholders
> P. Jones jnr., the Esquire of Mr. Hoskins bearing his shield
> Kedgwin Hoskins Esq. on horseback, supported on the right by
> Sir Geo. Cornewall bart. and on the left by the Rev. T.P. Symonds, surrounded
> by flags and banners from Ross, Leominster, Bromyard, Ledbury etc. etc.
> Mr. Hoskins' carriage
> The committee in carriages
> The carriages of T.A. Knight Esq., Col. Money, Dr. Meyrick, Dr. Evans,
> N. Morgan, Geo. Aveline, John Holder, J.W.R. Hall Esq. and a great number
> of others, together with post chaises and gigs filled with freeholders

Price and Hoskins were returned as members. The *Hereford Journal* also carried a report of the Reform Dinner held in Hoskins' honour at the Swan Hotel at Ross on 17 May, when eighty to ninety of the 'respectable' inhabitants of Ross attended. At the end of the meal there were Royal toasts; after that to the Duke of Sussex, Meyrick rose and said that 'his Royal Highness concurred with these views - it was a cause of estrangement from his brother George IV'. After relating how the duke had sat with his dying black servant, Samuel expressed his hope that when the duke visited Goodrich Court he would be shown honour for his conduct—'we will, we will' applauded the diners. After a few more toasts 'The worthy doctor then at considerable length ably and clearly defined the different forms of government, which exist throughout the world, and after some historical remarks on English history, said that the British constitution in its original purity, continued the advantages of every other description of government …'.

For those who remained awake after such an ordeal, 'there were a great many toasts, the bottle went round and round, cock began to crow before many of the guests had retired to their pillows'. Samuel wrote to his friend Pettigrew after the dinner that he had 'declined an offer from a deputation for him to stand for MP with certain success – but he was not sure he will be able to escape in future'.[4] If this sounds as if he would in fact be prepared to stand, his view by 1833 was different: 'I have never felt a wish to be in Parliament and indeed differ from the general opinion, conceiving that the constituents are indebted to those who undertake the office in a reformed house of Commons'.[5]

His change of heart may have been the result of a virulent attack on him published in a broadsheet in July 1832.[6] It is signed 'Crito', which was the pseudonym of a Rev. Duncombe writing for the *Gentleman's Magazine* in the late 18th century. As this Rev. Duncombe was dead by 1832, one can only presume that this unpleasant diatribe was written by the Rev. John Duncumb, that well respected historian and founding author of the first comprehensive history of Herefordshire. In an address to a meeting of the Freeholders of Herefordshire[7] Samuel had expounded on the iniquity of supporting the aristocracy in the guise of Charles II's illegitimate descendants. More to the point, he pointed out the injustice of the variable nature of the income of the clergy, leaving some to manage on £200 a year, while others had £4,000 or more. Duncumb may have taken umbrage at this, as he held the rectory of Abbey Dore and the vicarage of Mansell Lacy, though he was resident in Hereford all the time he held them.

Addressed to Samuel Rush Meyrick Knight 'Green grow the Rushes O', Crito says:

> … Alluding to Reform, you say - 'If we are satisfied with this, we are content with the cloth spread on the table without the dishes to form the banquet' - And is it come to this? After the bitter and long protracted struggle in which we have been engaged, we did believe the Reform Bill was something more than a table cloth … But the dishes you propose to serve up are still more extraordinary. Do not the people 'wish to give the lords spiritual the opportunity of paying their whole attention to things spiritual' &c. Do they not wish to destroy the temptation to pride and avarice in the inferior 'clergy &c?' Yes, Samuel, they do wish this - and now permit me, in turn to ask *you* a question. Do not the people wish also, that

all useless sinecures, overpaid by the extravagant patronage of a prodigal prince, should be abolished - especially when the hard cash comes from the pocket of the country, and the only return they get is to see a set of old spears standing up in chronological order? Had the people always been in this reforming humour, how far would the *wings* of Goodrich Court have extended? - The young sparrows which broke the shell last week in the second holly bush in your garden will give the dimensions ... It is true, reform is wanting here, for many of those exemplary men toil through a life of poverty and neglect, and when they sink to the grave from their sphere of usefulness, worn out and broken in spirit, and noticed and beloved alone by the poor and unhappy, their savings, in many instances, with their complicated duties and economy, do not amount to the sum you received for cleaning an old boot top!

… And now one word before we part. I have heard you are a good tempered man, and, on enquiry, I find you are well known in the neighbourhood of Ross, and have a curious taste for antiquated anecdotes. I will therefore translate for your amusement from Theodosius de Artificibus.

There lived about this time, in an obscure part of Rome, a Polisher of ancient Brass and Coins - a poor, but ingenious man. By some good fortune he obtained an introduction into the Imperial Household, and had the honour of burnishing the helmet of Caesar, on his return from the Dalmatian conquests. The helmet was much admired, even the Imperial Visitor condescended to notice its splendour, which so turned the poor man's brain, that he began to imagine himself somebody, and went about obtruding his advice amongst those who did not know him, and boasting of his noble acquaintance - the people pitied him, and said, 'What is the matter with the poor old brass Polisher?' Happily, however, he regained his senses; and, it is said, he saw his former folly, and died a respectable man.

Samuel! - take the hint! and do not offer advice where the only return is, 'What is the matter with the old brass Polisher'.

In view of later events, the most important early visitor to the Court was Francis Douce. By the time that Douce arrived on 10 September 1831 some three hundred friends or sightseers had signed the visitors' book, though presumably since the Armoury was not finished the collection must have been dispersed around the other public rooms.[8] Douce hated staying away from home—he said that 'when a man pays a visit to a friend in the country he must reckon on sacrificing his independence to the forms & habits of his host and be content to suffer numerous privations of his domestic comforts'.[9] Although he would have been happy enough when inside the

Court, he was by this stage rather too old and stout for much walking. Unfortunately Llewellyn had taken the 'chariot' on a tour of Devonshire, accompanied by old neighbours of theirs in Cadogan Place.[10] An untrained young horse was pressed into service to draw the gig slowly around the grounds. The inevitable happened—the horse went too fast and stumbled, Douce was thrown out and badly shaken up, breaking his watch in the process.[11] The accident could have given him a disgust of the place, but he had seen enough to be confirmed in his opinion that Goodrich Court would be a worthy setting for his great collection of antiquities.

By the end of 1831, Samuel's cup was almost overflowing. He had become a big fish in the relatively small pool of Herefordshire society. In the larger world, his chronological arrangement of the armour at the Tower was much admired, and he was recognised as *the* authority on arms and armour. The king was very pleased with the decorative effect of the displays of armour at Windsor. Only one thing was missing— some sort of official recognition of his labours. Douce had hinted to him in a letter back in 1829 that his labours should be rewarded by the King with some honour or other,[12] but the year passed with no such intimation. It could hardly be expected before the work at Windsor had been more or less completed, which in the event had not happened until July 1831.[13] Samuel's only recourse was to lobby the king at two stages removed, via the Duke of Sussex and his librarian Pettigrew. Only in one letter to Pettigrew does this become particularly pointed: 'I wish most exceedingly [exceedingly double underlined] that His Majesty could know that while every other decoration at the Castle has been expensive in the extreme what I have done here and at the Tower of London has put the country to no expense'.[14]

In due course the king returned the unpaid favours—on 20 January 1832 Samuel was able to write to Pettigrew that 'His Royal Highness was pleased to speak to the King on the subject of the Guelphic order, and wrote me word that His Majesty would confer it "with pleasure". Sir Herbert Taylor has this day announced that the King has been pleased to create me a K. H. and directed him to write to Lord Melbourne that I may have conferred on me the English order of Knighthood'.[15] Pettigrew's part in the honour was duly acknowledged: 'I have now, my good friend, to return you my most sincere thanks for the kind part you have taken in the matter and the valuable advice you were pleased to give me, and I beg you to receive them as warm as it is possible to conceive'.

The Royal Hanoverian Guelphic Order was founded in 1815 by George IV while he was still Prince Regent, and was not conferred after the death of William IV in

1837. Many of the recipients were members of the military. The order had three divisions, Knight Grand Cross, Knight Commander and Knight. As a Knight, Samuel was entitled to wear his insignia of a golden Maltese cross, enamelled in blue with white edges, with the white horse of Hanover on a red enamel ground in the centre. In between each arm of the cross were lions. The whole was circled with pale blue enamel bearing the motto *Nec Aspera Terrent*, surrounded again by an oak wreath. Sir Samuel is shown wearing the insignia in the portrait of him in the second edition of Skelton's *Engraved Illustrations of Armour*. Skelton had

Fig. 68 Sir Samuel wearing his order of knighthood, by Skelton

engraved this portrait and added the insignia before the end of 1833[16] from Briggs' painting of 1826.[17]

Sir Samuel must have been aware that the award of a knighthood was an expensive business; Sir Walter Scott was advised to set aside £400 for various registration fees for his baronetage.[18] On the same day that Sir Samuel wrote to Pettigrew that the investiture was set for 22 February 1832[19] another letter was despatched to Byham, secretary of the Board of Ordnance at the Tower of London.[20] After informing Byham of his knighthood, Sir Samuel reminded him that the work at the Tower was done free of charge and at his own expense. He had the 'presumption to hope that the Honble Board will not allow me to pay for my reward by defraying the fees from my own purse. I should not have made this application but being engaged in building at great cost every sixpence is of its full value'. His presumption was not rewarded—the Board being duly aware that he 'offered his assistance gratuitously in the first instance'.

Most people would at least make sure they were in London the day before their investiture, but Samuel proposed to 'arrive in London by the Mail on the morning of the 22d; go to the levee that day, on the next return thanks at Kensington Palace, and on the Friday to the drawing-room, leaving town that evening for Herefordshire'. In the event he was at St. James' Palace on the right afternoon with assorted officers, civil servants and the Mayor of Norwich to receive his honour.[21] Hopefully, in spite of her great age, Sir Samuel's mother Hannah was able to understand and celebrate the recognition of her son's achievements. John Meyrick's ghost might even have allowed that his son had brought lustre to the Meyrick name, in spite of his disastrous marriage. Perhaps Sir Samuel was just too proud—because the gods punished him swiftly for his *hubris*. In his exaltation they tempted him into a small act of foolishness, for which he paid with years of illness and a shortened lifespan.

On one of those two nights in London he contracted gonorrhea. The symptoms are unmistakable: within a few days of his return he was laid low by a fever, a purulent discharge from the urethra, an incessant desire to urinate and, later, pains in the joints. Without modern treatment, the initial symptoms of gonorrhea will abate after some months, but the disease often leaves the male sufferer with narrowing of the urethra (stricture) which can block the flow of urine totally. Often there is long-term damage to the kidneys. Sir Samuel's disease followed a classic path. His first recourse was to his friend Pettigrew who had just helped him to his knighthood. Presumably he didn't wish to involve a local doctor who would have been very well aware of the cause of his disease. The initial letter to Pettigrew is missing from the collection in the National Library of Wales, probably it was destroyed because it was too explicit about the cause of the malady. Only two weeks after his return from London Sir Samuel had finished the course of pills supplied by Pettigrew, but he was a very bad patient, often changing the recommended doses.[22] With occasional remissions the acute phase of the illness lasted through the summer, but gradually the symptoms lessened, though for the rest of 1832 there are regular letters giving Pettigrew progress reports about his bodily functions.[23]

In spite of his physical weakness Sir Samuel continued to work about the Court, helping with hammer and nails where he could. How he explained his indisposition to his son can only be imagined. He excused himself to John Nichols, editor of the *Gentleman's Magazine*, for a lack of material owing to 'my present circumstances', and said that he had had to fob off the editor of the *Cambrian Quarterly* with material written many years before.[24] In truth it must have been his state of health as much as the state of the Court which made life difficult. He was not to begin another major publishing project for eight years.

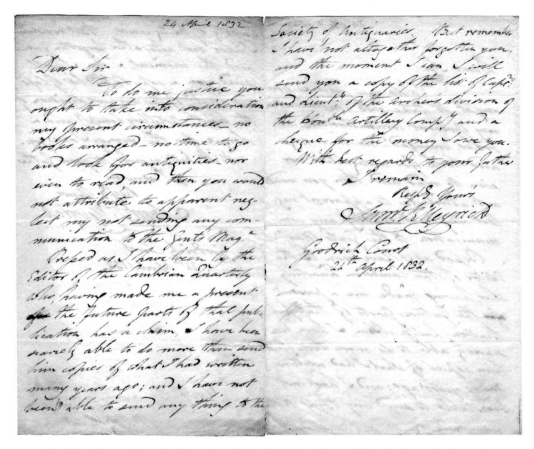

Fig. 69 A letter from Sir Samuel to John Nichols, editor of *The Gentleman's Magazine*

The final fitting up at the Court continued unabated. Sir Samuel was very hopeful that the Duke of Sussex would visit during the summer, as he had written to the duke personally to invite him. There is no record that the duke ever did so, but there was a continual stream of sightseers. By April 1832, the funds that had been allocated for the building of the Court had run out, and it must have been extreme reluctance that Sir Samuel applied to his mentor Francis Douce to borrow a further £1,500.[25] By this time, Llewellyn was well into his twenties, and so should have inherited the vast fortune left him by John Meyrick. There was just one problem—John Meyrick's will specifically left his estate to be invested in public funds, the interest to be paid to his widow Hannah for her natural life. Against all odds, Hannah was still alive at the advanced age of 88.

Although Douce turned down Sir Samuel's request, he wrote on the letter in his minute hand 'it was not convenient for me at this time to comply with Dr. M.'s request, but I afterwards regretted I had not done so as I know him to be a most honourable & friendly man'. In the end, Sir Samuel borrowed £1,000 from a third party, using as collateral his interest in his mother's inheritance from her father Samuel Rush.[26] Within a few months of his request to Douce, Hannah Meyrick was dead. She had made no will, and her property in Littlehampton devolved on her only son, as well as £850 in securities, cash and presumably jewellery and other items inherited from her step-mother.[27] The death duty registers show that John Meyrick's estate had risen in value to more than £57,000 by this date[28] but the final disposition of it of it could have presented some problems. As long as Sir Samuel was alive, it was theoretically possible that he could father more children—and John Meyrick's will had specifically stated that his estate should be divided between Samuel's lawful offspring. The executors evidently agreed that the legacy should be paid to Llewellyn as he was over twenty-one, a fortunate circumstance in view of later events, as John Meyrick had specified that in the event of Samuel having no surviving children the estate should go to the female children of his sisters and his sister-in-law.

At long last extra funds became available for adding to the armour. The collection belonging to Sir Samuel's friend, Bernard Brocas, was up for sale, but he had not known about it, and so had missed the opportunity.[29] Domenic Colnaghi, who had sold him the original fine suits in his collection, seems to have been instrumental in letting him know about another armour sale that was to be held by the dealer Gwennap, and indeed advancing him some money.[30] Sir Samuel managed to obtain by Planché's agency the dress of a mounted rajah brought from India by a Captain Grindley, which was mounted in the ante-Asiatic armoury at the Court.[31] He missed two horse figures which were bought by John Isaac and Swabey Bentley & Tuck at the Gwennap auction in early 1833. Originally Sir Samuel had been prepared to offer £150 each, and although they were now on sale for 500 guineas he told Isaac that he was only prepared to increase his offer to £400 for the two.[32] The most desirable piece he missed acquiring was an embossed suit, supposedly of Henri IV, which was bought by Lord Ormilie; 'If I had got that I should consider the collection complete'.[33]

The acquisition of the armour could have been totally academic, for Sir Samuel had very nearly lost an early battle with his disease. In June 1833 he had asked Pettigrew to buy him a 'caoutchouc' or rubber 'urinal' costing 10 shillings from Hancock's in the Strand, and send it with the unsuspecting William Skelton, Joseph's brother, who was coming to Goodrich anyway.[34] By the beginning of August his flow of urine had become completely blocked, and an emergency operation to relieve his condition was necessary. 'Cutting for the stone' was a well-known procedure for the removal of bladder stones, surgeons' reputations being gained according to the speed with which they could cut a path into the bladder to relieve the obstruction. A similar operation could relieve stricture of the urethra, but it was extremely hazardous, and only a life-threatening emergency could justify the excruciating pain and risk of complications. The local doctor Henry Ward had been called in the first instance, and had apparently hesitated to suggest to Sir Samuel that a catheter could relieve the problem as he was afraid of Sir Samuel's known irascibility.[35] He called in the Cheltenham surgeon John Fosbroke, who was the son of Thomas Fosbroke of Walford. Possibly John Fosbroke told his father the cause of Sir Samuel's problems.

In after years Sir Samuel described his treatment at the hands of Fosbroke to his friend the Rev. John Webb of Tretire as 'most unfeeling and brutal'.[36] For four days his life hung in the balance. The incision made in the perineum to drain the urine was still open when he wrote to Douce in late October.[37] He refused his doctors' suggestion that he wear a rubber catheter, presumably as a permanent safeguard. Considering his unhealed wound, and the tender state of his health after the operation, it is incredible that he told Douce that he had just returned on the 12th from a fortnight's trip to France. This was no rest cure, for he made the rounds of the museums and was particularly impressed with the way that coins were laid out in 'shew-glasses' rather than locked up in boxes as at the British Museum. Barely had he returned than Sir Jeffrey Wyatville arrived from Windsor, just before an 'incursion of barbarians [which] took place on the 15th October at seven o'clock at night. They were not finally expelled till 10 o'clock on the morning of the 17th'.[38] The so-called 'barbarians' included Planché, his wife and Charles Dance the playwright, one of Planché's theatrical associates.

Without regret Sir Samuel said goodbye to 1833 and looked forward to a much happier 1834. He would be instituted as High Sheriff of Herefordshire at the Lent Assizes, whilst the Court was virtually finished apart from a few articles of furniture, and his health was much improved.[39] In his Christmas letter to Douce Sir Samuel passed on some interesting observations on local customs:

> The farmers in my neighbourhood on old Xmas eve light twelve fires in a circle in a field of new sewn wheat with a larger one in the midst over which is suspended a female effigy of straw called the old witch.
> .... in the evening of the same day an ox is brought before the kitchen fire and a cake placed on his horn, when the party go on their knees and drink to it,

saying 'here's to thy pretty face and thy white horn. God send thy master a good crop of corn. Both wheat, rye and barley and all sorts of grain, and next year if we live, we'll drink to thee again'. If on the animal moving the cake falls forward the augury is favorable, if backward the reverse.[40]

On 14 February he swore his oath as High Sheriff at Ross, in front of Messrs. Evans and Bridgman, Justices of the Peace for Herefordshire. The oath included a declaration that 'I do from my heart abhor detest and abjure as impious and heretical that damnable doctrine that princes excommunicated or deprived by the Pope or any authority from the See of Rome may be deposed or murthered by their subjects or any other whatsoever'. His attorney William Hooper of Ross and Thomas Tyndale Gough of Hereford were appointed as undersheriffs.[41]

He wrote to Douce that he was looking forward to an unusually long visit to London from the middle of February until early March, and as soon as he had bought a new pair of boots from Hoby's he would proceed to a session with his old friend. It was not to be, for although he went to Douce's house as soon as he could after arriving in London and called twice more Douce was always too ill to see him. His friend laboured under 'some affection of the head which his medical man thinks may prove serious'.[42] Sir Samuel returned to Herefordshire saddened, but with the preparations for the Assizes on his mind. The necessary advertisement had been placed in the *Hereford Journal* on 5 March:

SIR SAMUEL RUSH MEYRICK, Knight of the Hanoverian Guelphic Order, SHERIFF of the County aforesaid, by virtue of divers writes of our Lord the King, to me directed, do hereby give Notice, that the Commission of Oyer and Terminer, to be in and for the County of Hereford aforesaid, will be opened at the Shire Hall, in the City of Hereford, on Saturday the 22nd day of March, instant. That on Sunday the twenty-third of March their Lordships, the Judges of Assize, will attend Divine Service, and on Monday the 24th, they will proceed to the Shire Hall to commence the public business, of which all Jurors, Chief Constables, Prosecutors, Witnesses, and others interested therein, are desired to take notice, and give their attendance accordingly. - but I do give further Notice, that the Grand Jurors will be called on Monday Morning the twenty-fourth instant, in the Crown Court, at nine o'clock precisely; and that the Petit and Party Jurors will be called over in the respective courts for which they were summoned on Monday Morning the twenty-fourth instant at eight o'clock precisely.

Sir Samuel had chosen to resurrect the custom of the Sheriff being accompanied by javelin-men who would escort the judges to the Assizes. He designed their costumes himself, in the style of the time of Henry VIII, and gave them £5 each to buy the clothing—though one *Hereford Times* correspondent later claimed it was a bribe for appearing in such a ridiculous garb.[43] The opening ceremony for the Assizes was preceded by the arrival of the High Sheriff from Goodrich, in a coach accompanied by twenty-six javelin-men and two trumpeters all on horseback, followed by a numerous escort of his friends, comprising more than two hundred highly respectable individuals in carriages and on horseback.[44] A large number of the population came to see the spectacle, as 'there seemed to be an expectation, founded probably on no other ground than Sir Samuel Meyrick having written so much on costume and armour, that his javelin-men would have some ancient style of attire ... The good citizens of Hereford could not, therefore, be disappointed when they saw the trumpeters and javelin-men of the time of Henry 8th, in green and buff, the colour of the livery, with the family badge of the ragged staff fixed to their backs and breasts. Sir Samuel himself, to do honour to His Majesty's Judges of Assize, wore a full dress court suit, and the chaplain appeared in his canonicals'.[45]

The javelin-men were drawn from among the people of Goodrich, including some of the workers who had helped to build Goodrich Court. Owing to the fact that the High Sheriff had to submit a claim for expenses at the end of his term of office many details are recorded, including their names, the cost of some of their garments, the tolls charged at the various gates as they rode from Goodrich, the amounts charged for their refreshments and that they were paid one guinea each for their pains.[46] The trumpeters—Lewis Jones and James Preece—were paid three guineas each. After Sir Samuel had been escorted to his lodgings in St. Owen Street, the javelin-men had time for 'a sumptuous repast' provided by Mr. Russell at the Bowling Green before re-mounting to escort Mr. Justice Parke to the Shire Hall. A similar performance was gone through when it was time for the Justices to leave Hereford—and an equally sustaining repast. Sir Samuel's accounts were not finally settled by Treasury Minute until 14 January 1836,[47] almost a year after his term came to an end on 9 February 1835.

Douce did not recover from his illness and died on Easter Sunday, 30 March 1834 at the age of seventy-seven, and was buried on 7 April in St. Pancras churchyard.[48] Pettigrew wrote to Sir Samuel shortly afterwards with the news, and told Sir Samuel that he was a beneficiary in Douce's will but not the details of the bequest. Probate was speedily granted, though the will was unwitnessed and more like a draft with alterations and a codicil. As a result of Nollekens' legacy, Douce was an extremely rich man. His specific cash bequests amounted to almost £10,000, whilst the residuary legatees shared an estimated £50,000.[49] His magnificent library of books, manuscripts, prints and drawings was left to the Bodleian Library.

The greatest surprise was the bequest to Dr. Meyrick of 'all my carvings in ivory or other materials, together with my miscellaneous curiosities of every description, including Greek, Roman, Egyptian and Oriental antiquities or other articles … in the fullest confidence that he will think it worthwhile to devote some small apartment in his noble mansion of Goodrich Court to their reception, either as a present museum, or as the foundation of a more extensive one …'. The will had been written in August 1830, more than a year before Douce had even seen Goodrich Court.[50]

If Sir Samuel had coveted anything belonging to Douce, it was surely his wonderful collection of early manuscripts, books and prints, rather than his 'miscellaneous curiosities'. The ivories were a different matter, dating from the Roman period to the reign of Henry VIII. Sir Samuel had already collected some ivories, and he was particularly interested in caskets or boxes which showed costume or armour of early periods. Douce's collection had many religious items in addition. His executors must have been in a quandary when it came to framed drawings, paintings and miniatures. In the event those also went to Sir Samuel rather than to the Bodleian Library.

To put it plainly, the bequest was something of an embarrassment, as Goodrich Court's public rooms and their contents had all been designed in advance down to the last detail, leaving little room for major new acquisitions. There wasn't really a suitable room to house the treasures that Sir Samuel knew were coming his way, let alone those which Douce probably had secreted in boxes all over his house. Just one room was set aside initially, but by the time that the catalogue of what he termed the Doucean Museum was published there were three rooms crowded with Douce's treasures, plus a few of Sir Samuel's own. Some choice items from the bequest were displayed in the other private rooms. Douce probably thought that his 'museum' would be open to the public, but it did not always form part of the regular tour.[51] It must have been very exciting when the boxes started arriving at the Court, and the relative dearth of letters from Sir Samuel in 1834 probably reflect the effort he put into examining the objects and then writing the catalogue. This was published in the *Gentleman's Magazine* between March and December 1836, when in the introduction he admits that he regretted that he had not been left the illuminated manuscripts.

Although Sir Samuel was too busy in the early 1830s to undertake any major published work, his pen was not still. Except for one isolated article, he contributed no more to *Archaeologia*, and his letters to the *Gentleman's Magazine* had virtually dried up, but he contributed substantial articles to the *Cambrian Quarterly* and the *Analyst*. The *Analyst* was a magazine for Worcestershire, Shropshire, Gloucestershire and Herefordshire first published in 1834, which Sir Samuel used as a vehicle for some historical articles. Sir Samuel wrote a long letter printed in one of the first issues about the house called Rudhall near Ross-on-Wye, and the families who had lived there.[52] Further articles followed: on Kentchurch Court and the Scudamore family in 1835[53] and a very long piece on Wigmore Castle, split over two issues in 1836.[54]

One consequence of Sir Samuel's removal to Goodrich was that he was even more removed from any original source material and reliant on his own reference books. It is almost possible to trace in his early works the contents of his library, except where he made extensive use of those belonging to others such as Douce. Even where he quotes from manuscripts in the British Museum, for example, he must often be using published transcriptions and illustrations which became widely available in the early 19th century. Indeed, it would hardly have been possible at that time to do anything else, and although he quotes authorities in his larger works he does not do so in articles for the *Gentleman's Magazine* or the *Analyst*. He didn't have the opportunity to work with a large quantity of original material again until 1840.

The most important publishing venture for Sir Samuel during the mid-1830s was a collaboration with Henry Shaw, a very talented architectural artist and engraver who had originally started as a draughtsman working with John Britton on the *Cathedral Antiquities* series. He became very interested in all manner of medieval decoration and costume, and published a number of beautifully illustrated books on the subject from the 1830s onwards. Sir Samuel may have been acquainted with Shaw through Thomas Willement, his stained glass artist. Willement had introduced Shaw to Francis Douce in early 1830, as Shaw wanted Douce's advice on his forthcoming publication, *Illuminated Ornaments*, about the decorations of the middle ages.[55]

Shaw was often travelling around, drawing specimens of medieval art, architecture and furniture, and in the summer of 1834 he visited Goodrich Court.[56] He must have stayed for some days, as he made drawings of an ornate mirror, a napkin press,

Fig. 70   A mirror at Goodrich Court engraved by Henry Shaw

two beds, various candlesticks and inkstands and fireplace furniture. These he engraved for *Specimens of Ancient Furniture* which was published in parts by William Pickering. Sir Samuel wrote the twenty-six page introduction to the work which he dated 10 July

1835, plus notes on the individual pieces which were shown in seventy-four plates. In 1837 Pickering published *Ancient Plate and Furniture from the Colleges of Oxford and the Ashmolean Museum*, a slim volume consisting of highly coloured versions of ten of the seventy-four plates from the *Specimens of Ancient Furniture*, with their accompanying descriptions.

The work was dedicated by Shaw to Thomas Lister Parker, an old friend of Sir Samuel and fellow admirer of the medieval arts, who had visited Goodrich Court only a few weeks before Shaw. The introduction is interesting, as it sets out one of Sir Samuel's governing principles: 'in an historical component, correctness in the auxiliaries is scarcely less important than in the more prominent parts, for the introduction of a wardrobe or a chair of the time of Queen Anne in the representation of an apartment of the reign of Henry Sixth, is as glaring an error as to depict soldiers at the battle of Cressy in the uniform and with the weapons of the dragoon guards of the present day. Extreme accuracy, even in the minutest detail, can alone produce that illusion which is requisite for the perfect success of a work of art'.

It must be remembered that accurate descriptions of domestic medieval architecture and furniture had not been published to any great extent. Sir Samuel's authorities were contemporary documents which described, usually in passing, decorations of apartments—admittedly those of kings or nobles. One document, dating from 1236, directs that 'the great chamber of the king at Westminster [should be] painted with good green colour, in imitation of a curtain, ... and also the little wardrobe of the king to have painted in the fashion of a curtain'. Perhaps this was the inspiration for a similar design in Llewellyn's bedroom.

In fact, Sir Samuel's remarks presage the later colourful re-creations of the medieval by the gothic architect and designer William Burges:

> Instead of fancying with the mind's eye that we behold the stately knights and dames of old sitting within bare walls, and resting their feet on rushes, - instead of imagining that we imitate their greatest splendour when we confine the decorations of rooms in modern Gothic buildings, to oak and stone relieved with a little gilding, - we must now do them the justice to allow, that while their tables glittered with plate and jewels, their beds dazzled with the richness of their hangings, and their seats were decorated with refulgent draperies, the Gothic carving of their furniture became brilliant by scarlet, blue and gold, and the walls of their apartments had the most interesting, as well as most effective appearance, from the grand paintings or the rich tapestry which were placed upon them.[57]

Fig. 71   Moustachioed helmet later owned
by William Burges

Burges was born in 1827, and after attending King's College in London was articled to Edward Blore. It's not too fanciful to suppose that the Meyrick collection helped to foster his love of the medieval, and he later acquired one of the ivories and some of the arms and armour. These included various helmets including one with a visor in the form of a moustache, breastplates, weapons and a buckler.[58]

To a modern mind, Shaw casts his net too widely, furniture and artefacts up to the reign of Queen Anne being included in the scope of the work—they could hardly have been called 'ancient' in 1835. As his avowed aim was to draw from the life, he had little choice because of the dearth of truly ancient furniture, although in fact some illustrations are copies of other documents. For once, artistic licence would have been preferable to show the furniture in its likely setting, rather than sitting in splendid isolation. The quality of Shaw's engraving is, however, superb.

The Douce bequest meant that Sir Samuel had had very little time to think about his own collection, and indeed he seems to have been tempted only by an apparatus for weighing armour from Isaac, which the dealer offered for £35.[59] As well as the constant stream of visitors to see the armour and the Doucean Museum, there were more illustrious arrivals. Prince George, son of the Prince of Cambridge and nephew to the Duke of Sussex had visited the Court, and Llewellyn had afterwards been hunting with him in Sussex.[60] Sir Thomas Phillipps and his daughters had been shown round the armour personally, and Sir Thomas had been grateful enough to send Sir Samuel a copy of one of his Middle Hill publications.[61] Otherwise Sir Samuel was busy setting up a tableau of Charles I in the Armoury, and getting Henry Briggs to make the face and hands.[62] He was also planning to improve the approach road from Pencraig.

As 1837 dawned Sir Samuel's only real worry was his son. Llewellyn had been complaining of indigestion for some time and had been losing weight, but he had refused to see a doctor. Finally a bout of influenza brought him so low that he consented to do so, but even then his medical attendants did not think he was in any immediate danger. Just a week later on 14 February he was dead, having told Sir Samuel the night before that he could not live. In the morning the 'poor dear fellow ... took an affectionate leave and expired on my breast'.[63] Llewellyn was only thirty-two, but his health had caused concern since the early 1820s. His father thought that it was 'some organic derangement about the heart', whose beat had become 'very languid'. The overt symptoms of pulmonary tuberculosis were well known but not always present: another possibility is rheumatic fever which often left a weakened heart muscle.

Llewellyn was buried on 21 February, close to the north wall of Goodrich church. In spite of the fact that he had often spent considerable periods away from home, there is no reason to think that the ties of affection with his father were other than close. Sir Samuel must have been heartbroken. According to Robert Curzon, Llewellyn was 'a remarkably fine handsome man, six foot high'.[64] Although two portraits of him are known to have existed, their current whereabouts are unknown. One was a miniature painted by Simon Rochard when Llewellyn was fifteen, dressed in his 'gentleman commoner's' gown at Oxford.[65] The other was a full-scale portrait by Richard Westall which hung in the banqueting hall at Goodrich. Llewellyn was depicted in the 'act of thanksgiving', supposedly at a moment when 'his young mind was calm and serene, pouring forth his "Hymn of Praise" for the bounteous goodness vouchsafed by Providence'.[66]

In spite of his ill-health, Llewellyn had made no will—or at least none was produced by Sir Samuel for probate. Administration of his estate was granted to his father in April 1837, with Francis Martin and Joseph Hawker, also of the Heralds' College acting as bondsmen. The monetary value alone of his estate was nearly £66,000—equivalent to more than £3 million pounds today. Although

Fig. 72 The Meyrick grave before restoration in 1942

144

it must seem to posterity unfortunate that he had no heirs, the fact remains that he had plenty of time to marry had he so wished. In 1827 Sir Samuel had replied to an enquiry on the subject by Joseph Skelton, 'Llewellyn is but three and twenty, so has still three years to search for a better half, but I have never heard him admire animated antiquities'.[67] Why he had 'still three years' is a mystery. When Llewellyn died, Sir Samuel himself was only fifty-three, and possibly still capable of fathering children in spite of his illness.

It seems strange that so little can be said about Llewellyn himself. An early turn for scholarship may be an illusion fostered by the powerful influence of his father, as his career at Oxford was not particularly distinguished. Until he came into the income from his fortune, there was little he could do in exerting his will. The first departure from Sir Samuel's plan was that he did not stay his year in Göttingen, and the remainder of his life was spent in the pleasures of an affluent young man. Although he showed a passing interest in the design of Goodrich Court, his main concern was the garden—according to the testimony of his father and his friends.

Sir Samuel's response to the terrible shock of Llewellyn's death was two-fold. One involved his unfailing nostrum—a trip to Paris to see the sights, and to look around the dealers' emporia. He took as an adult companion Francis Martin, the herald. Martin had lived in Paris for nearly three years before the Revolution, and had re-visited it in 1821, when he had been shocked by how the people were 'so altered and brutalized'.[68] He approved the new public buildings, and had the opportunity of seeing them by private introduction, as Sir Samuel's 'work on Antient Armour has gained him great celebrity throughout Europe'. Indeed, Skelton's *Engraved Illustrations* had already been published by Fincke of Berlin in an abridged German edition. On their way back, they went from Brighton to Portsmouth to see the dockyard, and then via Wilton House and Berkeley Castle back to Goodrich Court. Martin stayed but a fortnight before the death of William IV summoned him back to London. Sir Samuel's other companion on his trip to France was a young teenage boy—Edwin James Coward.

Edwin's story begins more than twenty years earlier, only a year after Mary Meyrick's death in 1818. In 1819 Sir Samuel acquired a new cook, Mary Williams, who was a native of Shropshire. She had lived with him for three years when she married James Coward at Kensington in September 1822.[69] Their son Edwin was born in February 1824, a decent interval after marriage, and as Mary was working as a housekeeper for an auctioneer at the time[70] there seems no reason to doubt that Edwin was James Coward's son. It is a coincidence, however, that he was named Edwin James, as this was also the name of Sir Samuel's little brother who had died in 1792, aged three and a half.[71] In 1868 Robert Curzon wrote that Samuel 'lived with his late wife's maid and she wore all her late mistress's dresses. I remember her in Cadogan Place'.[72] Curzon is not altogether reliable as he incorrectly attributed Samuel's being cut out of his father's will to this fact, and he was only eight when Mary Meyrick died, but he did know Sir Samuel by the time he was sixteen, and possibly earlier.[73]

The Cowards soon moved back into Upper Cadogan Place with Sir Samuel, but it was not a happy arrangement. Sir Samuel allowed Mary's husband to 'come and sleep upon the premises'[74] but 'in consequence of Coward's behaviour becoming irksome he was compelled to order his removal'.[75] Mary Coward remained as Sir Samuel's house-keeper until 1841. From 1826 Sir Samuel mentions a 'Miss Williams' in the odd letter, and in the summer of 1826 she accompanied him and Llewellyn when he visited Sudeley Castle and Tewkesbury, and he left them both behind at Brand Cottage, the cottage that he had rented in Malvern, when he returned to London.[76] 'Miss Williams' could have been Mary Coward, but it's possible that Mary had a sister who was house-keeping for Llewellyn.

In mid-November Llewellyn was still in Malvern,[77] but it's unfortunate that Mary Coward's whereabouts are unknown as she conceived another son at this time. Henry Coward was born on 17 August 1827 and baptised the next day at Colwall church, allegedly the son of James and Mary Coward of Brand Cottage, servants.[78] Sir Samuel was staying with Llewellyn at the time, and had been there earlier in the year, when Mary Coward may have been taken to Brand Cottage to await her confinement. Just seven weeks after the birth, Sir Samuel happened to mention to Joseph Skelton apropos Brand Cottage that '... he [Llewellyn] and Miss Williams have now with them Mr. Martin ... and Mr. Lister Parker, with young Buckler'.[79] Was James Coward truly Henry's father? Had Henry lived an answer may have been forthcoming, but he died the following February and was buried at Kensington.[80]

During the early years at Goodrich Court the Cowards fade into the background, although Mary was often the person who conducted visitors around the Court. The shillings paid for this privilege were enough to earn her about £50 a year, which paid for Edwin's education. This all changed in 1836, when a scandal erupted which must have caused severe embarrassment to Sir Samuel, and shone the spotlight on their rela-tionship. Mary had a younger brother, Enoch, and he had come to live in Ross. No doubt Sir Samuel's influence had been responsible for getting him a job as a clerk with the Hoopers, Sir Samuel's own attorneys. One of the suppliers to Goodrich Court was a butcher living in Ross, one Wellington. Because Sir Samuel had come to believe that Wellington was charging him too much for his meat, he decided to stop patronising him. Wellington took umbrage, and wrote a letter to Sir Samuel claiming that someone in his house was passing on some of the meat to a person in Ross, and that Wellington's delivery man was taking it to him. Although no names were quoted, the implication was that Mary Coward was supplying her brother Enoch with the meat. Sir Samuel then flew into a rage, and apparently dismissed Mary immediately, in spite of her length of service with him. The next turn of events was unexpected, and unfortunate.

The absent James Coward sued the unfortunate Wellington for £2,000 damages, a ridiculous amount, alleging loss of income for Mary Coward because of her dismissal. It seems unlikely that Mary Coward herself would have started the action, and the suggestion was made in court that it was a way Sir Samuel could punish Wellington for his insolence. If his conceit was such that he thought that his standing in the county would shield him from awkward questions he was sadly mistaken.

The case came to trial in Hereford in the middle of August, when Wellington was found guilty, but the damages were assessed at a derisory shilling. The accounts of the case in the local papers were fairly anodyne. However, someone friendly to Wellington (or inimical to Sir Samuel) must have decided that a full account of the trial should be spread abroad. Fortunately a copy has survived in Hereford Library, and so Sir Samuel's humiliating cross-examination can be witnessed. The account is one-sided, naturally, and the verbatim answers may not be accurate, but it's clear that Wellington was well served by his advocate, a Mr. Phillips. Phillips' tactic was to disprove that Mary Coward had in fact been dismissed, and that the case had been unwisely concocted by Sir Samuel and Mary's brother Enoch. James Coward, he said 'had no more knowledge of the case than the man in the Moon'.

Mary Coward had wisely taken herself off to stay with her father who lived in Tong in Shropshire two months before the case started. Although Wellington and Enoch Williams had to take their turn on the stand, in the account Phillips' questioning of them was mainly related to facts. The court enjoyed the spectacle of Powel Hooper, Sir Samuel's attorney's son and junior, being unable to tell the court who had instructed his firm and who was going to pay their bills! When it came to Sir Samuel's long spell in the witness box, Phillips' main weapon was innuendo. He started by doubting that Sir Samuel could have turned off Mary without allowing her to state her case, after so many years in his service. Was it not a fact, anyway, that Mary had returned to Goodrich Court a number of times after her dismissal, walked in the gardens with Sir Samuel, and even spent a number of nights there? (Laughter). Phillips even managed to put the thought into peoples' heads that maybe the accusation had come at a convenient time when Mary had to be sent away for a few months—she was, after all, 'ill' during this time. By his adroit questions, Phillips had managed to make Sir Samuel expose himself as bad-tempered, mean and somewhat less than truthful.

Eventually Mary did return to Goodrich, though where her son Edwin had been in the interim is not known. What is quite clear is that Edwin was not a typical servant's child, kept out of sight and out of mind. Taking a charitable view and absolving Mary Coward of manipulation, it is still remarkable that within six months of Llewellyn's death in February 1837 Sir Samuel had decided to adopt Edwin and give him the surname of Meyrick.[81] There's no doubt that Edwin himself was a very taking little boy, totally lacking in guile. Later events would prove that, though foolish and gullible, he was certainly not calculating. The herald Francis Martin calls him amiable and delightful, and 'a pet of mine since he was three'.[82] In fact, Edwin managed to charm all Sir Samuel's middle-aged friends, and they willingly acted as surrogate uncles.

Matters moved on apace. Sir Samuel's will had to be rewritten following Llewellyn's death, when he took the opportunity to make Edwin his heir. Francis Martin must have raised some objection, and Sir Samuel consulted his legal friend Kirkmann, typically without offering to pay.[83] Martin's letter had contained the mysterious phrase 'only think so and so has married his servant maid', which is extremely intriguing.

The process of turning Edwin from a sow's ear into a silk purse was begun. His name was put down for Eton, and then it was planned that he should go to Christ Church, Oxford. At no stage does a hint of doubt as to whether he was doing the right thing for Edwin enter Sir Samuel's mind. Edwin was to be groomed and moulded into a substitute Llewellyn. There was just one fatal flaw in this plan—Edwin was neither clever, nor cunning enough to appear so. Indeed, the spelling in his letters to Sir Samuel from Eton is poor, and it's possible that he suffered from dyslexia.[84] It's very touching that Sir Samuel saved these six letters, in spite of later events. He underlined the spelling mistakes in pencil, and the one letter which contains more than re-iterated commonplaces, in which Edwin mentions seeing the Queen and her 'intended', is sadly labelled 'the best'.

The plans for Edwin ground remorsefully on, in spite of his Eton tutor's unfavourable report.[85] How much his Eton fellow pupils knew of his background is difficult to say, but Sir Samuel's largesse enabled him to acquire a boat, so he probably followed the time-honoured practice of buying friends. A fellow pupil at Eton was Augustus Meyrick, the son of Sir Samuel's cousin, William Henry Meyrick, and his natural heir. This may have been the first intimation to the Meyrick family that Sir Samuel's riches were not to come their way.

Sir Samuel had wished to send Llewellyn to Christ Church College, Oxford, though in the end he had been thwarted—but Edwin did start there in the Michaelmas term of 1840. Fortunately Edwin does not seem to have been a sensitive child, and his happy-go-lucky nature must have spared him from the dread of social ostracism, and the academic torture to come at Oxford. Sir Samuel himself escorted Edwin to his rooms in Peckwater Quad in October 1840, in spite of illness and a prior claim of Sir Thomas Phillipps to his time. Edwin and the academic requirements of Oxford did not agree. The adjectives describing his set work during the Michaelmas term must have caused painful scenes during the Christmas vacation —'absurdi', 'omnium nihillisme'.[86]

Worse was to come for the Cowards, for Mary died at the age of forty-three on 13 March 1841. She had suffered from indifferent health for some time, and the cause given was 'decline'. It's possible that it was tuberculosis, or indeed that she suffered from the complications of gonorrhea. After all, Sir Samuel had told his friend Pettigrew just a few months after his infection in 1832 that he 'much more frequently ... *militare non sine gloria*. Methinks I see you smile ... but at my age this is something. I am almost forty-nine'.[87] One could assume from his remark that he 'marched not without glory' that he was still sexually active. The only candidate for his attentions was Mary Coward, and it would not be the first time that a housekeeper had satisfied her employer's needs. There is no proof of this, and we should not apply modern standards of sexual continence (or lack of it) to Sir Samuel. The fact remains that he was a passionate man who may have found his natural urges hard to suppress.

Mary's flat tombstone lies hard against the railings of the Meyrick tomb, which hopefully signifies the affection in which she was held, rather than Sir Samuel's disinclination to lash out on a new plot. Edwin came home briefly from Oxford for the funeral,[88] but before long his whole future began to unravel. The Hooper family, aware of the contents of Sir Samuel's will, had encouraged Edwin to dangle after their daughter Penelope. It was while Edwin was away from home with them that bills began to arrive from Oxford: for music lessons, clothes, a flute, jewellery, hire of a tennis court—the dunning continued through the autumn and winter. Although theoretically Sir Samuel was not responsible for Edwin's debts, he was to shell out more than £500.[89]

Edwin could not have chosen a better place to wound Sir Samuel—his wallet was ever a tender spot. But this is unkind, for it is evident that the railing over Edwin's debts in his letters to Kirkmann and other friends conceals a deeply wounded heart. He had loved Edwin, and Edwin's ingratitude and careless cruelty hurt him to the core. Did he now appreciate how his father felt when he had been similarly betrayed? His reaction was as swift—he immediately made a new will, making Augustus Meyrick his main heir, and giving Edwin a small annuity. Poor Edwin's heart had always governed his head, and now he was cast off by his 'father', and indeed by Penelope Hooper since his prospects were gone. He was surely more sinned against than sinning.

Sir Samuel never let Edwin come near to him again, and his letters were ignored. It's this behaviour that surely gives the lie to the possibility that Edwin was his son. He did make Edwin an allowance, and left him an annuity of £200. By raising Edwin's aspirations, Sir Samuel had given him a taste of a gentleman's life, and so Edwin was to describe himself (and his father) when he married Jane Jones, a farmer's daughter at Llanfoist near Abergavenny, when still only eighteen. In a short time they had a large family of daughters, before Edwin died of consumption aged only thirty in 1854. By then he was penniless, and his wife lost what little income she had from the annuity. In 1860 she was still trying to find out if Llewellyn Meyrick had left a will, presumably hoping that Llewellyn might have left something to Edwin.[90] Sir Samuel had destroyed Edwin, but it's doubtful if he ever acknowledged it, even to himself.

10   The Goodrich Court Experience

Imagine that you are a visitor to the Wye Valley—perhaps someone like Louisa Twamley, who had visited Ross-on-Wye in 1838, collecting material for a travel book to be entitled *An Autumn Ramble by the Wye*.[1] You describe your visit in a letter to a friend:

As soon as the Monday morning rain cleared we set forward in our carriage to Goodrich. Leaving Ross by the Wilton bridge, we bowled along in the direction of Monmouth. Glimpses of Goodrich Court began to appear along the road, and at Weir-end the Sussex tower could be seen filling a gap in a noble avenue of trees. But at Glewstone ferry about three or four miles from Ross the Court suddenly came into view in full majesty, appearing to command all the contiguous country, with the romantic ruins of Goodrich Castle in the vicinity, the meandering Wye hurrying towards the rock on which it stands, and Coppet Hill forming its background.

The horses struggled up the incline to Pencraig village, but shortly the carriage drew up at the

Fig. 73   The gatehouse to Goodrich Court
from Nash's guidebook

Fig. 74   The approach to Goodrich Court from Fosbroke's *Wye Tour*

Fig. 75   The front door, by George Shaw

Fig. 76   The Court's front door knocker

impressive entrance to the grounds of Goodrich Court. We learnt that the gatehouse was completed rather later than the Court itself, in 1837.[2] It is called 'The Monmouth Gate', and indeed it does resemble the fortified Monnow bridge there.

We drove through the open parkland, judiciously planted with maturing trees under the direction of Llewellyn Meyrick, Sir Samuel's late lamented son. As we passed the top of a ravine leading down to the river the Court sprang into view again, the brightness of the red sandstone rather spoiling the effect to my mind. We passed a small tower which proved to be the brewhouse, and swept over the bridge across a dry moat and through the principal gateway with its portcullis into the quadrangle or courtyard.

As we waited for the door to be answered, I looked around at the courtyard. I should guess it is about seventy feet by fifty feet, and on one side there is a great blank wall which turned out to belong to the Armoury. The doorknocker is particularly fine, made in bronze to the design of Giovanni of Bologna, representing the destruction of the Philistines by Samson.[3] On either side of the front door there is stained glass in the windows, and also in the window above the porch. A most polite footman admitted us and asked us to leave our cards.

As soon as I entered the hall, Sir Samuel's ruling passion became obvious. Displays of ancient weapons and stags' heads ornament the walls. A low arch leads towards the stairway, which is lit by an ancient bronze hanging lamp found in the ruins of

Fig. 77   The front hall, by Skelton

Fig. 78   Roman lamp in the front hall, by Skelton

Herculaneum, wonderfully cast with horses heads. The morning sun shone through the stained glass on the stairs, which Sir Samuel had painted by Mr. Willement to represent Meyrick ap Llewellyn, Esquire to the body of King Henry VII and one of his ancestors, I believe.[4]

The housekeeper having informed Sir Samuel of our arrival, we were so fortunate as to be conducted around his collection personally. Sir Samuel told me that sometimes there are as many as nine visitors' carriages outside, and that when there were too many seeking admittance they were limited to half an hour's tour. Usually the housekeeper or a housemaid escorted the visitors, almost a full-time job in the summer. He took us firstly to the Asiatic Ante Room, where he has a figure dressed as an Indian rajah in armour called Pindarrie, mounted on a carved Arabian steed.[5] He told us that Captain Grindley had brought the armour back from India. Next to him is a man in ancient Moorish armour, and all around the room are glass cases holding arms and armour from Asia. Sir Samuel told me that a number of the arms were collected by Mr. Claudius Rich, the famous author of books on Babylon and Perseopolis.[6] A beautiful Indian chess board in the room, inlaid with ivory and metal, was left to Sir Samuel as part of the bequest of Mr. Douce's treasures.

Figs. 79 & 80   The Asiatic Armoury with right, Polygar's armour, both by Skelton

The ante room leads into the main Asiatic Armoury, a circular room in the south-east tower, which I suppose is about twenty feet across. Sir Samuel has decorated the walls in Moorish style, with a blue ceiling scattered with gold stars, and over the fire-place is embedded one of the tiles from the Alhambra Palace at Granada in Spain. There are Chinese coloured drawings and glass cases filled with Hindoo idols and other curiosities from Mr. Douce's collection, such as a large carved box of coral. The room seemed almost too small for the two mounted warriors, one a Marhatta in a crimson velvet war dress, the other dressed as one of the Mogul's guard. There is also the armour of a Rajah from Northern India which once belonged to H.R.H. the Duke of York. Sir Samuel has displayed there the great standard of the Janissaries, which was

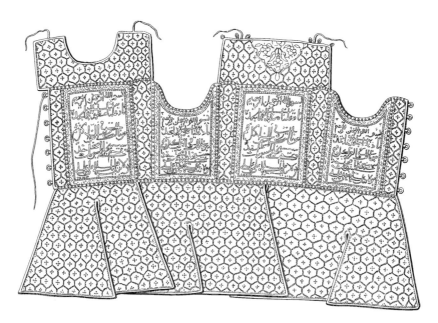

Fig. 81   Rajah's armour-plated rhinoceros hide, by Skelton

hung from a pole surmounted by a brass crescent. The flag is made of pale buff silk surrounded with a crimson border on which are written Arabic characters in gold.[7] The Janissaries were massacred at Constantinople by the orders of Sultan Mahmud II in 1826.[8]

The next room is the South Sea room, which is filled with weapons and clothing made from natural materials and feathers, from the people of the Pacific Islands. Sir Samuel told us that a war cloak made of feathers had been brought back by Captain Cook himself, and had been given to the collection by Lady Sarah Napier. Since his boyhood Sir Samuel had always been very interested in the Cook voyages, and the stories of the people of that part of the world. He had written for the *Gentleman's Magazine* on the subject of the Tahiteans some years ago.[9]

Fig. 82   Banner of the Janissaries now in the British Museum

156

Among his other curiosities was some wooden body-armour from the Sitca islands on the north-west coast of America, which were visited by Captain Cook.

The South Sea room leads into the Banqueting Hall, some fifty feet long with a minstrel's gallery over the entrance and also a most extraordinary thing, a billiard table on a raised floor instead of the high table. Sir Samuel seeing my surprise, explained that there were early examples of such a contrivance. In the three windows which look down onto the Grand Quadrangle are shields with arms of people associated with Goodrich, those of Valence, Warrine and Marshall. The east window which looks towards Goodrich Castle has the Comyn arms, appropriately as Elizabeth Comyn brought the Manor of Goodrich as her dowry to Richard Talbot on their marriage.[10] In niches under the gallery are statues of Edward II and his mother, copied from their effigies, both holding orbs and sceptres.[11]

The walls are papered crimson with gold fleur-de-lis which set off portraits of historical personages, as well as those of Sir Samuel himself by Briggs, and of his late son Llewellyn by Westall. In the dwarf bookcases lining the walls are many rare and valuable books, and on their tops lie a number of the exquisite ivory caskets left by Mr. Douce, each in itself a wonderful object and worthy of display cases of their own. On a lectern stands a copy of the Nuremburg Chronicle in its original binding of 1493. In the oriel window are representations of William and Aylmer de Valence, owners of Goodrich Castle in the reigns of Henry II and Edward I.

The entrance to the Hastilude Chamber lies alongside the billiard table, a room open on one side to the Armoury. I asked Sir Samuel what the name of the room meant, and he told me that it meant, in Latin, literally 'spear play', and that there were historical precedents for tableaux of such events. It was a pity we had not entered the Armoury from the far end, as when the Hastilude Chamber is viewed from that direction, there is the most perfect representation of a Tournament, complete with list, a royal box, figures dressed as heralds and all manner of jousting armour and lances from the period of Henry VI to Queen Elizabeth. Opposite the entrance appears the heraldic tree, from the branches of which are suspended the seven shields of the combatants, of various shapes, according to the dates of their armour.[12] The two heralds are dressed in their tabards, with black velvet caps on their heads and red stockings. One holds a casque,[13] the other a sword.

The armour of the different combatants being taken from the periods of the reigns of Edward IV to Elizabeth, it is a tournament which could never have happened in reality. Two combatants are already engaged in the list, Frederic Von Hurnheym of

Fig. 83   The Hastilude chamber as drawn by Skelton

Swabia from 1543, and William V, Duke of Bavaria from 1585. The former is wielding an enormous lance, and his horse is richly caparisoned in crimson and amber silk damask, with the word Hurnheym occurring four times on a black velvet border. On the chanfron[14] are his arms, and around the horse's neck a row of bells. William's horse wears the arms of Bavaria, which William also bears in relief on his shoulder-shield. His helmet has a little door in the face. It was through such that Henri IV of France suffered a terrible injury with a lance during a tournament, and died after some days of agony, never being allowed to see his beloved Diane de Poitiers.

On the back of the royal box is a piece of tapestry of the time of Henry VI, and standing outside the lists one of Sir Samuel's newer acquisitions, an armourer's anvil of the time of Benvenuto Cellini, embossed with the design which would appear on the finished article.[15] Sir Samuel has added figures in costumes he designed and had made for the javelin men who accompanied him on his installation as High Sheriff in 1834. They are of the style of the time of Henry VIII. They are accompanied by the two trumpeters with beautiful banners to their trumpets.

You can visualise the Grand Armoury when I tell you that it is eighty-six feet long, and very high. It is lit by great glass skylights, but I imagine it could be dark on a winter's day. The floor and roof beams are all made of oak, and so is the gallery which runs around three of its sides. In the galleries are ten large glass cases, which Sir Samuel had constructed to hold his many rare examples of ancient armour and his complete series of the gun from its invention to the firelock. Above the glass cases are twelve emblazoned banners of ancient owners of land in Herefordshire, such as Roger de Mortymer and Henri de Pembrugge.[16] Between the cases Sir Samuel had arranged eighty-four halberds, in chronological groups for better instruction. All the arms and armour have been labelled with descriptions on small cards written by Sir Samuel - I was surprised to see how many of the pieces had been donated by well-wishers.[17]

I found standing with the mounted armour on the floor of the armoury almost overwhelming. I was surrounded by the colour of the draperies and the cold gleam of the steel armour. I could have wished that the faces of the dummies inside the armour were rather better made, and also that careless members of the public had not forced Sir Samuel to put notices telling them not to touch in many places in the public rooms. This is a minor annoyance compared with the wonderful display which seems on the verge of coming to life.

Mr. Nash's guide book is invaluable in helping me remember some of the most interesting pieces. Sir Samuel has arranged them in chronological order, as far as possible, so that one can see the development of the features of the armour through the ages. His intention, as ever, is instruction. On the left as one enters from the hastilude chamber is one of the earliest pieces, the suit of an English man-at-arms, dating from about 1360, mounted on horseback. Its right hand rests on the crest, put with its furniture on the helm of Sir Richard Pembridge. Opposite rides a mounted knight in German armour dating from 1445.

Fig. 84   Hand-written cards that accompanied the armour displays

Sir Samuel has clothed his horse in a caparison bearing the arms of an ancestor of Sir Gelly Meyrick.

Then there was a Genoese cross-bowman of 1420 wearing the kind of helmet called a *salade*, with a moveable vizor, winding up a stirruped cross-bow. In a niche stands an Italian guisarmier wearing a jazerine jacket, covered with crimson velvet and ornamented with brass studs, is followed by an armed knight from 1490, equipped for battle and wearing one of the earliest examples of fluted armour. The next suit, that of a German infantry officer from about 1500, was so wonderfully decorated that I could not believe it could ever have been intended for war, but only for display. One of the scenes depicted on the armour shows Hercules lifting a giant, and strangling the Nemean lion. Of the same date is a suit that belonged to Albert IV, King of Bavaria. Sir Samuel told me that it was worn by the King's Champion at the coronation of King George IV in 1821.[18]

I had heard of this ancient ritual, whereby the Royal Champion rides on horse-back into the Coronation banquet held at Westminster Hall and presents himself to the newly-crowned sovereign. The last two sovereigns, William and Victoria, have dispensed with the ceremony, much to Sir Samuel's disgust. There are some amusing stories about this ceremony, but not told by Sir Samuel as he seems to take it very seriously. One of the traditions is that the Champion should challenge any supposed pretender to the throne by throwing down his gauntlet three times. Each time one of the heralds accompanying him picks the gauntlet up again, but on two occasions (in 1689 and 1761) it has been seized by somebody who made off with it! Even worse, at James II's coronation in 1685 the champion had flung his gauntlet so vigorously that he had fallen off his horse in pursuit of it, and had lain helpless like a stranded beetle, his limbs thrashing about. The Queen had snorted and the King had laughed openly.[19]

Sir Samuel told me that the last time the ceremony had been planned, at the coronation of George IV, the hereditary champion was the Rev. Dymoke, but as a clergyman he had sought to have a deputy to play the part for him. Initially this was to have been Mr. William Reader, one of Sir Samuel's antiquarian aquaintances, in which case Sir Samuel's late son Llewellyn would have been one of the pages. On Sir Samuel's advice, the horse of the Champion should have been covered in red velvet with a broad scroll border, and the Champion himself should have worn a highly polished fluted suit with a scarf of cloth of gold, and a plume of fourteen falls of white ostrich feathers. In the event only the row of ostrich feathers next to the horse's head were white, then there were blue feathers, then red, surmounted by black feathers from a heron.[20]

Fig. 85   Ceremony of the Champion at George IV's coronation

I remember reading in the *Times* that the Rev. Dymoke's son, Henry, had finally taken his father's part as the Champion, and had spent many hours practising at Astley's Amphitheatre on their piebald horse 'Cato', which was used in the ceremony as it was accustomed to crowds. His practice armour and the one used at the banquet were borrowed from Mr. Gwennap's stock at the Gothic Hall in Pall Mall. At his dress rehearsal Mr. Dymoke must have been considerably disconcerted to have an audience of nobility and gentry including the Duchess of St. Albans and Lady Caroline Lamb. Indeed, while Mr. Dymoke was changing his armour Lady Caroline entertained the crowd by showing that she, too, was capable of riding Cato backwards.[21] I have read that as the armour was borrowed for the occasion and the champion could not claim it from the monarch as his right, a brand-new suit was made to give to him.

The next suit of armour which took my eye was one which more nearly than any other follows in metal the style of the clothes of the day. It is so-called *puffed and slashed* armour, of an infantry officer of about 1510. Sir Samuel told me that he had been offered £600 for it, but had refused the offer.[22] Another suit had belonged to William IV, the successor to Albert IV, Duke of Bavaria, and like Albert's suit had been looted by Buonaparte's armies in their campaigns across Europe, and had come from his imperial residence.

I was surprised to see that not all the plate armour was burnished brightly, but some was black and some russet coloured. Sir Samuel explained that steel armour had always had a problem with rust, and various means had been used to overcome it. Sometimes the armour was left with the blue-black colour from the heat of the forge, and sometimes it was painted with black paint.[23] Finer armours were decorated with gold or silver which also helped to protect them. He was so kind as to tell me how to clean armour.[24] He recommends the use of a lathe with several wheels, either with brushes inserted into them, or with leather pads. If the rust has very much eaten into the armour, in places where there is no engraving or decoration then the leather wheel or *bob* should be dressed with emery and fine corn; next with flour emery and then it can be polished with the brush wheel and flour emery. When the rust is on parts covered with gilding, engraving or etching a hard brush on the lathe should be used, with fine corn emery, and then finished with a brush and flour emery, but the leather bob should not be used. In places that the lathe cannot reach, he recommends the use of walnut or mahogany sticks, covered with buff leather and dressed with the same materials as the bob. When I asked him how armour was 'browned', he said he had a recipe but it involved nitric acid, among other strong chemicals.[25]

One black suit in particular had a striking red cross emblazoned on the breastplate (see plate 15). The suit was made for a German knight of the Order of St. George of

Ravenna in or shortly after the year 1534. The Order was instituted by Pope Paul III at this date to counter the Barbary pirates.[26] A fluted suit of about the same time belonged to Ferdinand, King of the Romans, brother of the Emperor Charles V. This figure holds a fine sword which has an ancient German inscription which runs down each side of the blade and over the cross-bar.[27] The meaning is

Beware you – Have a care of me – If I find you – I will mince you
Look up and observe – have a care of one who will harm you –
Want of faith is prevalent

Some of the items in the collection now became more highly decorated. Sir Samuel showed me a suit of Genoese demi-launcers' armour of 1535, decorated in a curious fashion which was the prototype of embossing. The ground of the armour is black, but the foliage decoration is raised about a tenth of an inch, and made to shine. The pauldrons, elbow-pieces and knee-pieces have raised lion's heads upon them.[28] Remembering portraits from the time of Henry VIII, I was amused to see that the armour of the period followed the fashion of the clothes, perhaps of necessity considering the vast appetites of the period, in being *long-bellied* – Sir Samuel's words, not mine. Not only long, but capacious, the large surface offering plenty of room for the engraved decoration.[29]

A plain suit of an officer of demi-launcers is remarkable for the thickness and great weight of the breastplate, which is needed to resist pistol balls. I noticed that the thigh pieces or *cuisses* were made very large to accommodate the puffed breeches of the period.[30] Sir Samuel told me that at the beginning of Elizabeth's reign these trousers were so exaggerated that a sort of *scaffold* had been erected over the seats in the parliament house, 'for them to sit upon who used the wearing of great breeches stuffed with hair like woolsacks'.[31] Equally amusing was the information that there had been a proclamation in Queen Mary's time that no man should were his shoes above six inches wide at the toes! This affectation can be seen on some suits of armour. I suppose the armourers were kept as busy as seamstresses altering armour into the current fashion.

A figure of an officer of men-at-arms leans upon an ancient war-saddle, covered with crimson velvet, with prettily engraved steel plates. Sir Samuel told me that a splendid mounted suit of russet armour inlaid with gold dated to about 1550, and had belonged to Helionorus, Duc de Longueville, of the Chateau de Coulommiers en Brie, who was born in 1542 and died in 1573.[32]

The next beautiful suit from about 1560 belonged to Alexander Sforza, Count Burgonuovo. This is a superbly decorated gilt suit, with an equally costly saddle. With it is a baton which is said to have belonged to the Duke of Alva or Alba, which is made of russeted steel covered with figures inlaid in gold within silver lines. The figures allow calculations about the formation of different number of troops in an army, and the interior is hollow to contain papers, probably the muster roll of an army.[33]

Having seen so many magnificent pieces of armour from the Continent, reflecting the high level of craftmanship of Italian and German makers, it was an interesting contrast to examine the brigandine jacket of a humble English archer from 1590. It is made of a number of rudely shaped flat bits of iron quilted between two pieces of canvas: the exterior is sky-blue in colour, possibly faded I suppose. The quilting cords form triangular patterns on the outside, and are tied at each intersection. I shall pass over the remaining armour, as Mr. Nash has listed them in his guide book, though he only mentions a tenth of the treasures in the Armoury, and says nothing of the many smaller pieces. There were the most marvellous round shields or targets, embossed with intricate classical tales, or historical events; powder horns engraved with well-known legends; all manner of weapons finely engraved. I suppose the most astonishing thing to me is that so much artistic endeavour has been used for hundreds of years to decorate what were originally utilitarian battle items. When I mentioned this to Sir Samuel he laughed, and said that we must not suppose that the finer pieces were ever used in anger, or even at the joust. They were seen as symbols of the status of their owner, and were worn in parades and on ceremonial occasions. Even so, there was no reason why utilitarian items should not be decorated – he hoped the day would never come when the function of an object would outweigh all considerations of its beauty.

At the extreme end of the Armoury is a group of Charles the First, attended by his standard bearer issuing orders to two pikemen who are in black corselets with large collars and goffered cuffs. Mr. Henry Briggs, the Royal Academician and Sir Samuel's friend, was responsible for the most lifelike representations of the face and hands of the monarch, and supplied his boots and leathers.[34] The final piece I examined was a German saddle[35] of wood covered with stag's bone which is partly coloured in red, green and black, on which are carved in relief in the costume of the 15th century two lovers, as well as a love sonnet in German which translates to:

Woman: I am here, I know not how,
             I go hence, I know not where,
             Well-a-day! Willingly thou art never forgotten

Man: I go, I stop, the longer I stop
             The more mad I become,
             Thine for ever, the world o'er your betrothed.

Woman: But if the war should end?

Man: Should rejoice, be always thine.

From the ground floor of the Armoury we passed into the ante-room of the Chapel. The ante-room contains some interesting monuments which belong to the sixth century, brought by Sir Samuel from Tregaron in Wales.[36] Two stone figures

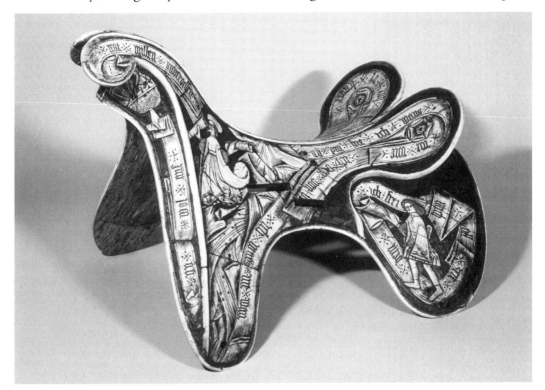

Fig. 86   German saddle with inscription

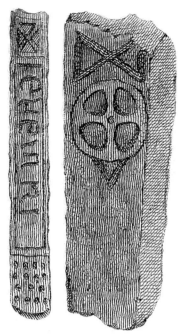

Fig. 87 Tombstone
from Tregaron

Fig. 88 Sextus Valerius
Genialis

about three feet high of the time of Henry II, which had formerly been at the palace of the Bishops of Hereford at Stretton Sugwas, had been donated to the collection. One is a man in long robes with a cap on and a crutch, the other a female with a hood and wimple pointing to a book – Sir Samuel thinks she was a schoolmistress.[37] There is also a most unusual Roman tombstone, of the equestrian figure of a Roman knight called Sextus Valerius Genialis. He appears in the act of thrusting his lance into the body of a vanquished Briton. It was found at Watermore near Cirencester in 1835, and an engraving of it was published in the *Gentleman's Magazine* in 1837.[38] Sir Samuel had it brought to Goodrich in 1843 – he took much delight in telling me that though the relic had cost him but five pounds, the carriage by his tenant farmer had cost three.[39] I did not question him on the propriety of removing it from where it had been found.

Sir Samuel pointed out the column between the twin arches into the chapel, which he had specifically requested his architect Mr. Blore should have made of cast iron.[40] A small stone figure of the time of Henry VII is inset in the wall above the column.

The Chapel is fitted up according to the original Catholic ceremonial with altarpiece, confessional, font and eagle lectern. In the altarpiece are four female saints, carved in oak of the time of Edward IV. The altar itself is covered with crimson velvet, and on it stand a large, gold Maltese cross, six large candlesticks and many rare ornaments. Croziers and procession crosses are distributed about the altar. Mr. Douce's bequest included the head and ferrule of a French crozier of the eleventh century, enamelled on copper and decorated most beautifully with scenes from the story of

Fig. 89   Effigy of de Mauley

David and Goliath, but Sir Samuel has two other croziers in his own collection; one with Adam and Eve with the tree of knowledge,[41] the other the coronation of the Virgin by Christ.[42] A large bronze dish, almost two feet across, is decorated with the scene of the Annunciation, and around the rim is the inscription *Al zeit geluch iam hart* which means 'Hail, lucky among women'.[43] The lectern was designed by Mr. Blore, and executed by Sir Samuel's own workmen.[44] The stone font was carved by one of his masons.[45]

In the floor is inlaid a brass figure in armour of the time of Richard III, and in the windows are painted effigies of St. George, and St. Barbara who is the patron saint of warriors. Sir Samuel told me that he had for a long time had a special affection for England's patron saint. The first sod had been cut for Goodrich Court on St. George's Day 1828, and the last stone put on the exterior on the same day in 1831. He was always very meticulous in raising the saint's standard on St. George's Day, and he said I would find other depictions of St. George as I walked around the house.

In the chapel also are parts of the stone effigy of Sir Robert de Mauley, originally in York Minster. There is a curious story of how they came to be at Goodrich Court. Sir Samuel had recommended two of his friends, Mr. Shaw and Mr. King, to examine the monument in the Minster as it shows an example of double and single mail together. To their surprise they could find no trace of the effigy. Mr. Shaw set enquiries in motion, and it transpired that the effigy had been broken into pieces when the Minster had been set alight by the arsonist Martin in 1829. The fragments found their way into a gentleman's garden where they held up the rockery, and he very kindly bestowed them on Sir Samuel.[46]

From the gallery of the Armoury Sir Samuel led us into the Doucean Museum, three adjacent rooms over the main gatehouse. I could not conceal my surprise and wonder at the veritable treasures literally crammed into these small spaces. There are altar-pieces, miniatures, seals, caskets in wood and ivory, many boxes, diptychs, paxes and other liturgical objects. The walls are hung with religious paintings of the masters, and with tapestries. Sir Samuel told me that the *Gentleman's Magazine* had published the catalogue of the Doucean Museum in parts two years ago. Such was the number of items that he could not accommodate them all in these rooms. Also, some were so valuable or delicate that he could not risk their exposure to the public. He promised to show me some of them where he had placed them in the private rooms.

I was struck with a richly painted altarpiece of the eighth century, from the days before much attention was paid to perspective. There are paintings from every century from the thirteenth to the eighteenth, by Pisano, Cimabue and Giotto. Among the several portraits I noticed a drawing of Garrick, taken from the life by Sherwin in 1775. In honour of Mr. Douce, Sir Samuel has hung his portrait presiding over the whole, drawn by Mr. Catterson Smith at Sir Samuel's command in 1830. Many ivory carvings are so ancient or beautiful that even their fragments have been worth preserving. I lost count of the diptychs, altarpieces, paxes and figurines.

As I admired an enamelled copper shrine, perhaps six inches long, Sir Samuel told me that there was one similar in Hereford Cathedral. It had been thought that the scenes shown on the Hereford shrine depicted the murder of King Ethelbert, but Mr. Douce had asserted that they were both made shortly after the murder of St. Thomas à Becket, which is borne out by the style of costume (see plate 31).[47] In order to make sections of the museum as complete and instructive as possible Sir Samuel has used pieces from his own collection wherever necessary.

Mr. Douce had a number of miniature cinque-cento bronzes on classical subjects, as well as candlesticks and seals. Some miniature Sicillian bronzes of youths show interesting shield shapes, as in the Bayeux Tapestry. I was taken with a bronze of a naked youth sleeping, his left hand on a decapitated boar's head, only 3 inches long, but most of them seem to have cruel subjects. Mr. Douce's coin collection was left, with his books and manuscripts to the Bodleian Library in Oxford, so Sir Samuel has exhibited

his own somewhat miscellaneous selection.[48] I was pleased to move on past
the plaster casts of many interesting
antiquities to the varied oddments
which Mr. Douce had accumulated in
his long life, many no doubt given by
friends who knew his taste for the
curious. He was very interested in the
history of playing cards, and so there is
a good selection, some dating from the
fifteenth century. The objects could

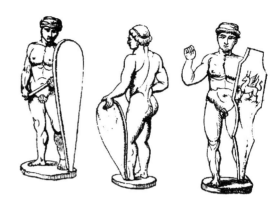

Fig. 90   Sicilian bronzes in the Meyrick collection

have been found in a 'cabinet of curiosities' in a previous age.

The museum ended with a large collection of antiquities from Egypt, Rome,
Greece, India, Persia, China and even Mexico. By this time even my indefatigable host
was beginning to flag, and we returned to the entrance hall for the promised tour of
the private rooms. The sun now creeping round, we could appreciate the stained glass
in the windows of the entrance hall, depicting arms of Meyrick ancestors: Rowland
bishop of Bangor, Sir Gelly Meyrick and Sir Gelly's daughter Margaret with her
husband John, Earl of Carbery.[49]

Leading towards the Sussex Tower from the entrance hall is Henry VI's Gallery, its
scarlet walls decorated with the ancient Meyrick badge and motto on scrolls, and which
is more than one hundred feet long terminating in the housekeeper's room. One of Sir
Samuel's most valuable suits of armour stands in this gallery. Magnificently embossed,
it belonged to Alfonso II, Duke of Ferrara, who died in 1597.[50] In the library we saw
the gilded depiction of the suit in Sir Samuel's great work on armour published in 1824.
It is not a large room, only some nineteen feet by fifteen, and this is why Sir Samuel's
books cannot all be accommodated here. Immediately my impression was of the
warmth of the colour of the oak and the refined carving of the frieze and the pendant
ceiling. The wallpaper was perhaps not to my taste, being of yellow with a shaded trellis
and fleurs-de-lis in black. The miniature bookcases hold mainly historical and antiquarian works, though there are some classical authors too. There is an oak figure of an
ecclesiastic holding a jousting helmet, and on either side of the looking glass over the
fireplace stand ancient German terra cotta figures in armour, between an astrolabe
which belonged to King Henry VIII and a German clock shaped like a summerhouse.

A large table in the middle of the room displays caskets, inkstands and candle-sticks. Sir Samuel showed me a small box in steel, beautifully embossed with biblical scenes, and with ormolu columns. The keyhole is concealed under the Cross, which is liberated by moving a skull. There are six bolts to the lock, skilfully fashioned by German craftsmen. It was once the property of Mr. Beckford of Fonthill.[51] Two candle-sticks of grotesque male and female figures and an ancient sundial with a compass also belong to the time of Henry VIII. The group is completed by some cinque-cento bronze inkstands, and another in old Limoges enamel.

Hanging on the walls are other treasures: an enamel of the Adoration; a carving in wood of Anthony and Cleopatra by Hans Schaufelin; a portrait of Martin Luther and his wife bearing upon them the monogram of Lucas Kranach; and a lady of the period of Mary, Queen of Scots. There is also an ancient portrait of King Henry VIII, and a St. George in armour on horseback of the time of Maximilian I. Two of the greatest treasures left by Mr. Douce are in this room – the miniatures by Hans Holbein of Henry VIII and Anne of Cleves (see plate 24).[52] It is believed that this is the very

Fig. 91 The steel box which once belonged to William Beckford

portrait of Anne which induced Henry to chose her as a wife. It is enclosed in a beautiful ivory box carved with a rose. Sir Samuel values these as beyond all price, though he did add that Mr. Douce had bought them for fifty guineas many years ago!

Fig. 92   Samuel's sketch of the dining room window

From the library we passed into the dining room, almost double the size of the library. The ceiling is painted a warm stone colour, and is divided into three sections by open oak spandrels and moulded beams supported by corbels of the same design as those in Goodrich Castle. The walls are covered with crimson flock wallpaper, patterned with fleurs de lis in a trellis. I was impressed by the beautiful paintings, the most striking being a depiction of the killing of the dragon by St. George, which Sir Samuel told me had been painted by Andrea Mantegna about the year 1488, which from the label on the back had been in the Royal collection of Charles I (see plate 28).[53] Sir Samuel drew my attention particularly to the depiction of St. George's armour. Over the sideboard is a picture painted by Benjamin West, president of the Royal Academy, for Sir Samuel's grandfather Samuel Rush in 1769. It shows the introduction of Helen to Paris after his combat with Menelaus – Sir Samuel said that Mr. West was usually chronologically correct in his depiction of costume, but in this case Paris is in the armour of Julius Caesar.

The oak sideboard was copied from one in Harewood Castle, of the time of Edward II, and it is decorated with ornamental shields, Sir Samuel's herald friend Mr. King having made sketches of the arms of England, France, Valence, and Angoulesme[54] which were later emblazoned by Mr. Willement.[55] The sideboard took several months for Sir Samuel's carpenter to make. Upon it is a handsome Hirlas or drinking horn with silver gilt mountings, and a salver, ewer and chalices. The chairs are made of oak of the same style of architecture with fitted seats embroidered with the family arms.[56] Among the other objects in the room are two exquisite wooden carvings of mendicants, about thirteen inches long by four high. One has seven beggars, mostly female, the other has eight, mostly men, and by their costume they seem to be from the seventeenth century.[57] Other carvings are representative of the legend of St. Agnes, the fable of the Countess di Vergi and the romance of Sir Tristram. The carvings came from Mr. Douce. Sir Samuel told me that the curtains, amber coloured with a pattern of scrolls in crimson, were made of old Italian Brocadillo. He had obtained the material from a dealer friend of his for twenty pounds, a very good price as Mr. Pugin was also interested.[58]

We moved into the small breakfast room which is decorated in the style of Queen Anne, a most salutary contrast to the dining room. The walls are panelled in silk tambour work, set in panels with gilt arabesque frames. The ceiling is finely worked in plaster en grillette with gilt flowers and intersections surrounded by leaves of Corinthian columns rising from a deep pendant moulding. It has been beautifully painted by Mr. Briggs in two compartments – the first depicting Venus riding on waves in her car attended by Nerieds, the second Neptune drawn by horses. In a glass case there are some family items – a gold knife & scissors, a fawn's foot stopper and a French needle case of the period which belonged to Sir Samuel's great grandmother.[59] She also owned a pair of foliated gilt candlesticks, another pair of sconces as well as the beautiful old Dresden branches for candles. Sir Samuel told me that a couple of Sèvres vases on the mantle-piece were valued at one hundred guineas. Even the handsome clock and looking glass are in strict conformity to the period of the room. The draperies are of green satin, and the window curtains the same with rich and deep borders of clustered fruit, all of French manufacture.

In a recess are the miniatures of Sir Samuel, his late wife Mary and that of his late son Llewellyn, taken when he was aged fifteen in his commoner's dress at Oxford by Simon Rochard. Other pictures include that of his father John Meyrick of Peterborough House, Middlesex as Colonel of the Fulham Light Infantry Volunteers, and that of Sir Samuel's grandfather, James Meyrick of Eyton Court in Herefordshire, copied by Darby, though he did not know the name of the original artist.[60] There is also a facsimile of Sir Gelly Meyrick's arms.

The final room on this floor is the Drawing Room, which lies in the Sussex Tower, and so is octagonal in shape, but only nineteen feet across. In furnishing the room Sir Samuel had in mind the style of the time of Edward II, and the medieval romances of chivalry. To this end he had four of the recesses in the room painted with scenes from the romances by Mr. John Coke Smyth, a most clever young artist.[61] The characters depicted are Syr Tristram, Syr Agolane, St. George and the Dragon, the Duke and Duchess of Bourgoyne, the Tournois du Cleft Blanc, and La Boyne Iscelt Brengrwain.[62] The fireplace was designed by Mr. Blore from a specimen dating to the end of Edward II's reign in Prior Crawden's house at Ely. In a recess is a piano by Broadwood, the oak case of which was designed by Mr Blore and built by Sir

Fig. 93   Coke Smyth's sketch of St. George and the dragon

Samuel's own craftsmen while the Court was being fitted out.[63] The keys are supported by corbels, one of which is a monk singing from a book, the other an abbess chanting from a roll. In the centre of the room is a large octagonal table made

Fig. 94   Table in Salisbury Cathedral
used as a model for one in Goodrich Court

of pollard and maiden oak and taken from the only existing specimen in Chapter House at Salisbury.

The walls are papered with a pattern of fleurs de lis in gold on a light pink background and the pattern of the seats is a large broad foliated design in crimson on a French white ground. To complete the atmosphere Sir Samuel has displayed some medieval treasures in the

Fig. 95   Lion inkstand

room. There are a number of beautifully illuminated missals. On the table are my attention was caught by a pair of spiked, enamelled candlesticks some seven hundred years old.[64]

Sir Samuel admitted that the inkstands on the table were not of the period of the room, but are very fine specimens. One is most interesting as a bronze lion acts as the handle by which the lid is drawn backwards. It was made in Italy in the reign of King Henry VIII.

It could be expected that the treasures in the house are restricted to the reception rooms, but this is very far from the case. Sir Samuel has designed the main bedrooms to act as instructive examples of different styles through the ages, and furnished them accordingly. We followed Sir Samuel up the stairs to Sir Gelly's chamber, and as Sir Gelly was executed in the year 1600 the furniture within comes from the reign of Queen Elizabeth. The room is not large, but fitted with panels of oak delicately carved with a most beautiful linenfold design. This panelling came from the house near a canal at Malines or Mechelen (now in Belgium) where Peter Paul Rubens used to paint. The doorway is supported by a pair of carved Corinthian columns, bearing painted cartouches. The ceiling, frieze and crimson walls are strikingly powdered with a pattern of a crown surmounting the letter E in gold. The chimney piece is of oak, beautifully carved with Sir Gelly's badge, a ragged staff fired, and the Welsh proverb which translates to 'Genius without wisdom is fire in the hands of folly'. The furniture for the fireplace is all in period, consisting of a backplate of cast-iron, which although it has Queen Elizabeth's arms is dated 1605, two years after her death. The andirons and brass fender date also from her reign.

The hangings of the bed are of a green pattern on a white ground, and the white satin counterpane of the same period contains £14 worth of gold thread. This last has a similar design to that of Queen Elizabeth in the British Museum. Sir Samuel told me that he had attended the sale of effects at Rudhall, a very old mansion the other side of Ross, which had belonged to Herbert Westfaling, son of the Bishop of Hereford in Queen Elizabeth's time. As well as the portrait of Herbert Westfaling himself which hangs in the next room, he bought the carved oak napkin-press in Sir Gelly's room. At the same time he bought some table linen of the time of Elizabeth, which had been traditionally used for the Christmas feast given every year by the owners of Rudhall for their tenants. The two tablecloths were marked H.W. 1598 and H.W. 1601, the twenty-seven napkins marked H.W. 1622.[65] These are preserved in the next room we visited, and it was most interesting

Fig. 96   Fireplace in Sir Gelly's room, drawn by Shaw

to reflect that those same napkins were no doubt pressed in that very napkin-press more than two hundred years ago!

A glazed armoire in the room protects a man's costume of the reign of Queen Elizabeth. On the right of the bed a finely painted head of Spinola by Otto van Veen is let into the panelling. One of the tables in the room is covered with a cloth of tapestry on which appear the names of Sir Gelly Meyrick and Margaret Lewis, his wife, with their armorial bearings and the date A.D. 1596. Upon this is a very curious clock, her Majesty's own copy of the Statutes of the Garter, and the original manuscript of Silver's Paradoxes of Defence, presented to the Earl of Essex with his arms.[66] A valuable emblazoned pedigree of Sir Philip Sydney is preserved in a case.

We moved on to James the First's room, which has an unusual bedstead which came to Sir Samuel from Mr. Douce. The posts are mainly of some very dark foreign

Fig. 97   The napkin press from Rudhall   Fig. 98   The bed inherited from Francis Douce

wood, inlaid with mother-of-pearl. It has plain panels behind the bolster, a dome top with sky-blue figured damask curtains, and a splendid counterpane of the same colour embroidered with flowers. I noticed a candlestick of iron with brass ornaments,[67] and a brass warming pan engraved with Royal arms, I. R. and the legend GOD SAVE OVRE KINGE JAMES, 1620.[68] The bellows in the fireplace are inlaid with mother of pearl and silver.

The next bedroom is called the Charles the First bedroom. The bedstead has the date 1628 carved upon it, and it is made of oak very dark from age. The panelling of the apartment which is from the same time only reaches halfway up the walls. The costly counterpane on the bed is made of white satin, elegantly worked with gold flowers. On the carved work over the mantlepiece under a coat of arms dated 1640 may be read details of Sir John Meyrick, knight, and under another dated 1644 those of Sir John's second wife. Above the mantlepiece is a sword found at the site of the battle of Edgehill, in Warwickshire, on the pommel of which is a portrait of Queen Henrietta Maria. Below is the exquisitely chased steel guard of a Milanese sword. The iron fireback has the arms of the City of Bristol cast upon it, and was presented to Sir Samuel by Mr. Banfield. The firedogs, fender and shovel tongs are all made of brass, and were presented by Mr. William Hooper, the attorney in Ross. There is a warming pan with a cover showing a figure with sabre & target, and the legend WHO BVRND YE NOBODIE, 1635 around the outside.

A sconce by the window which once belonged to the Reverend Thomas Swift was also presented by Mr. Hooper. On a table is a small backgammon board on the outside of which are the squares for chess, and on the other a table for the game of counters called *merelle*, which came from an old house in Herefordshire. Emblazoned on vellum are the funerary achievements of Richard, Earl of Carbery, whose father married Sir Gelly Meyrick's daughter Margaret. There are various portraits on the walls. The beautiful door has the date 1653 carved upon it.

In William the Third's room the bedstead came from Letton Court, seat of the Blisset family, with a counterpane of crimson and amber lutestring. The brass grate was given by the Reverend Powel Symmonds of Pengethley, and the tongs by his brother-in-law Mr. Hooper. There are the arms of William III painted on glass, and the glass and china ornaments on the mantlepiece belonged to Mrs. Rush, Sir Samuel's grandmother. There is the portrait of her husband, and the armorial bearings of his elder brother above. A splendid backgammon table has pieces with the portraits of the European princes of the time. The open carved oak folding doors came from an ecclesiastical building at Louvain in Belgium.

We walked along the Charles II gallery, where there is a picture of the Merry Monarch himself, supposedly painted by Lely, which was found in an outhouse at Pengethley and was also presented to Sir Samuel by the Reverend Symmonds. Unfortunately it had suffered somewhat from the damp during its enforced banishment from the house. There is also a portrait of Nell Gwynne from the late Lord Bristol's collection, also by Sir Peter. Two frames of miniatures include one of Sir Samuel's grandfather Samuel Rush, and there is a portrait of Louis XIV of France.[69] There are high-backed chairs, a marquetry wardrobe and a table with the twisted columns of the period. The picture of Charles II opens as a door.

The bedroom above the octagonal sitting room in the Sussex Tower was prepared with magnificent and costly appointments, in anticipation of a visit of the Duke of Sussex, but unfortunately this never took place owing to the duke's ill-health. Sir

Samuel has displayed here three curious illuminated manuscripts that belonged to the duke, as well as his favourite Highland broad-sword with a very ancient blade. Samuel acquired this at the sale of the duke's effects in 1843. The duke himself gave Sir Samuel the presentation copy of the catalogue of his library written by Mr. Pettigrew. In painted glass in the windows are the mottoes of the duke's several orders of knighthood, encircling his arms and initials. From these windows there are marvellous views to the Malvern Hills and to Ross. The stairs next to this room lead to the Page's and the Leech's chambers.

The Page's vestibule has chastely carved doors of open work, of the time of Henry VIII, and a contemporary figure of a priest holding a helmet and a crown of thorns. The Herald's chamber is decorated in a modern French style, and is named after Sir Samuel's friend Mr. Francis Martin, Norroy King of Arms. It has his herald's crown, sword, shields and tabard on display, as well as sketches by Sir Thomas Lawrence and other well-known artists.

We retraced our steps to the last suite of rooms on our tour, which had belonged to Sir Samuel's son Llewellyn, sited in the south-east tower where the windows look over the ferry crossing and Goodrich Castle. The curtains of Mr. Meyrick's bedstead are of Genoa velvet, and came from Wanstead House; the counterpane is of elegant German work. One of the wardrobes has a remarkable *trompe l'oeil* of a festooned curtain – most realistic. The dressing room is hung with a number of crayon and watercolour drawings. The sitting room is known as the Greek room, as it contains some good facsimiles of the Elgin Marbles, and several Greek and Etruscan vases as well as numerous antiquities.

After giving Sir Samuel our most heartfelt thanks for his great kindness, the housekeeper took us back to the entrance hall, telling us on the way that even the servant's hall was designed to look like a crypt on Mr. Llewellyn Meyrick's express orders![70] Sir Samuel had apologised for the lack of a suitable place of refreshment in the village, but we had decided to return to Ross by way of Kerne Bridge, after such a fatiguing morning. As we passed the remains of Flanesford Priory, and made our way back towards Ross, I looked back at the towers of Goodrich Court, and made a resolution to persuade you to visit it with me – such a treasure house can hardly be found in the capitals of Europe, and certainly no kindlier or more knowledgeable host.

Plate 23   George Shaw's painting of the chapel at Goodrich Court,
© Saddleworth Historical Society

Plate 24   Holbein miniature of Anne of Cleves once owned by Sir Samuel,
© Victoria & Albert Museum (CT67449 P.153:1 - 1910))

Plate 25 Portrait of Sir Samuel by Brockedon
circa 1830 in red and black chalk,
© National Portrait Gallery

Plate 26 Possible portrait of
Mary Coward, from a folio of drawings
attributed to Sir Samuel,
© Victoria & Albert Museum
(CT89872 E.260 - 1910)

Plate 27 St. George, ascribed by Sir Samuel to Mantegna,
from a private collection by kind permission

Plate 28 Portrait of Augustus William Henry Meyrick, Sir Samuel's cousin who eventually inherited Goodrich Court, by kind permission of Torre Abbey Historic House & Gallery, Torquay & the Meyrick family

Plate 29 Arms of Meyrick
as depicted in Strong's
The Heraldry of Herefordshire, 1848

Plate 30 An illuminated letter 'S' from
Critical Inquiry, 1824

Plate 31 Enamelled medieval chest owned by Sir Samuel,
similar to one held by Hereford cathedral, © British Museum

Plate 32 Mounted Nuremburg armour which belonged to Count Otto Heinrich,
once owned by Sir Samuel and now in the Wallace Collection (A29), © Wallace Collection

Plate 33 Armour made for Lord Buckhurst of Greenwich, once owned by Sir Samuel and now in the Wallace Collection (A62), © Wallace Collection

Plate 34 The Witham Shield, 400-300 BC, from *Horae Ferales*, © British Museum

11   A True Welshman

The dominating interest of Sir Samuel's later years was not, in fact, his armour but his *Welshness*. Before he set out on the journey that led to his marriage and sojourn in Cardiganshire in 1803, he had purchased a copy of Richards' *Welsh Dictionary*, and Evans' *Specimens of Welsh Poetry*, 'that I might have some notion of the names of places, and the language of the country I was about to explore'.[1] During his years in Cardiganshire while he was researching his *History* he must have increased his proficiency in Welsh considerably, though all the gentry that he visited would have spoken to him in English. It's quite possible that Llewellyn had a Welsh-speaking nursemaid as Sir Samuel calls Welsh the 'language of his [Llewellyn's] infancy'.[2]

It's impossible to know how fluent Sir Samuel was in speaking Welsh, but with his dictionary at hand he was quite competent at translation. Early in his correspondence with Angharad Llwyd, she took him at his word and sent some heraldic information to him in Welsh. He did manage to translate her letter without a dictionary to hand, but she was not one to suffer fools gladly and he had to accept her gibes about his mistakes. He was after all 'Meurig Sais'[3]—'Meurig the Englishman'. In his library there was only a handful of works in Welsh.

There is apparently a Welsh expression that translates as 'the best Welshman is one who lives outside Wales'. One of the most active expatriate Welsh communities was in London, and there had long been societies that catered for it. The Honourable Society of the Cymmrodorion was founded in 1751 by Richard Morris, who had come from humble beginnings in Anglesey to find work as a clerk in London. Sir Samuel was later to become an honorary member of both the Cymmrodorion and the Gwyneddigion, yet another Welsh literary society. It wasn't until the early 1820s that Sir Samuel's 'descent' from Sir Gelly took hold of him, and he could consider himself to be truly Welsh. He sent Douce two volumes of printed Welsh documents in 1822, and asserted that 'if you wish to have any part translated, it is so simple that I may volunteer my services'.[4]

One of the most controversial figures of this time of Welsh literary outpouring was William Owen, later William Owen Pughe.[5] Born in Merionethshire, he was yet another Welshman who went to live in London, in 1776, but a fortunate inheritance from a relative some thirty years later enabled him to return to Wales in some style. He became a leading light in the Gwyneddigion from 1783 when he was thirty-four, and from about this time he began to compile a Welsh-English dictionary which was finally published in 1803. In 1792 he published the poems of Llywarch Hen; was editor of the *Myvryian Archaeology of Wales* published in 1801 and 1807; edited the *Cambrian Register*, an English magazine, in 1796 and 1799 and was one of the editors of the journal of the Gwyneddigion—*Y Greal*. All these works were in Sir Samuel's library.[6] Pughe was regarded very highly as a lexicographer and was a principal authority on the Welsh language in the first decades of the nineteenth century.

Unfortunately his belief in 'improving' the language he was describing made him less than rigorous and sometimes misleading in his work. This led later writers to dismiss him as a quack, but he successfully explained many obscure words by reference to the original manuscripts. Pughe strayed progressively into the wilder reaches of visionary fervour, and he became one of the twenty-four elders of Joanna Southcott, a servant girl who believed that she was the 'woman clothed with the sun' prophesied in Revelations who would be sent to deliver mankind. Sir Samuel himself was a follower of Pughe's etymology, as in the preface to the *History of Cardiganshire* he thanks Pughe for interpreting the Welsh passages that Samuel had sent to him, and for historical information that he had furnished. Pughe may have regretted his kindness to the young Samuel, who continued to badger him with questions about Welsh history after returning to London in 1809, as well as pursuing him for favourable reviews and the price of his copy of the *History of Cardiganshire*.[7]

Two other important figures[8] in the revival of Welsh culture at this time are Iolo Morgannwg (Edward Williams) and his son Taliesin or Taliesin ab Iolo. Iolo was a contemporary of Owen Pughe and had helped found the Gwynneddigion. His fanatical devotion to Welsh literature and to the revival (or invention) of Welsh ceremonial combined with his fertile imagination have left an enduring legacy. He was instrumental in the creation of the gorsedd or guild of bards in 1819, and they still preside over the National Eisteddfoddau to this day. He came up with the arch-druid's thrice-repeated cry to the gathered audience at the eisteddfod—'A oes heddwch'—'Is there peace?'. The crowd (hopefully) answers each time 'Heddwch'—'Peace'. Unfortunately his enthusiasm for ancient Welsh manuscripts led him into 'finding' some of his own manufacture. After Iolo's death his son Taliesin, who ran a school in Merthyr, was left in charge of his father's manuscripts.

One of Sir Samuel's particular Welsh friends was John Jones, whose bardic name was Tegid. He was born in 1792 in Bala of middle class origins, but studied at Jesus College, Oxford where he graduated with a second in mathematics in 1818.[9] He then took holy orders, and became precentor of Christ Church in Oxford. From an early age he had been involved in the bardic movement, and had written a number of poems. His chief reputation was as a scholar and translator of ancient Welsh literature, but in orthography and etymology he was a follower of William Owen Pughe. In 1828 Tegid prepared an edition of the Welsh New Testament for the SPCK, and in doing so opened up the debates on orthography which raged between the followers of Pughe and those of William Bruce Knight. Knight and Tegid published several counter-arguments in the years following. Time has favoured the theories of Knight over Pughe.

Tegid edited the poems of Lewis Glyn Cothi, a Welsh bard from the beginning of the fifteenth century, in co-operation with the Rev. Walter Davies of Monavon or Gwalter Mechain, which was published by the Cymmrodorion between 1837 and 1839. Sir Samuel was delighted with them and he wrote to Charles Hartshorne that Cothi narrated 'many remarkable circumstances connected with ... Border history, as giving us a great insight into the pyrgological transactions of that age, beside much that is highly interesting regarding the mighty dead who lie entombed in the Church at Abergavenny'.[10] Hartshorne sent him drawings he had made of the tombs.[11] There are several striking wooden effigies in that church: that of George de Cantelupe dates from 1275, and that of John de Hastings or his son. It seems that Sir Samuel was so taken with one of the effigies that he tried to persuade the vicar that it should find its way to Goodrich Court. Fortunately he did not succeed, and he wrote to Kirkmann that after a period of no word from the vicar 'it is quite clear that all thought of the wooden effigy at Abergavenny must be abandoned'.[12]

The re-establishment of the traditional literary and musical forum of the eisteddfod by the Gwyneddigion towards the ends of the eighteenth century brought together supporters of Welsh culture from opposite ends of the social scale. The English-speaking gentry and iron-masters of the industrialised valleys of South Wales were generally scornful of Welsh language and culture. There were a number of honourable exceptions, among them the English-born Lady Charlotte Guest (née Bertie), and Augusta Hall of Llanover.

Born in 1812, Lady Charlotte Bertie was the eldest child of the ninth Earl of Lindsey, and from an early age had shown an aptitude for study. She learnt Italian and Latin as was usual, but also taught herself Arabic, and was widely versed in medieval stories. From the age of ten, Lady Charlotte kept an intimate and voluminous journal for nearly seventy years, with only occasional lapses. In July 1833 she married the much older John Guest, owner of the Dowlais ironworks, and immediately threw herself into the cultural life of her adopted country. Within a week of arriving in Wales that August she was taking lessons in Welsh from the rector, and beginning an intensive programme of reading on the subject. In November of the same year, the Cymdeithas Cymreigyddion y Fenni or the Society of Welsh Scholars of Abergavenny was formed. The Guests were founder members, as were the Halls of Llanover.

In contrast to Lady Charlotte, Augusta Waddington's roots were in Wales—she was heiress to the Llanover estate near Abergavenny. Ten years older than Lady Charlotte, she married Benjamin Hall of Abercarn in 1823. He became a prominent politician, was created a baronet in 1838, a peer in 1859, gave his name to Big Ben and, perforce, much of their time was spent in London. It seems extraordinary now that the hierarchy of the established church in Wales fought against their ministry being conducted in the native tongue, and did not foresee that by this they would lose ground to the non-conformists who did just that. The triumph of non-conformism in the lives of the ordinary people had the side-effect of emphasising the religious in Welsh writing and music, and all too often suppressing the natural exuberance of the Welsh cultural tradition. Benjamin Hall was a strong advocate in Parliament of the use of Welsh, but he was over-shadowed by his wife's enthusiasm. By 1834 she had learnt enough Welsh to carry off a prize at the Cardiff eisteddfod for an essay written in Welsh under her pen-name 'Gwenynen Gwent'—the Bee of Gwent.

Lady Charlotte and Augusta Hall both had the same feeling about Wales as Sir Samuel—the romance of Welsh history, and the bardic tradition affected them deeply. The Celtic has a romantic power of attraction that the Anglo-Saxon still does not have today. The year 1837 was important for both ladies—the Halls held a grand house-warming party for Llanover Hall, newly built in a Jacobean style, and at the same time the Cymreigyddion y Fenni held a very successful eisteddfod. As a result of discussions during these events, Lady Charlotte embarked upon the project for which she is best known—the publication of the *Mabinogion* in English.[13]

The Halls had a number of guests at their new house apart from Lady Charlotte and her husband: Angharad Llwyd had been tempted away from her seclusion in Rhyl; Lord and Lady Hereford; Lord and Lady Rodney; the Foleys of Stoke Edith; the Misses Williams of Aberpergwm; Arthur Johnes (the translator of Davydd ap Gwyllym); Tegid and Carnhuarnwc—the Rev. Thomas Price of Cwmdu. Carnhuanawc was one of the most respected scholars of his generation, a few years younger than Sir Samuel whom he outlived by just seven months. A tall, handsome man, he always wore clothes made entirely of home-made materials. After the death of Taliesin Williams he edited the Iolo manuscripts for the Welsh MSS Society.

Lady Charlotte recorded in her diary for Wednesday, 18 October 1837: 'we all went to Cymmreigyddion which was brilliantly attended & so numerously that the heat was almost Stifling and I was very glad to leave my honourable position near the chairman (Mr. Hall) and sit with Miss Williams & Mr. Port at an open window. Every thing went off well & satisfactorily – the Duke of Beaufort was announced as a subscriber and a great many prizes were promised for next year – But it seemed to me that there was not the same display of genuine and native enthusiasm among the lower orders of Welsh Literati themselves which had been so animating and gratifying in 1835. I am afraid the Society is beginning to be tamed, down to the conventional rules of English taste'.[14]

The eisteddfod saw the award of a number of prizes for Welsh compositions, but Sir Samuel was not among their number. He had submitted an essay in the summer of 1837 under his bardic name of Prên Tanlwyd or 'burning brand'—a reference to Sir Gelly's device—but it did not arrive in time to be considered for the 1837 session, and he was advised to submit it in the following year.[15] He did however agree to lend the society 'his feeble support'.[16]

On the Thursday Lady Charlotte arrived late at the eisteddfod, where it was so crowded that 'we found an entrance by a scaffold that was placed against a window just within which a plank was introduced (high above the heads of all the assembly) for me to sit upon, & where I remained ensconced seeing nothing but hearing everything'.[17] Sir Samuel was there also, having left Goodrich Court 'in the carriage at eight o'clock for Abergavenny, pushed into the Cymrygyddion [*sic*] meeting where I stood squeezed for several hours, then walked about the town and examined the interesting monuments in the church, dined, dressed in uniform at nine, started for Lanover[18] at ten, continued there from eleven till three on my legs, got into bed by five, rose at eight, breakfasted, drove home and entertained a party of two persons and a young lady from Wales for a week without feeling the least inconvenience'.[19]

One of the most popular recipients of a special medal for composition at the eisteddfod was Lady Coffin Greenly, whose family lived at Titley in the north of Herefordshire but who owned property in the Abergavenny area. She was yet another multi-talented female devotee of the Welsh language and music. Rather older than Lady Charlotte and Augusta Hall, she became friendly with Carnhuanawc in 1825, and unlike them was a fluent Welsh speaker.[20] She supported Iolo Morgannwg financially for many years, and for that act alone should have had as much right to a place in the *Dictionary of Welsh Biography* as Sir Samuel. If all this sounds rather serious and high-minded, Angharad Llwyd was the life and soul of the Llanover party, causing much merriment by proposing to marry the fiery Irish politician Daniel O'Connell so that within two years she would either 'convert him or kill him'. The joke was carried even further when a letter purporting to come from him, and actually franked by him, was sent to her by one of the amused guests at the party.[21]

The fancy dress party at Llanover was the social occasion of the year in Gwent, reported in the local newspapers—though they didn't mention Sir Samuel as one of the well-known guests. They were impressed with the lavish display of food, which was constantly re-supplied until the last guests left at seven in the morning. Banners of green and gold emblazoned with the arms of the Principality—taken from Sir Samuel's seal of Owain Glyndwr—were suspended from the minstrels' gallery. Rather incongruously, the motto surrounding the arms was *Brenhines Victoria* as well as the old inscription of *Tywysogaeth Cymru*.[22] Each day, carriages transported the Llanover party to Abergavenny, and their horses' heads were decorated with green and white ribbons. Girls in full Welsh costume presented guests with silver leeks as they drove through the gates.

Many of the outsiders came to the party as the usual 'variety of Turks, Greeks and Swiss peasants', but the Llanover guests came to the party dressed in adaptations of Welsh costume. Lady Guest was in 'a dress exactly to what the peasants wear about Merthyr except that the material instead of woollen was satin wove to the proper pattern on purpose, the hat was black velvet instead of beaver and that the whole had a sprinkling of gold over it to give it candlelight effects'—though according to her journal she did change later into her favourite Catherine de Medici costume (which the newspaper described as Mary Queen of Scots!). Her husband wore 'a regular old grey coat farmer's dress, with olive velvet shorts & immense silver buckles'.[23] Mrs. Scudamore of Kentchurch was in a 'strictly correct' Cardiganshire costume—of rich satin, with diamonds on her hat. Lady Greenly was in a Gwentian costume and Angharad Llwyd appeared in the green and white full costume of North Wales. Augusta Hall's Gwentian costume was made of satin, and she glittered with diamonds.[24] In all about two hundred and fifty guests attended, 'comprising all the principal families in Gwent and Morganwg, and many visitors from north Wales'. There is no record of the presence of other stalwarts of the Cymreigyddion, such as David Morris, a cobbler from Tredegar and prolific writer of poetry and prose.

As well as being the genesis of the project to translate and publish the *Mabinogion*, the eisteddfod was the occasion for the Halls, Lady Charlotte, Tegid, Carnhuanawc and Arthur Johnes to discuss the Welsh MSS Society, which had been founded to promote the publication of important Welsh documents.

After the Llanover house party broke up, some of the guests found their way to Goodrich Court. Sir Samuel had been introduced to Carnhuanawc at Llanover, and he, the Rev. Walter Davies (Gwallter Mechain) and his daughter, and Angharad Llwyd took advantage of Sir Samuel's hospitality for a few days before leaving on 16 November.[25] Rev. Davies lived in Montgomeryshire, not far from Lord Clive's seat at Powis Castle, where in 1810 Sir Samuel had seen some elephant armour in good condition.[26] The next time he went during his tour of north Wales in 1821 'the elephant was falling to pieces and the armour on it in a state of neglect'.[27] In fact, he rated the elephant armour so highly that he told the Rev. Davies that he would be prepared to swop the Battle Abbey sword given him by Lord Gage for it. Incidentally, Sir Samuel's fame had spread so far that his autograph was cut from one of his letters by the Rev. Davies and sent to the president (*sic*) of Ohio![28]

The next year Sir Samuel again submitted his long essay 'on the influence which Welsh traditions have had on European literature' for consideration by the Cymmreigyddion y Fenni, but it was unsuccessful, and he asked for it to be sent back. It was acquired by his friend Thomas King and is now in the National Library of Wales[29] along with the other entries.[30]

In the late summer of 1837 Sir Samuel was joined at Goodrich Court by his friend Thomas King, the herald. King was a meticulous record keeper, and for a number of years kept a journal of his holidays at Goodrich.[31] In 1837 he left London by the Mazeppa coach at 6 a.m. on 24 August, and arrived at the Court at 10 p.m. His record of costs is interesting:

Expenditure	£	s	d
Coach hire London to Ross	1	6	0
Breakfast at Wycombe at nine	0	2	6
Coachman at Witney	0	2	0
Dinner at Cheltenham at half past 5	0	4	6
Coachman at Cheltenham	0	2	0
ditto at Ross	0	1	0
Guard at Ross	0	2	6
Return			
Servants at Goodrich Court	0	16	0
Coachman at Ross	0	1	0
Coach hire to London	1	6	0
Coachman at Cheltenham	0	1	0
ditto Witney	0	2	0
Dinner at Oxford 3pm	0	4	0
Wine at Wycombe	0	0	6
Coachman & guard London	0	5	0
Porterage etc	0	2	0
Total	4	18	0

The autumn of 1837 had left Sir Samuel feeling restless, and he set off for a tour around South Wales in January 1838, where he was 'much impressed with the improvements at Tenby and Swansea and the royal dockyard at Pater, but grieved to behold Milford, of which I witnessed the first dawn, going rapidly to decay'.[32] Apart from trying to buy some plain halberd heads, his main purchases early in the year were books for his library, though he did ask his friend Kirkmann to get some Portugal onion seeds for his vegetable garden.[33] He bought from his dealer friend John Isaac a volume on the Ambras collection of armour, rather expensive at £9 10s., but 'I must have the work'.[34] He also asked Isaac to find him 'the lower parts of arms of a common Charles 1st suit'.

Around this time John Sell Cotman was preparing a second edition of his *Engravings of Sepulchral Brasses in Norfolk & Suffolk* to be published in 1839, and Sir Samuel was asked to make notes upon armour portrayed in the plates. Dawson Turner wrote an introductory essay, Sir Samuel's old adversary Sir Nicholas Nicolas wrote some notes as did Albert Way, one of the younger generation of antiquarians. In truth it could not have taken him very long to do, but it did give him the opportunity to correct a mistake he had made in the *Critical Inquiry* abut the cords which connected chain mail to a helmet.[35]

King's summer visit in 1838 was the harbinger of things to come—he caught the Mazeppa coach as before, but only as far as the Great Western Railway station at Paddington. This was a wooden structure, some quarter of a mile to the west of the current station, which had been opened shortly before on 4 June.[36] He took the train as far as Steventon [he thought], when he had to rejoin the coach—probably the same one, as he got to Goodrich only seven minutes earlier than the year before.[37] He was met at Pencraig gate by Sir Samuel and Edwin, and did his best to entertain Edwin while he was there, helped by an exhibition of fireworks in the lower garden. Apart from the ubiquitous Hooper family, Sir Samuel's attorneys, the only dinner guest of note was 'Mr. Courbold the artist'. This was surely Edward Henry Corbould, who specialised in romantic historical pictures. Corbould had no doubt been making sketches of armour for use in his works, but the topic of conversation may have been an entry in the *Court Journal* on 4 August to the effect that Lord Eglinton was plan-ning to give a medieval tournament.[38] Corbould was one of the the artists who subse-quently produced paintings of the tournament, which were lithographed and widely sold. Sir Samuel had tinted copies of Corbould's lithographs, and it seems possible that they were a gift from the artist.[39]

Although the Eglinton tournament did not take place until the next autumn, the enthusiasm for anything medieval was already running at fever pitch.[40] A rumour that Queen Victoria was planning to hold a tournament after her coronation had proved false, but this had only momentarily depressed the public. In the summer of 1838 an opera by Lord Burghersh called *The Tournament* was produced at St. James' Theatre. Set in the twelfth century, it was a tale of knights and maidens, love lost and found again. The Royal Academy exhibition had just moved from Somerset House to the new National Gallery, and the best of the paintings were agreed to be those of Gothic subjects. For a number of years Sir Walter Scott's novels had provided inspiration, and that year there was *Ivanhoe, The Tournament at Ashby de la Zouch* by Allom, *Marmion* by Waylen and two illustrations for *Talisman* by Charles Landseer. Interestingly, a Mr. Landseer had visited the Meyrick collection in 1822 with a Mr. Hering when Sir Samuel had been absent, and had earned a severe reprimand from him as they had taken down the armour, handled it and scratched a table.[41] Other artists with medieval scenes in the exhibition were Wood, Morley and Severn.

There was of course the armoury at the Tower, where the price of admission had been reduced to one shilling, and then to sixpence. For those of a more robust taste, Astley's amphitheatre had for some time been setting its equestrian spectaculars in the Middle Ages, many drawn from Scott's works. One of the most popular entertainments was *Ivanhoe*, which boasted knights actually clad in armour. Soon after Edwin went to Eton in the autumn of 1838 he wrote to Sir Samuel that 'Mr. Martin ... had a very bad cold ... he caught it at Astleys', so probably Martin had been to see the show.[42] The other place to visit for armour enthusiasts in London was the display of arms and armour by Samuel Pratt, but in this case the visitors could buy as well as admire. Pratt was not above including fakes or seriously restored pieces in his collection, but he had a genuine romantic passion for his subject, as evinced by this sample of his first catalogue, where he describes 'the ponderous mace, yet encrusted with the accumulated rust of centuries'. He opened his gallery, a 'truly Gothic apartment', in 1838, when he was just thirty-three. His association with the Meyrick collection only ended with his death in 1878.

Lord Eglinton started to think about organising his tournament towards the end of 1838, aided in part by a copy of Sir Samuel's *Critical Inquiry into Antient Armour* which is known to have been in his library. He held a meeting in Pratt's showroom when about a hundred and fifty possible competitors showed up. The discussions of the possible dangers were enough to whittle this number down to forty. Although the harassed Pratt engaged to supply the armour, the burden of the organisation fell on Lord Eglinton. As the tournament was to be held at Eglinton Castle in Ayrshire, Pratt managed to convince his lordship that rehearsals should take place in London in the early summer of 1839, which would greatly add to the advertising value. Of course, the armour used by the knights of old were made to measure, but the noble lords taking part in the Eglinton tournament had to be content with off-the-peg. Hopefully they were provided with a copy of Sir Samuel's paper *Remarks on the ancient mode of putting on Armour*, which was read to the Society of Antiquaries in 1821.[43]

As none of the participants had attempted the tilt, or the quintain, or even tried to school their horses before the first rehearsal, the numerous spectators at the Eyre Arms on the Finchley Road had a most enjoyable time. Fortunately there were no serious injuries in spite of lots of tumbles, and the tournament was allowed to go ahead after a highly successful second and final dress rehearsal, which more than two and a half thousand guests, armed with Pratt's admission cards, enjoyed under cloudless skies. The date was set for 28 August 1839, but sadly the participating knights were already reduced to just nineteen.

Lord Eglinton had conjectured that possibly a few thousand spectators would make the long journey to Ayrshire. Owing to the publicity generated by the newspaper reports the final total was, unbelievably, about one hundred thousand, drawn from all over the country and even from the United States. The horrors endured in travelling to the site, and the stories of respectable people being forced to sleep in stables and byres were all too genuine. The valiant Pratt had provided medieval tents, and a huge Gothic grandstand for the ladies, including a royal box for the Queen of Beauty— otherwise Lady Jane Seymour. The procession from the castle to the lists was more than a hundred strong and half a mile in length, gorgeously costumed from the Eglinton Herald at the front, through musicians, pages, esquire, ladies, the knights in armour to the Queen of Beauty at the end.

The difficulties of organising the procession had made it three hours late—a fateful three hours, for as the Queen of Beauty left the castle there was a frightful clap of thunder, and lightning rent the sky. In medieval times, the tournament would have been postponed, but the luckless Lord Eglinton had no such option if he wished to escape the wrath of the waiting thousands. The disaster was compounded when the roof of the Gothic grandstand proved unequal to the weather, and the ladies and invited guests in their expensive fancy dresses were drenched. The bedraggled crowd

Fig. 99   The procession at the Eglinton tournament

was only raised to enthusiasm by the comic spectacle of two knights at the tilt who failed to hit each other in spite of several passes.

Lord Eglinton appeared to apologise to the crowd, and wish them a safe journey home. Those invited to a grand medieval banquet in a tent behind the castle, who had been congratulating themselves on the fact that they would be able to change into dry clothes, were horrified to learn that the banquet had been cancelled as the tent was also leaking. It only needs to be said that the burn which flowed around the site had become flooded and impassable to carriages, and the scene of misery was complete. Many left the site to find no shelter or food for miles around. Those guests fortunate enough to have a bed in Eglinton Castle or lodgings nearby were consoled for their suffering, because the tournament *did* go ahead. Two days later, in perfect weather, a large crowd watched a perfectly acceptable tournament, and the banquet was held for four hundred people. In a curious echo of the Llanover housewarming party of two years before, the guests wore their own interpretations of medieval dress, diamonds and all. One of the suits of Gothic armour used at Eglinton was purchased for the collection at Windsor Castle, and has turned out to be a very fine forgery that probably deceived even Pratt.

In Goodrich, 1839 started propitiously enough with an agreement that Sir Samuel could make a change to his pew arrangements in the church.[44] This may seem a trivial matter, but the allocation of pews in a village church often resulted in acrimonious debates, and even lawsuits. The position and number of seats that could be used by the inhabitants of a particular farm or house in the village was governed by its antiquity and status. When Sir Samuel had moved to Goodrich he had only acquired the rights of the Giddis estate pews. In no time he had persuaded the bishop to allow his masons to move an ancient tomb, probably belonging to one of the Talbot family of Goodrich Castle, so that he could build a pew more in accordance with his status.[45] Unfortunately the tomb either fell to pieces in the process or was deliberately shortened—and now it has only four bays to the arcade, instead of the original five shown by Bonnor's engraving.

Changes were also afoot in the display in the Armoury—or maybe the moth had been troublesome. Sir Samuel asked his dealer friend Isaac to go to a knacker's yard and obtain a white mane and a black one, both with the top-knots.[46] Isaac had to tell them to cut the manes with three or four inches of the surrounding skin, so that they could be fixed to the wooden horses. Poor Isaac would have to bargain with the knackers who

Fig. 100   The Talbot tomb in Goodrich church before truncation, as drawn by Bonnor

would be unwilling, but he was given leave to go to 10 shillings for the two. Certainly the young antiquaries Charles Hartshorne and Albert Way had been less than pleased with the appearance of the Armoury when they had made the journey to Goodrich. Hartshorne wrote to Way after his second visit 'Sir Sam¹ has made great improvements since we were there, the Grand Armoury is in beautiful order - many new banners by Willement and everything is well sustained, arranged and in good taste. If you remember we had formerly some misgivings on the latter point, but now there is no room for criticism. Be sure I made the most of my time there, & on the whole our conversation was martial. The table was well spread, & formed a contrast to our former repast'.[47]

It was at this time that Way had mooted the possibility with Sir Samuel of a second edition of the *Critical Inquiry into Antient Armour*. He had done this through Hartshorne, presumably because he felt nervous at suggesting the corrections that would inevitably prove necessary. In the event, Hartshorne reported that 'he rejoiced to hear of your project' and that 'he gave me to understand that he should attempt nothing further'.[48] Sir Samuel's feeling on the original edition were made clearer to Way after Hartshorne had paid the second visit to Goodrich Court: 'I could say much to you about Meyrick's Armour, but I must write it to Bohn. Sir Sam¹ is disgusted with the plates, to such a degree that he absolutely loaths the sight of them, and I am persuaded that he will never work at the new edition with alacrity and cheerfulness unless Bohn apprises him that the mezzotinta foundation plates can be made softer'.[49]

Sir Samuel set to work making additional drawings for Skelton to engrave[50]—for example the new frontispiece of the 'battle of the keys'. When the prospectus for the new edition of the *Critical Inquiry* was issued by Bohn it was described as 'formerly published at £21 – now at £10 10s. 3 volumes imperial quarto. Neatly half-bound morocco, uncut, top edges gilt'.[51] Bohn's edition was published in 1842, with Way's corrections, dedicated by Bohn to King Louis Philippe of France.

King arrived for his holiday earlier than usual in July 1839, accompanied this time by Francis Martin. All appeared well initially, with Sir Samuel consulting King on the tricky question of Edwin's change of name from Coward to Meyrick, which would be confirmed by royal licence when Edwin came of age. There was also the problem of how Edwin's arms were to be differenced, given that he was 'no relation of Sir Samuel'. But by the 24th Sir Samuel was 'suffering under the dreadful disorder which ultimately was the cause of his ever-to-be-lamented death'. It seems that again his flow of urine had been stopped by strictures in his urethra, but this time he considered himself fortunate that Dr. Ward was dead[52] and that Dr. Underwood now treated him. Underwood managed to pass a catheter, and gradually opened up a passage with increasing sizes of dilators. King says Sir Samuel underwent 'severe suffering' in the stretching of the strictures, and from a letter to Sir Samuel's friend the Rev. Webb of Tretire it seems that Underwood had to operate twenty-five times.[53] In spite of his health Sir Samuel read the service in the chapel the Sunday after his attack, but the burden of amusing Edwin and his friend Okeover fell on King and Martin. On 4 August they held a mock coronation banquet in the banqueting hall, to show the boys the duties of the Officers of Arms, wearing their old heralds' costumes.

By October 1839 Sir Samuel was well enough to attend the eisteddfod held by the Cymreigyddion y Fenni,[54] and no doubt this is where his last, great publishing venture was hatched. It's possible that the idea had been put into his head originally by one of his friends from the College of Arms during their summer holiday. At the eisteddfod the Welsh MSS Society committee would have been well represented, and given their enthusiasm and Sir Samuel's need for some Welsh historical research to win his spurs it's possible that the idea took on an unstoppable life of its own—rather like the Eglinton tournament, in fact. He told Hartshorne that although the Welsh MSS Society had 'wisely begun with the *Liber Landavensis*, the most annoying has fallen to my lot to edit'.[55] Probably if he had known just how tedious and difficult his new venture would become he would not have started, for like all perfectionists it was impossible for him to leave any stone unturned in his research.

Unlike his previous publications, Sir Samuel was to be the editor, not the author, of a collection of the genealogies of Welsh and Marches families made by Lewis or Lewys Dwnn, who had lived between about 1550 and 1616. From an early age Dwnn was interested in genealogy, at a time when many of the descents were handed down by the bards.[56] In 1585 he was fortunate enough to get the post as deputy to Clarencieux king-at-arms and Norroy king-at-arms of the College of Heralds, as deputy herald-at-arms for the three provinces of Wales. Apart from his other interest of poetry, the rest of his life was spent in compiling and writing pedigrees, both as part of his heraldic duties and for his own ends. By the time that Sir Samuel engaged on his project, Dwnn's original writings were distributed widely, and in some cases only existed as copies.

Sir Samuel had first made Dwnn's acquaintance in the 1820s, when he had visited Edward Evans of Eyton Hall in Herefordshire on the track of his ancestors. Evans had a manuscript copy of Dwnn's pedigrees made in 1689, and Sir Samuel wrote to the *Gentleman's Magazine* about it.[57] A reply was printed in April from Joseph Morris of Shrewsbury, who had copied a voluminous Dwnn manuscript, and was to prove of the greatest assistance to Sir Samuel.[58] Immediately Sir Samuel set about writing to all the possible people who could help him in his venture. Having made a firm friend of Rev. Walter Davies, whom Sir Samuel complimented as being 'the first Welsh scholar of the age', he put him to use in hunting out the Dwnn pedigrees.[59]

The political world outside had hardly been mentioned in Sir Samuel's letters since the success of the campaign for the Reform Act in 1832. This was to change in late 1839 when the agitation of the Chartist movement came much nearer to home. Chartism was so named after the People's Charter, published in 1838, which made six demands designed to make Parliament more responsive to the will of the people. Only one of the six—an annual general parliamentary election—was not granted by 1911. During 1839 unrest began to grow in different parts of the country where the working people were suffering cruel hardship. In the South Wales industrial heartlands the campaign exploded into open confrontation.

On 4 November 1839, the Chartists held a major rally at Newport in Monmouthshire, when about five thousand miners and labourers marched on the town. They were met by armed soldiers who fired upon the wet and tired participants, with a number being killed and many injured. The Chartist leaders were arrested, and initially sentenced to be hanged and quartered, but their sentences were commuted to transportation. Unlike the earlier Reform movement, it's difficult to know where Sir Samuel's sympathies lay, for Edwin may have taken his tone from him when he wrote from Eton in February 1840: 'I understand the chartests [*sic*] are to be transported and not to be executed, but I hope the latter will be put in action'.[60] What's even more macabre is that the Newport authorities 'presented' some of the insurrectionary weapons—poor improvised pikes and the like—to the Goodrich Court collection where they were displayed in the Armoury.[61] They must have formed a sad contrast to the glorious works of art therein, while no doubt valid as a record of a historical occurrence.

Sometime in the winter of 1839 the roof at the Court began to give trouble, and the books had to be moved out of the banqueting hall while it was repaired. In spite of all the other calls on his purse, Sir Samuel's appetite for books remained undiminished. His friend Kirkmann had a list of *Libri desiderata* to which Sir Samuel added titles by virtually every letter. Poor Kirkmann had to plough through all the booksellers' catalogues as they came out, remembering that Sir Samuel dearly loved a bargain.

One of the antiquaries Sir Samuel approached in his quest for Dwnn manuscripts was Sir Thomas Phillipps of Middle Hill. They had been acquainted since the 1820s when Sir Samuel was still on the search for his Meyrick ancestry and hoped Sir Thomas could help.[62] Phillipps was born in 1792, the son of a wealthy manufacturer from Manchester who had retired to a house called Middle Hill in the Cotswolds, not far from Cheltenham. From an early age he developed a love of old manuscripts and books, and the death of his father when he was only twenty-six gave him the wealth to indulge his habit. In contrast to Douce, who was of necessity very discriminating in his purchases, Phillipps would often buy whole libraries as they came up for sale, or the complete stock of a bookseller. It is reckoned that he had 60,000 manuscripts in his libraries at Middle Hill and at his Cheltenham residence, Thirlestaine House.[63] Apart from maintaining a voluminous antiquarian correspondence, Sir Thomas catalogued and produced edited editions of items in his collection, many of which were printed at his own press at Middle Hill. Small wonder that he often worked all night, snatching a few hours sleep during the morning. Sir Thomas and his daughters had visited Goodrich Court in late 1835, when the ladies would 'never forget the splendour and novelty of your halls of Armour and the Equestrian Warriors in particular'.[64]

By the beginning of May 1840 Sir Samuel was able to tell the Rev. Walter Davies that he had got quite a lot of information, though Dwnn's writing was very crabbed. Angharad had written with her list of manuscripts, but from Taliesin (Williams) he expected little, from Carnhuanawc nothing, and Tegid had his time too much occupied to assist him in deciphering and translating Dwnn's preface to his original work.[65] Mr. Morris of Shrewsbury had been very helpful, and Mr. Wynne had 'promised much'.[66] He had already transcribed a hundred pages out of the six hundred and sixty-five of Mr. Morris's copy of Dwnn's Glan-y-Wern manuscript—a vast undertaking in itself.

On 4 August 1840 Sir Samuel set out for North Wales to examine parish registers and manorial rolls to establish Dwnn's date of death—at least, he planned to do so in July, and after long acquaintance with him one can feel quite confident that he did so.[67] He was back by the 22nd to meet King, Martin and Kirkmann who had arrived from London, along with a new friend called George Shaw, a wool manufacturer from Saddleworth in Yorkshire.[68] Shaw was only thirty, but was already interested in architecture, antiquities and armour. He had a much younger brother, John Radcliffe Shaw, who was to join him in his newly established architectural practice. John was a talented artist who by the age of seventeen in 1845 was already expert enough to give Sir Samuel a picture of Tintern Abbey, and Mary Preece the housekeeper one of the 'ecclesiastical edifice' at Whitchurch.[69] Shaw went on to design numerous churches in Yorkshire and Lancashire, and 'gothicised' his own Georgian house in Saddleworth, calling it St. Chads.[70] He died in 1876, but St. Chad's survives because it was bought as council offices.

Sir Samuel's other friend from the north at this time was James Dearden, who lived in a house called The Orchard in Rochdale. He stayed at Goodrich Court several times in the 1840s, and Sir Samuel stayed with him at the Orchard in the autumn of 1845, on his way back from a visit to Raby Castle, one of the seats of the Duke of Cleveland.[71] At Rochdale Sir Samuel was introduced to the Rev. Francis Raines, whose first appointment after being ordained in 1828 was at Saddleworth, but who moved on to Rochdale shortly afterwards, then became the incumbent at Milnrow not far away.[72] From Raines we learn of his first meeting with of Sir Samuel—'his unaffected manner and real goodness of disposition evinced itself on all occasions during the evening, and I am sure he would make the same favourable impression on others which he did on me. There was nothing assuming - the great man never appeared - nothing dictatorial, nothing like Sir Pertinax ... and nothing like Sir Dogberry'.[73] Raines was an exemplary historian, antiquary and genealogist, and he went on to be a founder member of the Chetham Society, as well one of Sir Samuel's regular correspondents.

In only one aspect is he open to criticism, for a correspondent to the *Gentleman's Magazine* in 1852 excoriated James Dearden as he had 'devoted a portion of the sacred edifice at Rochdale to a series of medieval mockeries, and surely here the incumbent is as much, if not more to blame than the individual, whose vanity had led him into so great a folly'.[74] Sir Samuel wrote in 1843 to George Shaw that: 'I am glad Mr. Dearden liked what has been done for his chapel', so perhaps he had a hand in the 'medieval mockery'.[75] Since a handsomely carved screen decorated with armorial insignia had been erected to separate the chapel from the rest of the church, and a knight's effigy installed within, it seems possible. There were also reproduction incised slabs and brasses, 'in close imitation of styles of different eras'. Final corroboration of the hand of the Goodrich Court set in the affair would seem to be that the 'genealogical fiction' of James Dearden's descent was entered on the books of the College of Arms in 1841.

The convocation at Goodrich in the summer of 1840 was joined by C.J. Richardson, who made drawings of a number of Sir Samuel's precious antiquities.[76] The small party of antiquarians visited all the local haunts. At Goodrich Castle Kirkmann picked up a spur of the time of Charles I, where they also discovered a large portion of a human skeleton in the moat, which they conjectured to be one of the

Fig. 101 The title vignette from *Lewys Dwnn*

196

fallen during the siege at the end of the Civil War. While digging in the chapel Kirkmann and Shaw found a few encaustic tiles—'but nothing of much importance'. King sketched the arms of Wales for the vignette on the title page for the Dwnn book.

Sir Samuel's aim had been to make Dwnn's works as interesting as possible by means of historical footnotes and commentaries on the genealogies. In spite of this it is Sir Samuel's least accessible work, unrelieved except by rare illustrations of arms—in fact, before each major family's description a blank shield was printed 'to enable the possessors of the volumes to insert the armorial bearings and add the crests'.[77] The work was made more difficult by Dwnn's curious mode of spelling, as Sir Samuel says he was 'attempting to spell English words according to a Welsh orthography, and Greek and Latin, as the sound struck his ear'. For example, Dwnn rendered 'Justice of the Peace' as 'Dustus o'r Pies'. In view of all these difficulties it is amazing that Sir Samuel was able to write to his friend Walter Davies in March 1841 that the printer had already received from him six hundred and thirty folio pages very full of notes, and the manuscript was substantially complete.[78]

A mention must be made here of that heroic printer, William Rees of Llandovery, who was responsible for a large number of the productions of the Welsh MSS Society among others. His press became the most celebrated in Wales, and the quality of his productions was outstanding. He was responsible for the first Welsh MSS Society publication, the *Liber Landavensis*, and also for Lady Charlotte Guest's *Mabinogion*.

Fig. 102   Arms from *Lewys Dwnn*

There's no doubt that both his patience and his finances were sorely tried by the Welsh MSS Society. Subscriptions had been collected annually from the members, and not unreasonably they expected that there would be a steady stream of publications for their money. The *Liber Landavensis* came out in due course in 1840. The next publication should have been *Lewys Dwnn*, but the committee of the society decided that they would use £50 of their fund to pay Iolo Morgannwg's son Taliesin to copy his father's manuscripts. The unfortunate Rees was left with a number of the pages of Dwnn printed, but the society did not have enough money to pay for it to be finished and bound. Sir Samuel was quite disgusted with them—he told Sir Thomas Phillipps that 'you have yet to learn of the Welsh character ... enthusiasm at the commencement of an undertaking, all apathy afterwards'.[79]

In the event Taliesin ab Iolo became ill, and the society had to wait a long time for their material, which was not published until 1852. It took threats of withheld subscriptions, and emergency meetings of the society's committee when Augusta Hall had to browbeat them into submission before the printing of *Dwnn* finally got under way in earnest. Of course, the final stages involved proof reading and corrections, and was further delayed by Sir Thomas Phillipps' offer of pedigrees from one of his own manuscripts which he would not let out of his possession. Poor Rees was nearly driven mad by Sir Thomas's prevarications.[80] The *Heraldic Visitations of Wales and Part of the Marches between the years 1586 and 1613 under the authority of Clarencieux and Norroy by Lewys Dwnn* finally arrived in the middle of 1846, and Sir Samuel must have heaved a sigh of relief. The society made some recompense by offering him three free copies, and allowing him 10 guineas for binding.[81] In the event he declined the money and took only two free copies, which he gave to his friend, Thomas William King and to Joseph Morris of Shrewsbury, both of whom had helped him so much in the work.[82]

12   An Indian Summer ... and Fall

Sir Samuel's days of major purchases for his collection were over, but some additions continued to be made to the antiquities at Goodrich. It was evidently Kirkmann's practice to patrol the 'marchands des antiques' of London in advance of Sir Samuel's yearly visit, there to note down anything 'within a purchaseable price' for inspection.[1] Sir Samuel was having a large washstand made for the 'Elizabethan bedroom', and needed an additional Elizabethan white stoneware jug to 'hold water for the teeth', as he told Isaac the dealer who had sent him one which wouldn't do.[2] He also added some items to the armour collection from Samuel Pratt's sale at the Oxenham Rooms: 'a fine Greek helmet which belonged to Lord Byron, a pavoise of the 15th century, and an armourer's anvil with embossed figures on which [were hammered] plates of armour that were to be covered with subjects in relief'.[3] He 'did not get a third of what I sent for owing to the great prices that were given' nor did he try for any of the suits, 'not actually wanting them'. In the event he was disappointed with the purchases, except for the 'bicorne' which he though was so exquisite it could only have belonged to Benvenuto Cellini, dating to about 1525.[4] It is now in the British Museum.[5]

The Goodrich Court estate had remained largely unchanged in size since its original formation, and it did not have the income from rentals commensurate with the status of the Court itself. The farm of Giddis was let to a tenant farmer called Preece, and the park latterly to a farmer called Samuel Aveline, who had proved a thorn in Sir Samuel's side. As late as 1840 they were disagreeing about Sir Samuel's right to grow four bags of potatoes yearly for his own use, and over Aveline's obligation to cut down nettles and supply dung for the garden.[6] Sir Samuel had always desired the Flanesford Priory estate, but for the moment there was no prospect of acquiring it, so he set about buying other smaller parcels of land around the village. In March 1841 he purchased a cottage called Yew Tree House and its associated land.[7] In a letter to Kirkmann[8] about the acquisition he quotes another interesting Herefordshire saying: on St. David's Day 'whoever first opens the door of a house on this day will let in a host of fleas'—and speculates that the Welsh may have something to do with this!

Yew Tree House was a small cottage on the way to Coppet Hill, the great hump-backed common which looms over Goodrich, and it is known from King that he and Sir Samuel visited it in August 1843.[9] The house has an interesting later history, as Sir Samuel is believed to have given it as a wedding present to his housekeeper Mary Preece, daughter of his tenant farmer. In the process it was upgraded by Sir Samuel 'after the fashion prevalent in Queen Elizabeth's reign'[10] and pieces of early carved wood were built in, presumably from Sir Samuel's odds and ends box as they included two fragments from the Breda ceiling.

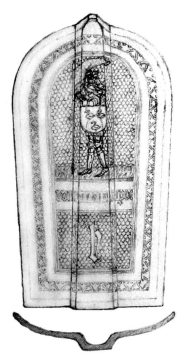

Fig. 103 Bohemian Pavoise, possibly that referred to on the previous page

Commencing with the purchase of Yew Tree House, Sir Samuel invested in real estate practically every year. In 1842 he bought some properties in Pencraig and Little Ash, in the Ross direction, and took over the copyhold of woodland near the Court, which cost him over £500 in total.[11] During 1843 he wanted to buy a little ruin of a building, where the old road from the Goodrich ferry came up a steep hill into the village. Unfortunately nobody could agree who owned it, although from a Goodrich manorial map of 1718 it was quite clear that it belonged to the lord.[12] After various parish commissions Sir Samuel finally gained it in October 1843, when his workmen set to excavating in the garden, though in fact they never found anything interesting because it had been set between two arms of the road. He told Kirkmann that the cellar was 'certainly 500 years old', and he was most probably right.[13]

Herefordshire is most unfortunate in that it was originally surveyed for the Historic Monuments Commission in the 1930s, at a time when anything after 1700 was ignored, and the surveyors often just looked at a building from their car before passing their judgement. In Goodrich this little house—now called Y Crwys—was dismissed as a nineteenth-century Meyrick fantasy, as indeed was the nearby inn. Sir Samuel believed that at the site there was originally a wayside cross, which was removed to a place near the Cross Keys inn on the main Ross-Monmouth road where it was known as William's Cross, where the remains were probably still visible in Sir Samuel's day. To replace the cross it seems a chantry chapel was built with a cross on top, which he says had been mutilated but which he replaced. In rebuilding the upper storey, Sir Samuel's masons found the arch of the principal window and one of the capitals of the door-frame built up in the wall.[14] The masons set about restoring the building, then the stone-tiled roof was repaired and new doors made.[15] A chimney was made in the same style as the Court, and the William de Valence arms engraved above the front door.[16]

Having complained about the slowness of the parish commissioners when he bought Y Crwys, Sir Samuel overcame his qualms in 1844 to set in motion another deal with them, this time for the exchange of some of his lands for the property called Gardyner's Charity, which consisted of a cottage next to Y Crwys and some lands which ran down to the Goodrich ferry. Gardyner's Charity had been left to the parish of Goodrich in 1622, the rents to be used provide for ornaments and books for the church, as perhaps like many others the Reformation had stripped the church bare and forbidden its usual sources of revenue. Although from the outside the house (now called Holly Cottage) looks like a simple eighteenth-century dwelling, the Gardiner

Fig. 104 Y Crwys from Nash's guide book

family are known to have lived there from the sixteenth century. There is a discernible strategy in these acquisitions—where a property was not actually contiguous to the Goodrich Court land it could be used in future exchanges. Sir Samuel was thinking ahead for his heir.

By 1845 many of the visitors to the Court may have arrived by road, or perhaps the Ferry Inn by the river was a little too rough for the carriage trade. Whatever the reason, Sir Samuel took the opportunity to acquire a former hostelry called the

Fig. 105   Decorative woodwork in Sir Samuel's
cottage on Coppet Hill

Crown and Anchor.[17] It had a history of rowdiness, but had been used latterly as the parish poorhouse before that function had been taken over by the Poor Law Union. Sir Samuel took up its renovation enthusiastically. There is a plan reputedly by Edward Blore for its modernisation,[18] but it may be that Sir Samuel's friend George Shaw, the architect, had the greater hand in it, or even Sir Samuel himself. According to another of Sir Samuel's friends, George Strong, the pointed chimneys and windows were 'scrupulously copied by Sir Samuel from an Illumination in a beautiful missal tem. Ed. I'.[19] In a letter to his friend Raines[20] dated January 1846 Sir Samuel drew a very fair sketch of the final design, although complaining that 'it is impossible to make anything picturesque ... one is confined to a straight line which will never admit of beauty'.

A is his house which has two shop windows, one on each side of his door, and two others over them, a comparatively low pitched roof and a red brick chimney at each end of the gable. Excepting a porch and my own style of chimney I am as yet undecided about the rest; which must I think be guided by the new building. B is the part to be added. Between the square tower and the old house will be a passage arched over 4 feet square,

Fig. 106   Sir Samuel's design for Ye Hostelrie.
The lettering is explained in the text alongside

for the *profanum vulgus* to approach the tap room. The tower as you see contains the entrance porch and a water-closet above it. Opposite the door is the stair-case and on its right a passage to the further end. There turning to the left, a door is seen on the right by which access is had to the bar on one side and the kitchen on the other. But if at the end of the passage you turn to the right you see another passage a door at the end of which opens into a parlour the double window to which is at F. Or if you turn sharp to the right there is a door to the parlour with the single window E.

The two dormer windows give light to a passage above stairs, where there are three bedrooms, or two and a sitting room, the two having windows backwards and the sitting room the pointed double window looking towards Copped hill which you see in the gable. These three rooms make one, by removing the wooden partitions, and then it is a club or ball-room. C is a double-coach-house, D a five stalled and loose box stable with loft over. Whether I shall go to the expence of the arched entrance to the stable-yard or not I cannot tell. To carry in hay & straw, it must be as high as that at the Court, which makes me hesitate. We are now digging a well, near where will be the kitchen, but you need a ground plan for the rest. I must therefore shew it to you when you come here.

Sir Samuel's design survives in essence, though there is now a ladies' water closet blocking the entrance on the ground floor of the tower, so that not only the *profanum vulgus* enter by the arched passage. In the 1851 census the inn was called the Meyrick Arms, but it has since always been known as Ye Hostelrie.

One of Sir Samuel's new acquaintances during 1841 was an unrelated William Meyrick, who smarted under some injustice of his father.[21] Very interested in armour, he was an attorney who went on to have a substantial collection, and indeed to acquire some of the Meyrick collection himself. The rest of the year was made

Fig. 107   An advertisement for Ye Hostelrie in 1896

tedious by Dwnn and horrible by the breach with Edwin, the only compensation being a continuous supply of books from London, and a full house of visitors in August. Apart from the ubiquitous Martin, King, Kirkmann and Shaw, Sir Samuel's old collaborator Colonel Hamilton Smith came with his daughters.[22]

As a compensation for all that he had endured, Sir Samuel promised himself some treats in the New Year. He planned to call in at Windsor[23] at the beginning of May 1842 on his way back from his usual sojourn in London, and then he would go to France in June.[24] On his return it would not be long before his friends arrived and they could console each other about Edwin. Thomas King continued his patronage of the railway—this year he managed to get as far as Cirencester before having to transfer to a coach. While he and Sir Samuel were strolling by the ancient Talbot Oak down at the Goodrich ferry Sir Samuel asked King to be one of the executors of his will—Kirkmann was the other—and he wrote it out himself in October.[25] Other guests were Mr. and Mrs. Meyrick, probably William Meyrick and his wife. The only incident of note was when King tumbled into the moat at the castle. King never mentions any celebrations for Sir Samuel's birthday, though it fell during the annual convocation of his friends at Goodrich. Perhaps he had begun to feel the years pressing—Sir Samuel was fifty-nine in 1842.

During 1843 the progress of beautification of the Court continued—it seems as if the Heiton tower was being altered, as Sir Samuel tells Shaw that the work on it cannot be finished because the wife of his mason Dix had gone mad, and after an abortive attempt to get her into Gloucester lunatic asylum Dix had been forced to put her in one at Whitchurch, presumably a private establishment.[26] Nothing loth to embrace new technology, he asked Shaw to see if he could find out how much a grass-cutting machine would be, as his 'gardener is wild for one'. They had been invented some eight or nine years before, and had begun to supersede the old way of scything, or letting sheep do the work with concommittant nuisance.

The Duke of Sussex died in early 1843 and Sir Samuel wrote to Pettigrew in May that he had seen in Christie's sale catalogue of the duke's effects that his Highland broad swords were for sale, and begged him to obtain one.[27] He would hang it up under a portrait of the duke that he hoped Briggs would paint for him. Pettigrew was successful and the sword duly arrived.[28] The same letter gave Pettigrew news of a major new venture on Sir Samuel's part. The previous night he had given his inaugural lecture on *The History of England* to the Mechanics' Institute of Hereford.

Mechanics' Institutes owed their origin to George Birkbeck, a friend of the radical Henry Brougham and a professor of natural philosophy at the Anderson Institution in Glasgow at the turn of the eighteenth century. He had started giving Saturday evening lectures to working men, and the idea led to the founding of the Glasgow Mechanics' Institute in 1823. Birkbeck had moved to London in the meantime, but he and an enthusiastic circle of friends took up the idea in London where they founded the Mechanics' Institute which later became Birkbeck College. The subjects covered were mainly scientific, but as time went on the range was considerably extended. It all went to prove that there was a great hunger for knowledge among both men and women with little access to higher education.

Given Sir Samuel's fervent belief in instruction, it's not surprising that he should become the first president of the Hereford Mechanics' Institute, and gave the inaugural address on 29 May 1843. He told Pettigrew that at that evening 'there were 300 men and women present, and many disappointed who applied for tickets', and at the first lecture there were five hundred. The venture was not a light commitment: 'it is a great expense and trouble to me, as there and back are 30 miles to post, and I do not get home til 12 o'clock at night, but as I have embarked I mean to keep on my voyage and spread all the canvas I can'. In all he gave thirty-three lectures covering the history of England from the earliest times almost to the current day, the last one only a few weeks before his death. The first few lectures were such a success that 'the Custos and Vicars Choral of the Cathedral have kindly offered the use of their college hall, of which I shall take advantage when giving my fourth lecture on Monday'.[29]

There was considerable preparation work, judging by the amount of column inches each occupied when printed in the *Hereford Times*. He must sometimes have wondered if the effort would prove as tedious as that of editing Dwnn. In 1844 he gave an illustrated lecture to the Newport Mechanics on the early history of shipbuilding,[30] and another to the Leominster Mechanics on *The conduct which the Jews have experienced from the Christians* or rather, as the text says, *An Historical Summary of the Cruelties experienced by the Jews at the hands of the Christians*. The lecture was printed as a pamphlet[31] by Edward Wemyss of Hereford, whose proposal to publish the history lectures as a set was foiled by Sir Samuel's death. Such an innocuous project as the historical lectures were not without their perils—he suffered a virulent attack in the letters page of the *Hereford Times* from 'an admirer of the Ninth Commandment' (thou shalt not covet they neighbour's wife) who said that he had held up 'the first churchmen in early British history to derision and obloquy'. Sir Samuel's comment was: 'I had at the beginning determined to avoid a paper war and therefore shall not reply. Indeed if I did I must fill a column of a newspaper with Latin quotations. ... My excellent uncle has characterised the history of professed Christianity in the following few pithy words: "The source was all purity but the stream grew sadly turbulent and filthy in it's course, and even now greatly requires a filter"'.[32]

Sir Samuel was somewhat intolerant at a personal level, as witness his remark that his stained glass artist Willement's only fault was 'a forgetfulness occasionally of the station he occupies in society, and a consequent disposition to be too familiar'.[33] Yet, when it came to the rights of oppressed groups of the population such as Catholics, Jews and women he was a modern man, despite his arch references to 'the fair sex'. The Leominster lecture started with a comprehensive history of the sufferings of the Jewish people from the time of the Romans to the present day, where Sir Samuel acutely observed that 'this atrocious conduct was cloaked under an outward feeling of religion, but examine it without prejudice, and it glares forth as the most shameful robbery'. He pointed out that Catholics and Non-conformists had now been rightly relieved of the former injustices against them, and that at long last Jews were taking their place in public life. Probably he had his dealer friend, John Isaac in mind when he said: 'I know myself some excellent honourable men who profess the Jewish religion'. His fervent request to his audience was 'show we are all good Christians, that we know the humanity taught by our divine Saviour, and look upon all created beings as our brothers'. That there was still some way to go was shown by an extract from a contemporary issue of the *Sunday Times*, which was printed at the end of the pamphlet. This told how Mr. Salomons, who had been high sheriff of Kent and was a magistrate, could not become an alderman of the City of London because he was unable to swear the oath, and unlike Non-conformists, Jews had not been given a dispensation.

This concern for his fellow men was manifest in another direction in 1843, when he was elected chairman of a meeting and dinner for the Anti-Corn Law activists Richard Cobden and Col. Peyronnet Thompson, which was held on 26 July at the Town Hall in Hereford. Sir Samuel made his feelings clear in a later letter to King: 'I must say a word or two on behalf of the league, which I never joined, for a reason I will give afterwards. I am as anxious to preserve peace as any of my friends in the Society of Friends. ... 20,000 landed proprietors and the clergy have for over 30 years been robbing 20,000,000 people ... I presided, when asked, at an Anti-Corn law meeting at Hereford, because I was convinced of the injustice of our laws, and the only reason I did not join the league was the uncertainty of its continuing strictly to that one point'.[34]

One of the Ross-on-Wye Quakers was a local banker, Nathaniel Morgan, who had proposed Sir Samuel as chairman of the meeting. From his journal we know that it was attended by more than two thousand people, though the cause was not necessarily very popular in an agricultural county like Herefordshire. Morgan had written a consoling letter to Llewellyn when Sir Samuel was not expected to survive his operation in 1833, and wrote in his diary when Llewellyn died that he was 'a fine handsome and most gentlemanly man as could be seen and very kindhearted'. He often took his visitors to Goodrich Court, so it seems extraordinary that he made no valedictory remarks when Sir Samuel died. He would at least have seconded Sir Samuel's belief expressed to King— that 'politicians should vote for the general good of all classes in the country'.[35]

One of Sir Samuel's earliest interests had been in so-called primitive cultures, which had been aroused by the artefacts brought back from the Pacific by Cook. In *The Costume of the Original Inhabitants of the British Isles* he wrote that the native 'Cimbrians' must have appeared to wandering Phoenicians as 'the South Sea Islanders to the celebrated Captain Cook'. In this book he showed that he was an advocate of the 'Helio-Arkite' religious theory, which he summarises as 'paganism appears in all parts of the world to have been at first merely a deification of Noah and the ark, and subsequently an identification of them with the sun and moon'.[36] The symbol of Noah's ark appeared to him and his contemporaries in all sorts of unlikely guises—Welsh cromlechs, for example. As scholarship progressed in the nineteenth century Helio-Arkism eventually went the way of many another pet theory. Sir Samuel held onto it until his death, and wrote to the *Gentleman's Magazine* on the subject.[37] In the usual way of things, the importance of the widespread Flood legend has resurfaced today as a possible folk memory of the world-wide inundation at the end of the last ice age.

In 1825 he had written in the *Gentleman's Magazine* about the Druids, and the cosmogony or world foundation legends of the Tahitians, and in the *Cambrian Quarterly* about the religion of the Irish. The Douce bequest brought him all manner of religious curiosities, including Egyptian mummies, and he had put his name down for Pettigrew's book on the subject.[38] Now his new friend Rev. Raines gave him a carved wooden figure which had belonged to a group sitting in a 'serpent boat'. The group was an ogdoad, or set of eight which was a common motif in early religion and art. Martin, his 'facetious friend, the Norroy king of Arms, has wittily termed the serpent-ship a cock-boat. It is a pity that such interesting confirmations of the truth of the Mosiac records, should from their non-conformance to our very proper ideas of decency, become neutralized, except to those of our sex as would view them in their illustrative character'.[39] Whether Sir Samuel was successful in acquiring the rest of the figures and the boat from the vendor isn't known—there is no mention in a later catalogue of his collection.

The years from 1843 to 1847 were something of an Indian summer for him. His health was relatively good, he had no money worries and no difficulties with his personal relationships. He had renewed his close relationship with his only surviving uncle, General George Meyrick, who now lived in Exeter. As Charles Hamilton Smith lived not far away in Torquay he visited them both in June 1844, arriving home in time to entertain Walter Savage Landor and Mr. St. John, who were closely followed by Augustus Meyrick's parents.[40] At the end of the year some extensive alterations were made in the Armoury, with new stone being cut and the floor having to be raised.

Fig. 108   Ewer and plate from the Meyrick collection
now owned by the National Museum of Wales

While King and Shaw had been at Goodrich Court in the summer of 1843 they had designed a silver gilt salver[41] which was made by John Samuel Hunt of the firm of Hunt and Roskell in Bond Street.[42] It arrived in November 1844, according to Sir Samuel's letter to King.[43] The National Museum of Wales at Cardiff has since acquired both the salver and a matching ewer, which is not mentioned in Sir Samuel's or King's letters. The design incorporates those of four gemellions or water basins for use during the Mass, dating from the thirteenth century, which were part of the Douce bequest but are now in the British Museum—King says the design was 'after those in the *Archaeologia*'. As well as the 'ragged staffs fired' of Sir Gelly Meyrick, there are scrolls bearing Sir Samuel's motto *Stemmata quid Faciunt*. Around the salver is inscribed the legend *Syr Samuel Rush Meyrick chevalier de l'ordere Guelphique de hanovre de Goderich Court dans le conte de Hereford / Nec aspera terrent.*

A major event was held at Goodrich Court as a result of Sir Samuel's involvement with the British Archaeological Association (BAA). The younger generation had become very dissatisfied with the Society of Antiquaries, and the BAA had been set up in 1843 by Pettigrew, Thomas Wright and Charles Roach Smith, amongst others. This had soon been torn by dispute, and the rival Archaeological Institute was formed by Albert Way and Richard Westmacott. Many local societies were also formed at this time, as the middle classes with free time for such pursuits burgeoned. One important event in the life of the bigger societies was an annual congress, usually lasting a week. Members would convene at some major town, and local representatives would arrange a series of day-time excursions to places of historical interest, which were interspersed with lectures on historical subjects.

In 1844 the BAA held their congress in Canterbury, and in 1845 in Winchester. Although Sir Samuel did not attend either of these, he sent an amusing account of how he had come by a piece of chainmail in his possession:

> A respectable tenant of mine between fifty and sixty years of age having informed me that when a boy he remembered on old rope-maker at Micheldean in the county of Gloucester using two pieces of what he termed coat of mail, but which as far as he recollected more nearly resembled the sculptured representation on the De Mauley effigy at this place than any of the shirts of mail, I was anxious to know a little more about the matter. The pieces he said were about the size of his hands and were laid in the palms of stout gloves and when clasped around the ropes were rubbed up and down to destroy the little knots in the surface.

The old man had been in the habit of using them for many years and alleged that they were portions of old armour, and had come out of a church in that county. This old man was dead, but I despatched my tenant to his son who still continued the business to make enquiries respecting these fragments. They were found one in a pretty good state of preservation, the other the reverse, and the possessor having been induced to part with that in best condition it is now at Goodrich Court. The drawing which accompanies this exhibits a small portion only with sufficient to give the general character and I think it may be regarded as a specimen of the earliest chain mail.[44]

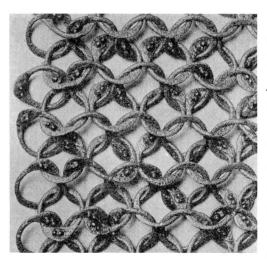

Fig. 109   Part of the chainmail found in Mitcheldean

The 1846 congress was due to be held at Gloucester, and Sir Samuel wrote to Pettigrew that he could 'give a *dejeuner à la fourchette* to between 50 and 60 ladies and gentlemen in the Banqueting Hall'.[45] The *Gloucester Journal* devoted a page and a half to the proceedings of the congress,[46] noting that in the absence of the president, Lord Conygham, Pettigrew chaired the opening session on the afternoon of Monday 3 August, not losing the opportunity for a dig at the Archaeological Institute. The papers read in the sessions that day and on the next were mainly about the history of the surrounding area, about a hundred ladies and gentlemen adjourning to the cathedral to peer into its darkest corners. On Wednesday the delegates went by train to Cirencester to examine the remains there and at Woodchester, and in the evening reconvened at the Grand Jury rooms at 8.30 for more lectures.

Sir Samuel did not put in an appearance until Thursday morning, when as vice-president he chaired the session, and gave a paper on ancient Pagan religion. Unfortunately this was so long that he had not finished at noon, the time designated for another trip by rail to Tewkesbury. The evening meeting to Cheltenham 'was not distinguished by that harmony and good feeling which have so favourably characterised the Gloucester meetings. By some unfortunate misconception in the arrangements, a local gentleman of talent and attainments as an archaeologist received a slight, and one of the gentlemen who represented the London association unfortunately is not sufficiently influenced by the *suaviter in mode* to respect or apply balm to wounded feelings. The consequence was that some unpleasant words were exchanged, which marred the pleasure which would otherwise have been experienced from the well written papers submitted to the meeting'.

Hopefully the ruffled feathers had subsided by the time the party made their way to Goodrich on the Friday. The delegates were pleased to sign the visitors' book, no doubt cursing under their breath at a very recalcitrant pen that had been provided.[47] The Pettigrews headed the list, and among the other guests were Thomas Crofton Croker the writer and Frederick Fairholt the artist, but many did not sign the book. Kirkmann and King were on hand to help shepherd people around. It must have been a festive occasion, as Sir Samuel had arranged for minstrels in the gallery of the banqueting hall to entertain the diners as they ate.[48] King sent a description of the entertainment to Charles Roach Smith the next day:[49]

> The party entered the Banqueting Hall as the harpers were playing *Gorhofedd Gwyr Harlech* or *The delight of the Men of Harlech*
>
> Song between *Yr Eos Vach* (the little nightingale) & Mr. Thomas: *Serch Hudol – The Enchantment of Love*
>
> Mr. Williams on the harp played, with a variation of his own composing:-
> *Y Bardd Awen – The Inspiration of the Bard*
> *Yr Eos Vach* and *Y Drw Vach* (the little wren) which Mr. Thomas sang, accompanied by the Harper the following songs:
>
> *Sir Harri Ddu* or *Black Sir Harry*
> *Deryn Pur* or *The Spotted Bird* (encored)
> *Morwyn Cevn Ydon* or *The Maid of Ydon Hill*
> *Callyn Serchys* or *Lovely Catherine*
>
> And by the vocalists *Y Gadlys* or *The Battle Tent*
> This was afterwards played by the harpers as the company left the table.

Antiquaries were made of sterner stuff in those days, and no doubt most attended the evening lectures on their return to Gloucester, and the highlight of Saturday which was a visit to Berkeley Castle. The reporter from the *Gloucester Journal* may perhaps be pointing the finger at Pettigrew as the guilty party at the *fracas* at Cheltenham, as he

Fig. 110   Arms of Wales drawn by Willement
for *Archaeologia Cambrensis*

omits him from his acknowledgement of 'the courtesy, kindness and assistance we have received at the hands of Mr. Wright, Mr. Smith, Mr. Crofton Croker, and the other metropolitan gentlemen who have upon this occasion so ably represented the Archaeological Association at the congress of Gloucester'.

In January 1846 a journal called *Archaeologia Cambrensis* was started with the express purpose of providing a forum for the publishing of articles (in English) about Welsh historical and archaeological matters. The editors included some of the Welsh MSS Society crowd, and they must have already solicited Sir Samuel's support. In the first issue they thanked Henry Shaw for superintending the plates, Thomas Willement for presenting them with the drawing of the arms of Wales in the style of the thirteenth century on the title page and Sir Samuel for giving them 'the honour of his valuable opinion'.

Hardly had the journal started than correspondents were suggesting that an archaeological association should be formed, and that the *Archaeologia Cambrensis* should be its journal. Surprisingly, many of the enthusiasts were neither Welsh, nor living in Wales, including James Dearden of Rochdale who became the treasurer. The two general secretaries were the Rev. Longueville Jones and the Rev. John Williams (ab Ithel). These gentlemen had become friendly during the campaign to oppose the amalgamation of the two dioceses of St. Asaph and Bangor, and they were able to call on all four Welsh bishops as the patrons of the new association. Of those who accepted their invitation to become vice-presidents Sir Samuel was in the illustrious company of Viscount Adare, the deans of St. Asaph and of Bangor, Sir Benjamin Hall and William Watkins Edward Wynne. The only person whose nose was put out of joint was Sir Thomas Phillipps, who complained to Sir Samuel that after his work on the history of Glamorganshire he should at least have been invited to join.[50] In fact, he thought he should be on the committee, if not a vice-president.

Although Sir Samuel might welcome the new opportunity to publish papers on Welsh subjects, as it happens he had nothing new to hand. His first paper was published in 1846 and was one that had been read at the Society of Antiquaries some years before, but never published in their transactions. It was called *Inscription at Llanfair Waterdine*, and was about strange characters inscribed on an ancient screen at the little Shropshire church. In itself, this might not have produced a long article, but he took the opportunity to present a potted history of music from ancient times, and the different notations used to write it down. His conclusion that the characters represented music was interesting, because he mentions music so rarely. When he lived in London there was more variety, but he told one correspondent: 'you would have found me at home had it been the Hereford music-meeting; for much as I admire music I detest the dull monotony of an oratorio'.[51] Evidently he preferred informal music making, for once he wrote to his friend Kirkmann: 'as I cannot get here any good violin strings and my fiddle de dee is often borrowed, [I] should be obliged if you could forward to me a good first and a good second, at your leisure'.[52]

The first annual congress of the Cambrian Archaeological Association was held at Aberystwyth from 7 to 10 September, 1847. Not given to irony, Sir Samuel cannot have had himself in mind in spite of his avowed Welshness when he wrote to King that it was difficult to make the congress attractive 'owing to the prosy nature of the Welsh'.[53] Again we see him re-hashing old material for a lecture there called *On the state of the Druidic Religion in Britain during the residence of the Romans*. Showing a touching faith in the coach timetables he told the committee 'he would arrive in Aberystwyth at '1/4 past 4 [when he] will get the British shield and weapons to the room and put them up with a muffled hammer so as not to disturb the committee'.[54] They formed part of a collection of antiquities exhibited for the interest of the delegates. Sir Samuel might have brought along the bronze socketed ribbed axe which had turned up in the field belonging to Yew Tree House, which now belonged to his housekeeper Mary, daughter of his tenant farmer John Preece. She had married a gentleman called William Sanderson at Goodrich in September 1846, when Sir Samuel had been one of the witnesses. He was presumably god-father to their first child, Emma Hales Sanderson, born the following July, as he bought in their joint names a bond for £100. When she reached her majority in 1868 she had to advertise in the *Times* that she was claiming the £100 in her sole name, a standard procedure.

By no stretch of the imagination could Sir Samuel be called an old man at this time, but his name does not appear among the excursionists who walked about the hillsides in search of stone circles, or went on the outing to Strata Florida Abbey.[55] He may have paid a visit instead to his wife's family, as he had written to her cousin's grandson George William Parry of Llidiardau that he might do.[56] The suspicion must be that his health was now restricting his activities. On his return from Aberystwyth there was at least some cheering news—the owners of Flanesford Priory had agreed to sell him the estate. It was finally conveyed to him in February 1848, at the cost of £12,500—the equivalent of about £650,000 today.[57] His friend King had given him five volumes of Marlborough's despatches, which he said he 'could not have afforded', although 'could but would not' seems rather the case.[58] The priory estate still consists of contiguous fields which run down from Goodrich Castle towards the Wye at Kerne bridge. It had belonged to the lord of the manor of Goodrich until it was sold in the mid eighteenth century, having been the endowment of the priory when it had been founded by Sir Richard Talbot in 1346. When Sir Samuel bought the estate, the priory buildings had long been used as barns, a new farmhouse having been built nearby. John Preece, Mary Sanderson's father, took over as tenant farmer.

As 1848 opened Sir Samuel was not very well—he had been 'obliged to live on slops and take medicine frequently. This has given me rather a cadaverous appearance'.[59] However, he was well enough to lash out on a cottage at the entrance to the lane to the castle, since demolished. He had become a great fan of *Dombey and Son*, and in his opinion 'Dickens beats all novelists the world has yet produced'.[60] His favourite doctor, Dr. Underwood, had been succeeded by Dr. Cockburn, who in early March was treating him for 'acid in the vesica'—in other words, in the bladder.[61] To make matters worse, his butler Davis died suddenly of a paralytic attack.[62] He took the precaution of making an updated version of his will on 11 March, but by the middle of the month he believed the worst was over, although he told his friend King that he was too ill to make a search in the minstrel's gallery for some information.[63] When he wrote to Rev. Raines on 22 March he was in a great deal of pain from internal inflammation, but gave no intimation that he thought he would not recover.

Sir Samuel's last letter to King on 24 March 1848 had to be written by Mary Sanderson from his dictation, though he added a final message in pencil: 'Many, many thanks for your very feeling and affectionate expressions'.[64] His letter is as jaunty as ever:

> The languid circulation of the blood consequent upon so much medicine and confinement to the house gives me cramp in the fingers so like other great men I have elevated our friend Sanderson to the post of private secretary. I hope you have returned safe and sound to the land of rational liberty without fraternity and are not the worse for your voyage.

You will receive from Mr. John Parry the second part of the Welsh Harper and I shall be obliged to you afterwards to call at 31 Great Russell Street and leave 18s. its cost for Mr. John Parry.

Wemyss is now oscillating between doubt & certainty a very flattering letter has come to him from a friend at the Queen's printing office to urge him to proceed and on that he places much reliance but should your cuttings be wanted I will let you know.

Mr. & Mrs. Sanderson join me in kindest regards.

Please to remember to Mr. Martin & Mr. Woods to tell the latter I thank him very much for the trouble he has so kindly undertaken.

King later wrote an account of Sir Samuel's last days from rough notes, but his anguish at the events had hardly been softened when he wrote it:[65]

The awful and melancholy occasion of this visit, so deeply in contrast with those happy excursions. ... The dreadful sufferings of my dear late friend, whose decease now forms the principal feature of these remarks, could only have been relieved by the hand of death. Organic disease of many years standing at length wore out a vigourous constitution: a serious attack in 1839 had then nearly, to all human apprehensions, terminated the valuable existence of poor Sir Samuel; but a kind and indulgent providence was pleased to spare him a few more years in comparatively restored health & a renewed constitution, which had given his friends the most sanguine hopes of a long life, till within a few weeks of his most lamented decease. He had, however, been declining from about October, and a severe cold, from exposure to the cold air a week or two prior to his death produce[d] a violent & at length fatal inflammation of the bladder, which baffled all medical skill to alleviate.

On Wednesday 29 March 1848 King received a letter from Mary Sanderson saying that Sir Samuel was asking for him: he and Augustus Meyrick set out that evening from London and arrived at Goodrich at 4 a.m. First Augustus then King went into see Sir Samuel for a few minutes, but he was too exhausted to do more than pat King's face. Although they sought a second opinion from Dr. Evans of Gloucester he could give them no hope, for by now Sir Samuel was debilitated by incessant and violent pain. King immediately sent for Kirkmann and Shaw, but when Kirkmann arrived the next day Sir Samuel was already slipping into unconsciousness. King's hopes for his recovery fled. The Sandersons were at his bedside constantly, and called

King into Sir Samuel's room at around 5 a.m. on Sunday 2 April, just in time for him to witness his old friend's last painful struggles. Only William Sanderson was there at the actual moment of death, retaining sufficient presence of mind to give King the key of the drawer containing Sir Samuel's will. A heavy thunderstorm during the afternoon completed their feeling of gloom. William Sanderson registered the death two days later, when the cause was given as 'chronic inflammation of the bladder'. Sir Samuel was just sixty-four years old.

Augustus's father, Col. William Henry Meyrick duly arrived, as did George Shaw. Martin by this time was probably too frail to attend for he died later in the year. One of Sir Samuel's cousins, Mr. Trotter, arrived for the funeral—hopefully not his cousin John, the 'ultra' Tory. King gave his account of the burial on 8 April:

> The Funeral of my dear respected and lamented friend took place this day about two o'clock in Goodrich Church yard, being buried in the same grave with his son on the north side and near the church. The funeral was attended by the Revd. H. Morgan vicar, Dr. Cockburn, Mr. Hooper, (who preceded the hearse in one mourning coach) - Col. Meyrick, and his son Mr. Aug. Meyrick (sole devisee & residuary legatee) and Mr. Trotter in the coach immediately following the hearse - Kirkmann and myself (the two executors) with Sanderson & Shaw in the remaining coach. Mr. Preece one of Sir Samuel's tenants (Mrs. Sanderson's father) and his son, and one of his sons-in-law followed on horseback.
>
> Col. Meyrick & Mr. Aug. Meyrick & Mr. Trotter left the Court immediately after the funeral.

Sir Samuel was universally lamented by all his friends and acquaintances in the antiquarian world, and many journals ran fulsome obituaries. His friend George Strong gives an affectionate (if qualified) portrait of him:

> The Library recalls him best to our recollection; with slight active figure, dry, yet polished voice, opening those curious miniatures by Holbein, or pointing out the beauties of the napkin panelling from Breda; there was a rapid and frequent production from the book-shelves, of a print or authority; and characteristic too, was the extremely natty way of placing a richly bound tome upon the desk before us, opening it at the very page, and carefully replacing it. His language was excellent and ready, and there hung a well-bred irresistible charm about the knight, when he wished to please'.[66]

13 The Meyrick Heritage

King left the Court for a few days, but soon returned and spent nearly two weeks with Kirkmann making an inventory of Sir Samuel's possessions. A number of copies of it were made by Hooper's clerks, and if there is a one lurking somewhere in a solicitor's vault it would be a very interesting document.

In Sir Samuel's will, proved promptly on 27 April, he left annuities to some of his female servants: Mary Sanderson received £300, her sister Elizabeth Lickfold £200 and Margaret Faithfull, the daughter of his servant Henry, £50. The last of these annuities did not fall in until 1890, when the cash set aside finally reverted to the estate. Edwin Coward's £200 annuity did not have long to run. Various family members received £100, as did Kirkmann and King who were to have the heavy duty of being executors. Other friends such as Francis Martin and George Shaw benefited to the tune of £30 and £10 respectively. Considering Sir Samuel's considerable estate the bequests to his friends seem a little on the mean side—Planché and Pettigrew were not mentioned at all. The other servants would have been pleased with their £10—the equivalent of about £500 today.

The remainder of Sir Samuel's considerable assets devolved upon Augustus William Henry Meyrick, who was now a very rich young man. From the estate duty records Sir Samuel left cash and investments, including the value of annuities, totalling some £43,000 or the equivalent of some £2,250,000,[1] of which much was taxed at 10%. Taxable objects such as the furniture, plate, books etc. were valued at £8,263. The armour is not explicitly mentioned, nor the Douce treasures. At this time land was not taxed, so the value of the Goodrich Court estate was also not included, nor presumably the lease of 20 Cadogan Place which is mentioned. The threat of increased death duties must have been the reason why Sir Samuel chose to by-pass Augustus's father, William Henry, in his will, and leave Goodrich Court and all its treasures to his son.

Although Augustus's parents Col. William Henry and Lady Laura did not own Goodrich Court, it seems to have been arranged in the family that they should have the use of it. They were quite different from Sir Samuel who rarely left the Court for very long, as they had a London house, and also travelled widely on the Continent. They were not at Goodrich for the 1851 or 1861 censuses when the house was being run by a skeleton staff. Lady Laura at least was sociable, and the local doctor and antiquarian George Strong dedicated his *Handbook to Ross and Archenfield* to her. Sir Samuel's death may have caused an upsurge in interest in his collection, but no visitors' books for 1847 to 1852 have been found. The newly-formed Herefordshire Philosophical and Antiquarian Institution made the Court and castle the subject of their second excursion in July 1850, when the members had to pay their shilling to see the collection.[2] In later years it seems that William Henry and Lady Laura were more frequently to be found at Goodrich, rather than Augustus the career soldier.

The last visitors' book runs from May 1852 but ends abruptly after 11 June 1868, one of the last entries being of the Goodrich family from Cleveland, Ohio.[3] In the 1850s and '60s Goodrich Court was as popular as ever, a number of visitors coming from abroad—one even from Kathmandu. One unimpressed visitor was the antiquary Thomas Wright. Although he admired the collection he could not say the same about the Court itself: 'built in not very good imitation of several styles ... and presenting the appearance of a large wooden toy ... in extremely bad taste'.[4] He was only seconding the opinion of William Wordsworth, who re-visited Goodrich in 1841 some forty-eight years after he met the little girl immortalised in *We are Seven*. In notes on the poem dictated to Isabella Fenwick in 1843 he said about Goodrich Castle: 'I could not but deeply regret that its solemnity was impaired by a fantastic new Castle set up on a projection of the same ridge, as if to show how far modern art can go in surpassing all that could be done by antiquity and nature with their unified graces, remembrances, and associations'.[5] Goodrich Court even appeared on souvenir china, probably part of a Wye Tour set.[6]

The collection was given another boost by the selection of many items for the Art Treasures Exhibition held at Old Trafford in Manchester in 1857. The exhibition was designed to bring together for public viewing rare and exquisite examples of art and artefacts which belonged to collections in Britain. It was opened by Prince Albert on

5 May, visited by Queen Victoria on 29 June and by the closing date of 17 October it had been seen by well over one million people.

A document found on the floor of Goodrich Court when it was later cleared prior to demolition is a list of items inspected by a Mr. Deane, who ticked the items he was interested in exhibiting in Manchester.[7] Lady Laura Meyrick, Augustus's mother, conducted Mr. Deane around the Court so that he could make his selection. There is a note on the list that: 'Col. Meyrick has a strong objection to take armour to pieces. Deane suggests send as they are. Suggestion meets his approval and he desires that the carpenter employed at Goodrich should pack the figures'. One of the other items found with the list was the card of Edward Jones, builder, surveyor, cabinetmaker and undertaker of Kerne Villa, Walford, with his bill for making:

1 case sufficiently large to contain a full-sized horse, its rider and accoutrements, now standing in the Armoury at Goodrich Court	£7-10s
Packing and conveying ditto to Railway Station Ross	£2-10s
	£10-0-0

The cost of packing and conveying the figures on one foot pedestals was £70. Sir Samuel's good friend Planché was asked by the Committee of Management of the exhibition to display the armour, and he determined to make a strictly chronological arrangement.[8] Augustus Meyrick had stipulated that the Meyrick armour should not be mixed with that from any other collection, there being pieces from the Tower, Windsor and other private collections also exhibited. The Dymoke family sent the suit of armour used by the hereditary champion at the coronation of George I, which had always been thought to have belonged to Edward the Black Prince from the fact that the armour was black and had the letter 'E' forming its profuse ornamentation. Planché was able to show that under the placate or extra breast-plate was the date 1585. Even better, he was able to demonstrate that the suit was the same design as a chanfron and part of a saddle from Windsor, and that the other part of the saddle was in the Meyrick collection, Sir Samuel having bought it from the Tower when it was being sold as part of a lot of 'old iron'.[9] Eventually this complete set of armour was reunited in the Royal collection, Sir Samuel's saddle plate being bought when the Meyrick collection was broken up. The suit was not acquired until 1901.[10]

Planché was responsible for the part of the catalogue of the exhibition describing the armour, and also wrote an article for the *Manchester Guardian* describing how the Meyrick collection had been acquired, and the pieces which had been selected for the exhibition. As the criterion was artistic excellence rather than rarity, there were only three items from the early periods: the Witham shield, and two tarians, or round bucklers. There was a display of eight headpieces arranged on a partition as one entered the 'nave' of the exhibition hall—these included the Pembridge helm and the masked bourginot with the vizor shaped like moustaches. Above them were displayed ranceurs and spetums, weapons of the fifteenth century. Beneath were two square targets, and the ivory saddle with German lovers. Next came some two-handed swords and a specimen of the 'morning star'—a spiked mace.

On the south side of the nave was the first mounted figure from the collection, the German suit from 1445, carrying a shield. Facing this figure was the fluted suit of bright steel with pass guards, dating from the time of Henry VII. The next two suits were those of Maximilian, king of the Romans and the gold one said to have belonged to the elector of Bavaria. In the south court stood a chronological sequence of all the best suits in the collection, and behind them the weapons of their respective ages. The Queen sent from Windsor the suit of armour which had belonged to Henry, Prince of Wales and brother to Charles I. This suit was decorated in exactly the same manner as Sir Samuel's gauntlet, believed to have come from a very similar suit, if not the same one. The authorities at Windsor Castle were given the chance of buying the gauntlet for £100 when the Meyrick collection was broken up, but thought it too expensive.[11]

Sir Samuel's portrait by Briggs was hung above the beautiful embossed half-suit of Alphonso, Duke of Ferrara. The armourer's anvil was standing on the floor below. Sir Samuel's collection of firearms, swords and daggers occupied a large glass case in the centre of the court. In this case the targets of Francis I and the Emperor Charles V merited a prominent place.

The armour was not the only Meyrick treasure to be displayed. Naturally the miniatures of Henry VIII and Anne of Cleves were included. Also exhibited were the 'fine Wynants'—a large landscape with cattle and figures, in a rich moulded burnished gold frame, dated 1672; the 'original' Nell Gwynne by Lely; the portrait of Mary, Queen of Scots 'believed by Sir Samuel to be authentic'; Queen Elizabeth's coronation gloves with one of her pattens and a number of the ivory carvings. Deane commented

Fig. 111   Augustus Meyrick with the sword now
at Torre Abbey, Torquay

that the Lely was 'the picture engraved in the Comte de Gramont's memoirs – it is a great fortune'. On the collection's return from Manchester, Planché re-arranged it at Goodrich Court.[12]

It seemed as if Augustus Meyrick might finally make his home at Goodrich, in spite of being a career soldier. During the 1850s and 1860s the Goodrich Court estate was considerably increased, every opportunity being taken to exchange or purchase adjacent property as it came on the market. The small glebe field lying inside the Flanesford priory estate was exchanged in 1851 and the Bryant's Court estate was acquired by purchase and exchange in 1853 and 1854. A man called William Roberts had been a thorn in Sir Samuel's side, preventing him from making an entrance to the Court from the Kerne Bridge direction. Roberts died in 1859, and his heirs sold the Croose estate at long last. The farmhouse was located between Y Crwys and Ye Hostelrie, and part of it still remains, now in the middle of a range of estate workers' cottages.

In 1859 the ancient right of the ferry was acquired by the estate after an exchange with some land across the Wye. This was to prove more trouble than it was worth—which was £13 11s. 7½d in 1865—as much traffic now went over Kerne Bridge but the obligation to provide the ferry remained.[13] It was not finally quashed until the 1940s. Other major purchases were the Knapp in Croose, and Ash Farm which was a substantial holding on the hill between Pencraig and Ross. Sundry cottages and odd fields were added, and even after Col. William Henry's death in 1865 Augustus carried on buying. The nett income from the estate in 1865 was £870,[14] but during 1865 Augustus raised £16,000 by a mortgage on the estate, and a further £4,000 later the

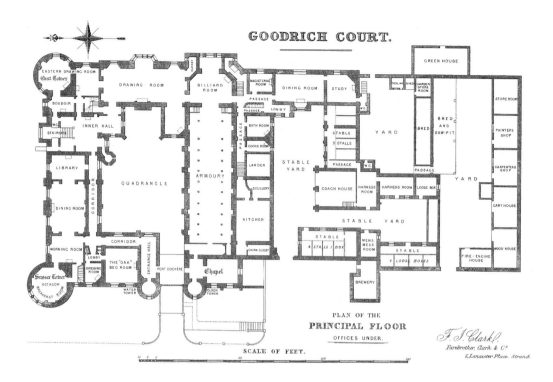

Fig. 112   The plan of Goodrich Court used in the 1869 sale particulars

same year.[15] His last major purchase was in 1867, when he bought Pencraig Farm, now called Home Farm, for £1,845.[16]

In his will Sir Samuel wished that Augustus would bear in mind 'that I thus leave and bequeath to him absolutely my dwellinghouse and estate of Goodrich Court my estate of Flansford Priory and my other freehold property in the confident hope that he will not sell the same but will retain them the armour books pictures ancient and imitated ancient furniture as nearly as possible in the state in which they came into his hands and hand down the same to his posterity and that I leave and bequeath to him my funded property principally for the maintenance repair and support of the same'. Despite the early promise, it proved a vain hope—four years after the death of Augustus's father in 1865 the Goodrich Court estate was on the market.

Augustus may always have wanted to sell Goodrich Court, but had refrained from doing so while his father was still alive, mindful that this was going against Sir Samuel's expressed wish to keep the collection together at the Court. Lady Laura was made of stern stuff and survived until 1882, and presumably she had no objection to Augustus disposing of his legacy from Sir Samuel. Whatever the reason, the sales particulars show that by the time of the sale some significant alterations had already been made to the Court as Sir Samuel had built it. The original front door in the corner of the quadrangle had been blocked up, and a new entrance led from under the gatehouse past the old vaulted kitchen, which was now the 'oak' bedroom. The South Sea and Asiatic armouries were drawing rooms, as was the large banqueting hall which had been extended into the quadrangle. The hastilude chamber was a billiard room, and a new range of reception rooms with bedrooms above had been built facing the garden front. Behind them, along the side of the Armoury was a whole new range of service rooms including the new kitchen. There was additional stabling and workshops beyond the previous stable court, though it is possible that some of these latter were added by Sir Samuel when he altered the Heiton tower.

The new use for the rooms formerly occupied by antiquities was made necessary by the conventions now governing after-dinner division of the sexes. The ladies needed to withdraw into their own room which was presumably next to the 'boudoir' that had housed the South Sea items. The gentlemen had a billiard room away from the ladies where they could smoke. The armour collection must have been squashed up into the Armoury to accommodate these new fashions. As the public could hardly traipse through Lady Laura's drawing room, the old circuit of the Court was curtailed with a new entrance to the Armoury in the gatehouse.

The sale included the fire engine and hose, which had their own house within the stable area. A major modernisation had been the building of a gas works, which burned Forest of Dean coal in two retorts, and stored the resulting gas in a gasometer. All the service rooms, the stabling and the armoury were now lit by gas, but how far it extended into the rest of the house is not known. The building which housed the gas works lies next to the road into Goodrich, out of smelling reach of the Court, and has been converted into a house utilising a chimney from the gatehouse. The original fresh water arrangements had been supplemented by the pumping station below the Court on the Wye.

Although the Court was not finally sold until 1871, no new owner would want to take over the Meyrick furnishings lock, stock and barrel. The biggest problem was the armour and the other treasures, and it does seem as if Augustus made a concerted effort to keep it all together in deference to Sir Samuel's wishes. In lieu of another exhibition to take it away, if temporarily, there were few places which would have the capacity to display it, but one such was the new South Kensington Museum. In fact, moves were afoot the year before Goodrich Court was put on the market, when a letter was written by Bruce Seton to Henry Cole, the Director: a 'number of MPs have asked that the Goodrich Collection of armour &c belonging to Colonel Meyrick may be exhibited in the Gallery at South Kensington where the National Portraits are [and] whether the Science & Art Dept. could undertake the removal of it'.[17] Cole had visited

Fig. 113 Mounted armour at the South Kensington Exhibition

Fig. 114   A decorated target at the South Kensington Exhibition

Goodrich Court in the summer of 1868, and he wrote on 5 June: 'Col. Meyrick knows nothing and cares nothing for the collection'.[18] The removal duly went ahead, and from 26 December 1868 the collection was opened to the public in the galleries facing the horticultural gardens, for three years forming one of the popular sights of London.

The indefatigable Planché was responsible for the direction of the display, aided by his assistants Mr. C. Pierce and Mr. C.C. Black, as reported by the *Builder*.[19] Planché's task was not an easy one, as this was no Art Treasures exhibition. He wrote the catalogue which is both exhaustive and exhausting, as it has 1,552 entries. A number of these relate to multiple objects, the last describing a case full of Etruscan, Greek, Roman and other antiquities which had yet to be arranged. In other words both

Fig. 115   A morion at the South Kensington Exhibition

the jewels and the dross were taken to South Kensington, but at least the catalogue can give some idea of the full range of Sir Samuel's collection. The only items missing would be those thought of as decorative fittings at the Court. It seems unlikely that the arrangements of armour and weapons on the posts at the foot of the main staircase would have been dismantled, for example.

The exhibition followed Sir Samuel's chronological arrangement, each reign being 'marked out by the livery colours of the successive Royal houses, separated only by a slight fence formed with weapons of the period'. This idea allowed the eye to wander from bay to bay, giving a more impressive effect overall. The *Builder* hoped that the lessons quietly taught by this arrangement would 'lead to the reform we have for so long called for in the national collection in the Tower of London'. Planché's introduction to the Catalogue shows that he was perfectly prepared to argue with Sir Samuel's attribution of dates to some items. He had the bright idea of displaying the plates and written descriptions of the decorated targets of Charles V and Francis I from Skelton's *Engravings* alongside the actual items. His closing remarks sum up the philosophy behind Sir Samuel's collection: 'the grand object of its founder was INSTRUCTION, and his old friend and grateful pupil rejoices in the fortunate occurrence which has enabled him to assist in its further development'.

The South Kensington Museum provided an appropriate home for the collection for the next few years, but after Goodrich Court was finally sold in 1871 there was no possibility it could ever return. Augustus was still desirous of keeping it together, and so the idea was mooted that it should be sold to the nation. He wrote to the South Kensington authorities in February 1872 that 'in accordance with the suggestion contained in your last official communication, I have had the armour small arms &c valued by a competent authority, and the result is that they (from no 1 to 1315) are valued at the sum of £40,469.18s.'. He offered the collection to the nation for that sum, or he would 'stand by my original offer viz £50,000 for the <u>whole</u> of my collection now on loan to the South Kensington Museum'.[20] He went on to say that 'I must however request an immediate answer having promised a reply to other parties at 12 noon tomorrow. I trust this country will be the possessor and not the foreigner'. Meanwhile the South Kensington authorities were having the ivories in the collection valued by an expert, W. Maskell.[21] They comprised items 1316 to 1391 in the catalogue, plus 1524, 1527, 1543, 1545 and 1549. Maskell also valued the miniatures of Henry VIII and Anne of Cleves, as they were in ivory boxes.

His comments on the items are interesting, as they show that the collection held some very early ivories which had not been recognised. For example, item 1339 was the head of a Pastoral staff, catalogued as northern European from the twelfth or thirteenth centuries. Maskell considered it a 'very important specimen ... no reason why it should not be regarded as English of the xjth or even earlier'. The most important item in his view was no. 1358:—'a pair of tusks of Walrus ivory: admirably carved, & in fine state of preservation. I shall make no guess as to the original purpose of this ivory. One fact is quite certain, the two were never a knife sheath: as they are so described. ... Possibly Anglo-Saxon 10th or 11th C'. A number of the ivory plaques were separated pieces of the same caskets—perhaps they had been muddled up by Douce's packers. In all Maskell valued these items for £3,230 including the miniatures at £600. In his opinion, the Meyrick ivories would complete the museum's collection (if this could ever be said) and no other museum would have one so comprehensive.

The items which weren't valued were the enamels, including the early candlesticks and the Bologna knocker from the original front door of Goodrich Court; other metal-work and bronzes; wooden carvings and presumably the paintings in Planché's catalogue, a number of which were fifteenth or sixteenth century. Neither the offer of the armour at valuation or the collection as a whole for £50,000 was tempting enough, and the note of the board meeting of the Museum committee held on 9 February have the remark 'Purchase refused' written on them in pencil.[22] The Meyrick collection was removed from the museum's premises, though they inadvertently held on to a pair of wooden bellows from Goodrich Court, and as this wasn't discovered until 1921 they decided to hold on to them but with a note that 'they should be given up to Col. Meyrick's heirs if necessary'.[23]

As part of the disposal of the contents of the Court, Sir Samuel's library was auctioned by Sotheby, Wilkinson & Hodge at their house in the Strand on Thursday, 20 July 1871 and the three following days. There were 1,451 lots, but a number of these consisted of long runs of journals, multi-volume sets and bundles of loose items. Incidentally, some reference books say that Sir Samuel had a librarian, Harry Evelyn Fell, whose daughter gave a number of items to the Wallace Collection. No mention of a librarian has been found during Sir Samuel's life. In fact, Fell was a chef, or 'artist in gastronomy', presumably to Col. William Henry Meyrick. He seems to have had two children baptised in Goodrich by one wife, and another large family in later life in London.[24]

Some of Sir Samuel's books were no doubt absorbed into the Meyrick family's own library, so the catalogue may not reflect his lighter reading matter. With this proviso, as might be expected Sir Samuel's interests ranged widely through history, costume, archaeology and travel. His copies of his own works, such as the *Costume*, *Critical Inquiry into Antient Armour* and Skelton's *Engravings of Armour* were bound by Hering in green morocco, gilded with his crest. Some of the volumes sold had personal associations with the family—for example, the volumes of the catalogue of the library of the Duke of Sussex were a presentation copy from the duke to Sir Samuel.

The bibliophiles attending the sale had to wait until the last day for the manuscript gems, but there was plenty of interest in the folio volumes sold throughout the four days, many dated before 1650. Lot 298 was the *Nuremberg Chronicle* of 1493; lot 344 Gaguin's *Les Grands Croniques* of 1514, which had been in the Duke of Sussex's library. Lot 948 was Rowlandson's *Loyal Volunteers of London and Environs ... in their respective Uniforms,* which had been published in 1799 when John Meyrick had been a subscriber. It is possible that some of John Meyrick's books had not been in his library on the day he died in 1805, and had thus escaped the sale. If so, this is a candidate as there were not many printed and it is described as 'rare' in the sale catalogue. As the plates were 'coloured and heightened with gold and silver' they were in some sense a prototype for the plates in the *Critical Inquiry.*

There were a number of rare French and German books dealing with warfare, quite possibly bought as bargains on the continent on one of Sir Samuel's shopping trips. One, Vegetius's *De Re Militari* with a large collection of early woodcuts, had been presented to Sir Samuel by Douce. The earlier works were usually concerned with military matters—for example Styward's *Pathwaie to Martiall Discipline* of 1581, or Sutcliffe's *Practice, Proceedings and Lawes of Armes* of 1593, or Saviolo's *His Practice*, on the use of the rapier and dagger of 1595. Even Sir Samuel's working textbooks were included, like Taylor's *Elements of the Civil Law*, with his own notes added.

The seventy-two lots of manuscripts covered a wide range. They included Sir Samuel's own unpublished manuscripts and various journals belonging to Llewellyn, as well as the *Catalogue of the Meyrickian Museum*. There were six volumes of Sir Samuel's commonplace books, and his collection relating to the loyal archers of Great Britain. Among the illuminated manuscripts on vellum were no less than five Books of Hours, one of which had been taken by Sir Samuel on his stay in Cardiganshire, as it too had been damaged by the shipwreck on his return. Lot 1398 was George Silver's *Paradoxes of Defence*, which demonstrated among other things that 'the short sword hath advantage of the longe Rapyr'. This was written for and dedicated to the Earl of Essex, Sir Gelly Meyrick's patron, the title page being richly decorated with his arms in gold, silver and colours.[25] The book by John Waunrin from John Meyrick's library was sold, and also four documents of the Court Leet of the Manor of Goodrich from 1635.

There were some thirty-one lots of drawings, presumably unframed: some of classical subjects by Italian masters; a sketch by Hogarth of Dr. Johnson asleep in a chair; humorous subjects by Rowlandson, and most frustratingly a 'large parcel' of sketches by Sir Samuel and his family. Thus were Sir Samuel's unpublished literary endeavours dispersed to the four winds, along with his carefully purchased volumes. Library sales were all too regular in the nineteenth century, but few that had belonged to an author of Sir Samuel's kind. Fortunately many of the manuscript works have survived in one archive or another, and doubtless there are more waiting for discovery.

The story of Sir Samuel's treasures and that of Goodrich Court part company to a large degree in 1871, with the purchase of the Goodrich Court estate by George Moffatt. But not entirely, as Moffatt bought a number of items from Augustus Meyrick, and of course there were many fixtures and fittings which remained in the Court to share its fate. Their history can wait for a later chapter.

14   The Fate of the Treasures

By 1871, Augustus Meyrick and his wife Fanny had four daughters: Fanny, Elizabeth, Laura and Louisa. He had had a successful military career, winning medals in the Crimea, and was still only forty-five years old. Although a number of family portraits from Goodrich and other minor objects could be accommodated in his London house, there was no question of giving a home to the armour or many of the antiquities. The South Kensington Museum would no doubt have been prepared to accept the collection as a gift had it been offered, but it was not and to universal expressions of regret much of it was sold. A few gentlemen did not share the general dismay—there was a very healthy trade in ancient arms and armour—and among them were Samuel Pratt and Frédéric Spitzer the Paris dealer. Planché was particularly affected—he wrote that 'these impeccable antiquities are fast leaving England, one Parisian dealer alone having bought to the extent of £12,000'.[1]

The market for arms and armour was very buoyant in Paris, and this is no doubt what inspired Spitzer to invest a substantial amount of money and take his pick of the collection. It is owing to his acumen, the tastes of Sir Richard Wallace and the generosity of Wallace's wife, that even the impecunious members of the British public can still admire Sir Samuel's taste, which would be some sort of consolation to him. Richard, the 4th Marquess of Hertford, had lived in Paris since 1842 and was a serious collector of beautiful works of art. He had the money to indulge his habit, and when he died in 1870 the heir to his collection was his illegitimate son, Sir Richard Wallace.[2] Sir Richard's taste extended to arms and armour, and within a short time he had formed a brilliant collection.

One armour enthusiast was the Comte de Nieuwerkerke, who had been superintendent of the Beaux-Arts under Napoleon III. On the collapse of the Second Empire in 1870 he fled to England and tried to sell some pieces from his own collection (which were on loan there) to the South Kensington Museum, but was unsuccessful. He returned to Paris in 1871, and in August he sold everything to Sir Richard Wallace for 400,000 francs.[3] Once Sir Richard Wallace had decided that he would move back to London with his French wife, he bought Hertford House from the 5th Marquess in 1871 and proceeded to renovate it. In the meantime, he lived in another house nearby, together with some of the Nieuwerkerke armour.

At some time in 1872 Frédéric Spitzer sold his entire stock of arms and armour to Wallace. This included pieces other than the Meyrick items, but where they were housed until Wallace finally moved into Hertford House in 1875 is unclear. Wallace died in Paris in 1890, but his widow Amélie-Julie-Charlotte continued living in Hertford House. When she died in 1897 she left his collection and Hertford House to the British nation. It opened to the public in 1900, and since then they have been able to admire some of the gems of Sir Samuel's collection free of charge. Items from the Wallace Collection cannot be sold, neither can the collection have any added. It reflects the very different tastes of Sir Richard and his father. The collection has more than seventy pieces from the Meyrick collection—a small proportion of it in total numbers, but they represent some of the finest specimens of the arms and armour that Sir Samuel had collected.

One of the later curators of the collection was Sir James Mann, who was very interested in Sir Samuel. The library at Hertford House has a number of Meyrick items including the journals of Sir Samuel and Llewellyn's trip to Germany in 1823, given by Miss Fell in 1937. Mr. H. Furnage presented a collection of drawings for an unpublished third volume of Skelton's *Engraved Illustrations of Armour at Goodrich Court* to the library of Hertford House in 1924. Bohn was the publisher of the second edition of Skelton in 1854, but there are no additional plates, although Sir Samuel had made some extra drawings now bound in a volume at the Wallace Collection.

The consequence of depleting the Meyrick collection of the best items was that it became progressively more difficult to sell the remainder. Samuel Pratt was still going strong as a dealer, and one of his customers was George Greville, Earl of Warwick from 1853 to 1893. Greville had bought odd items from Pratt since he had succeeded to the title, but in 1871 there was a disastrous fire at Warwick Castle. Some of the armour was saved, and he decided to refurnish the Great Hall with arms and armour with Pratt's help. In March 1873 Pratt was warning him that a quantity of 'bad and false' armour was being brought from Florence and Milan to London, and that he advised him to wait 'till the remr of the Meyrick Collection is to be dispersed – for tho we have sold more than 40,000£ there is still 30,000£ of worth to sell'.[4]

Sometime between March and September Pratt visited Warwick Castle, and was able to advise Lord Warwick what best to do, and to dissuade him from making up suits from odd pieces which did not go together. He recommended that his lordship could spend about £100 and get 'Gisarmes, Glaives, Ranseurs, Spetums &c [and] XVth century Halberds before they are sold because probably another opportunity may never recur of finding these rare weapons at the really low prices which are fixed on them'.[5] During his visit he had obviously persuaded Warwick that he needed some horse armour to make an impressive display, and he suggested the 'Fluted Horse Armour in the collection ... the Suit having been sold for nearly 1200£'. After some equivocation Warwick decided to take the horse armour at £450, and it seems one of the wooden horses as well, as he says 'I like the horse with his *foot up* the best',[6] indeed, the horse that the fluted armour stands on in the Great Hall at Warwick does have its foot raised. The assorted gisarmes and other pieces Warwick bought for £100, knocked down from £107.

As an aside, the whole question of the horses is interesting in itself. It seems unlikely that any horses were crammed into the house in Cadogan Place. Was it a common practice to buy horse armour with the horse—presumably not from a regular armour dealer who would need it for a later display. The horses from the exhibition in South Kensington may well have been sold with their armour as in Warwick's case. This raises the possibility that they are still together in their ultimate destinations, if the woodworm has not got to them in the intervening years.

In the middle of 1875 Pratt made a further selection of items from the Meyrick collection that he thought Warwick would be interested in acquiring. He had evidently made the arrangement of the armour at Warwick Castle himself, and said he was not totally satisfied with the result,. This led him to suggest the suit of the Knight of St. George of Ravenna for the Great Hall, supported on either side by halberds, glaives and swords of the fifteenth century. He recommended as well a tilting suit 'rare at the reduced price', and suggested that it could go in the other window of the Great Hall.[7] The St. George armour was on offer at £150, a bargain as 'much more was refused last year', and Pratt recommended it should be polished.[8] The St. George armour was black-painted, as is shown in Plate LXIII of the *Critical Inquiry*.

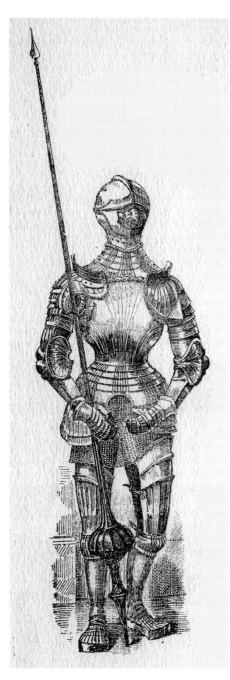

Fig. 116 The Champion's armour from the Meyrick collection which ended up at Eastnor Castle, Herefordshire

When the paint was removed, Pratt must have been horrified to find that the red cross of St. George 'had been repainted within the last 50 years'—or does he mean *painted* in the last 50 years? He recommended that it should not be put on again.[9] At the same time Lord Warwick bought a fifteenth-century painted shield, a stirrup cross-bow and various axes, maces and halberds.[10] The tilting armour was a snip, reduced from £400 to £300, and with extra pieces—a grande garde mentonne, garde bras, tilting gauntlets, saddle, caparison and the horse itself. Lord Warwick also bought some items from the Gurney collection when Pratt handled its sale in late 1875. Pratt's last mention of the Meyrick collection is in the spring of 1876 when various weapons were still on offer, and he sent to Warwick purchase recommendations with the note that: 'as far as I can [to] the numbers in Skelton's Meyrick ... I have added the *old* prices and the reduced'.[11] In April a 'portion of the remnants of the Meyrick collection [will be sent] to Paris for sale'.[12] Armour and arms with a Meyrick provenance appeared in a sale in March 1878, when they included a Philip and Mary demi-suit which sold for £20, the cross-hilted sword engraved by Durer which sold for £57 10s. and an Elizabeth 1st carbine for £31 10s.[13]

Some at least of the Meyrick armour is still in Herefordshire—the 3rd Earl Somers of Eastnor suffered from what he termed 'armouritis'. He had already acquired more than thirty suits from the armoury storeroom at

234

Milan before the Meyrick collection became available. Of the two Meyrick suits at Eastnor, one is the suit reputedly of Albert of Bavaria, worn by Mr. Dymoke as the King's Champion in 1821. The horse armour belonging to this suit is now in Warwick Castle.[14] The suit of William of Bavaria, which Sir Samuel bought at the same time is suit A29 in the Wallace Collection. Another Meyrick item is a seventeenth-century painted lance which was used with the tilting carousel, which had originally been in the Vienna armoury.[15] No other pieces are identified definitely as from the Meyrick collection, but it seems likely that this was the source for a number of the weapons. Unfortunately letters and accounts for the 1870s have not yet been found in the ongoing process of cataloguing the Eastnor archives, but it seems probable that they will come to light. Until then it is not possible to correlate Eastnor's pieces with the sketchy descriptions in the list of items in the South Kensington Museum.

Sir Samuel's name did not fade from the memories of armour collectors, because those who had seen the Meyrick collection and been inspired by it passed their enthusiasm down the generations. One was Robert Curzon, whose desire for early pieces unfortunately made him susceptible to forgeries. Another who was more in Sir Samuel's scholarly mould was Baron Charles De Cosson. De Cosson had gone to the Manchester Art Treasures exhibition of 1857 as a child of eleven[16] and it had fired his interest in armour. As a result of a conversation he had with Seymour Lucas, a painter of historical pictures and himself an armour collector, the Kernoozer's Club was formed.[17] The word 'kernoozer' requires some explanation. A somewhat illiterate Londoner, who was familiar in artistic circles because he had worked at one time as an artist's model, was wandering one day around Christie's saleroom looking at some armour. When approached by an assistant he disclaimed any knowledge, stating 'as the Frenchman says, I'm no kernoozer'.

De Cosson was elected president of the first meeting of the club, on 28 December 1881. The meetings were convivial affairs, but as the size of the membership threatened to increase the members voted in 1889 to limit their numbers to twenty. Probably as a result of this restriction the Junior Kernoozer's Club was formed in 1890 for 'the encouragement of research on the subject of arms and armour'. Seymour Lucas was one of the early presidents. The Senior Kernoozers often met at each other's homes, and in 1899 the club was divided over the moral dilemma posed by one of the members having a live-in mistress rather than a wife to act as hostess. It never really recovered from this dispute, and it was probably due to this that when the Junior

Kernoozers discussed a name change during their annual meeting of 1904 they decided on The Meyrick Society.

The Kernoozer's Club records were deposited in the British Museum, and are now in the British Library.[18] There are a number of photographs from the 1880s of the members' armouries, of their annual excursions and of them wearing armour. There is a photograph of a black and white suit which had formerly been in Sir Samuel's collection but was then owned by Seymour Lucas.[19]

One of the most colourful characters in the Society, twice its president, was Guy Laking. Laking had taken the metaphorical baton from De Cosson when he was a schoolboy, though he was already keen on armour. Perhaps it's true that all great armour enthusiasts become hooked as children on the romance of the subject, and they never lose that attachment be they ever so scholarly. Laking was the host of a remarkable dinner when Miss Green, his son's governess, dressed in a replica suit of armour to take a loving cup around the company. They ate peacock, of course. Laking was a friend of Edward VII, and lived an extravagant lifestyle to match.[20] At short notice, he was asked to catalogue and arrange the arms and armour at Hertford House before the Wallace Collection opened to the public in 1900. He set out the pieces decoratively rather than chronologically, which would have not pleased Sir Samuel, but returned in 1908 to repair this omission. Laking's greatest work was the five volume *A Record of European Arms and Armour*, the first work on the subject fully illustrated with photographs. Laking died prematurely in 1919 without achieving his aim of becoming the Keeper of the Wallace Collection, though he held many other posts such as Keeper of the King's Armoury.

The Meyrick Society continued to hold convivial gatherings, but was also active in providing finances for restoration of church armour where a parish was too poor to afford it. The president at the time of the society's fiftieth anniversary was Sir James Mann, one of the most important armour authorities of the day. At the celebratory meeting on 1 May 1940, it was reported that when a memorial wreath was laid on Sir Samuel's grave in Goodrich churchyard it had been found that the monument was in very bad condition. The railings around it were not requisitioned for scrap, but the inscribed slab was so far gone that a new one had to be cut, and the old buried underneath. The Society paid for the work to be carried out.

Just a few years later in 1946, a Society member walking through the graveyard of St. Luke's, Chelsea discovered by chance the gravestone of Mary Meyrick, so badly worn that the inscription was re-cut at the Society's expense. Apparently it has now worn smooth again.[21] The members of the Meyrick Society never visited Goodrich Court, where although Sir Samuel's armour was gone there was enough of his original building unaltered to make it worthwhile, particularly the stained glass by Willement. The Meyrick Society celebrated its centenary in 1990, its members still devoted to the study and enjoyment of armour.

Augustus Meyrick put some of Sir Samuel's treasures up for auction at Christie's in November 1872. They included the portrait of Francis Douce which had been specially commissioned by Sir Samuel, and which had hung on his bedroom wall.[22] Also sold was the painting of St. George and the Dragon attributed to Mantegna.[23] The portraits of Sir Samuel, Llewellyn and Augustus were kept within the family, as were some miniatures but whether they were the ones described in Sir Samuel's inventory isn't known.[24] Augustus kept a number of the other treasures—the miniatures of Henry VIII and Anne of Cleves, for example. These at least can be seen at the Victoria and Albert Museum, in spite of a chequered history. In his will Augustus left the Anne of Cleves miniature to a friend, and eventually it found its way into the ownership of George Salting. The portrait of Henry VIII was stolen and then recovered, and passed to J. Pierpoint Morgan.

The armour collecting fraternity were generally less interested in early weapons and in the artefacts from the Pacific, and there were besides all the other antiquities— the ivories, the enamels and all manner of odds and ends. Yet again another bachelor

Fig. 117   A montage of Pacific weapons in the Meyrick collection, drawn by Skelton

antiquarian's influence was crucial and coincidentally his name was also Augustus—Augustus Wollaston Franks. He was a contemporary of Augustus Meyrick as they were both born in 1826, and as both went to Eton their acquaintance may have started there. They were very different, however, for as Augustus Meyrick was starting his military career Franks was embarking on his life-long attachment to history at Trinity College Cambridge.[25]

In 1851 Franks was appointed as an assistant at the British Museum, with a special charge for the British and Medieval collections. By 1866, when he became Keeper of his department Franks had won himself a reputation as a formidable scholar of wide antiquarian interests. The timespan of his career marks the start of the replacement of the amateur scholar by the professional, and the beginning of specialisation. Franks retained a breadth of interest and expertise, and this basis of knowledge was complemented by another of his strengths—his 'eye' . He was renowned for being able to spot fakes, and therefore he must just as easily have seen the Meyrick treasures for what they were. Coincidentally, one of his closest friends in later life was Lady Charlotte Schreiber, formerly Guest, who had left Dowlais after she married her son's tutor and embarked on a second peripatetic career as a collector. It is largely due to Franks that her famous collections of ceramics and playing cards were given to the British Museum.

According to his own account, Franks had strongly recommended to the government that they should accept Augustus Meyrick's offer to sell the Meyrick collection to them for £50,000.[26] Franks goes on to say that the gift of the remainder of the Meyrick collection to the British Museum was due to General Augustus Meyrick's knowing that he had made that strong recommendation to the government. This is where the picture gets a little murky, for Franks seems to have made a selection for his own collection before the very substantial residue was passed on to the British Museum. For example, the Witham Shield, one of Sir Samuel's most prized early specimens, was given to the British Museum by Franks, not by Meyrick. In Kemble's *Horae Ferales*, published in 1863, Franks gives an account of how he was the first person to realise the significance of the holes punched through this ancient bronze shield covering. They trace the outline of a wild boar which is renowned as a courageous fighter, and would convey that the shield owner was similarly to be feared. Franks noticed this in 1856, when the shield was being prepared for the Art Treasures Exhibition in Manchester the following year. Franks also donated the two early round shields or 'tarians' from the Meyrick collection, and a helmet and feathered cape from the South Pacific.

The South Kensington exhibition catalogue of the Meyrick collection has some 1,552 entries, but the actual number of individual items was somewhat larger as the last entry was for a large group of antiquities. Augustus Meyrick donated some 686 items from the collection to the British Museum in 1878, and these were individually catalogued in some detail. In addition some purchases were made by the British Museum, and there were the donations or bequests by Franks and William Burges. Possibly the British Museum holds some thirty per cent by quantity of the inventory of Sir Samuel's collection, but a much lower proportion of the arms and armour. There are a few real treasures, as well as the broken ivories and imperfect spear heads that gave Sir Samuel and Douce so much historical information but were unsaleable.

The British Museum's items include the armourer's anvil[27] which Sir Samuel was convinced was by Benvenuto Cellini; the nutcrackers[28] in the form of a man and a key[29] bequeathed by Douce, and the curious ivory salt cellar,[30] which were illustrated by Henry Shaw; the enamel shrine[31] depicting Thomas à Becket; the putative foundation stone[32] of St. Mark's

Fig. 118   Douce's West African carved ivory salt cellar as illustrated by Skelton

Venice also bequeathed by Douce; and a number of Bronze Age axe heads. One of Douce's odder bequests which survives is a plaster cast[33] of three heads depicted on the Bayeux Tapestry, which had been taken by Charles Stothard, the artist. There are three hundred pieces[34] of oriental arms and armour, including thirteen shields and the sword of Tipu Sultan.[35] Among the ethnographic items[36] are some from Llewellyn's early catalogue, for example the woven fabrics from the Pacific islands and various weapons. Included is the iron-bladed adze which Captain Cook's armourer had made in imitation of the stone weapons of Tahiti.[37] There are some forged antiquities which presumably came via Douce.[38]

Douce's ivories can be found in the thirty or so which Augustus donated: a small but rather crude casket[39] depicting saints under religious arches; two paxes[40] and a satirical panel depicting 'Orator Harley' lecturing to an audience of animals.[41] One of Douce's most

Fig. 119 Drawing of the Virgin on a breastplate later owned by William Burges (© Ashmolean Museum, Oxford)

important pieces, a large ivory chest which depicts the story of Susanna and the Elders, is also now in the British Museum. The majority of the Meyrick items from William Burges came as a result of his bequest which came to the museum in 1881, and some can be identified as they appear in Skelton's engravings. They include a number of helmets of various kinds; breastplates and assorted weapons and accessories. Another Douce casket with scenes from the Romances is in the Metropolitan Museum of Art, which it reached via Spitzer and J. Pierpoint Morgan.

So it can be seen that the treasures of the Meyrick collection cannot said to be lost, but the whereabouts of many are still unknown. Those that survive, most importantly in the Wallace Collection, are not displayed in the same way as Sir Samuel had conceived at Goodrich Court. The 'first object' of the Wye Tour can be visited only in the imagination.

15   Goodrich Court

Goodrich Castle sits imperturbably on its headland overlooking the Wye, and probably Goodrich Court would still be doing the same had not the modernisation process started by Augustus Meyrick continued. Many of the country houses which succumbed to dynamite or the wrecker's ball in the 1950s had reached an ultimately unsustainable size. The booming economy of the late nineteenth and early twentieth centuries provided the money for grandiose building projects, and the exploding population supplied legions of cheap servants to keep these edifices going. The Goodrich Court that Sir Samuel had built was a somewhat unusual building for an ordinary family, but only the Armoury could have been described as unsuited for everyday purposes.

In late 1871 Augustus Meyrick sold the Court to George Moffatt, a wealthy businessman and sometime MP for Southampton who already had substantial property in other parts of the country. Moffatt was a very close friend of Richard Cobden, who had spoken at the Anti-Corn Law meeting in Hereford that Sir Samuel had chaired, and was instrumental in providing for Cobden's widow after his death.[1] When he bought Goodrich Court he was already sixty-one, and only lived to enjoy it for another seven years. Although the Meyrick collection, the books and other items were removed from the Court when Moffatt moved in, a large number of items dating from Sir Samuel's time were sold with the house, or were bought back by Moffatt at the later sales in London. Apparently the house was not thoroughly spring-cleaned before the Moffatts moved in, as Sir James Mann found various items dating from the period of the Meyricks' ownership on the floor when he visited just prior to demolition. George Moffatt himself was not of a particularly antiquarian turn of mind, though he did have a good eye for unusual furniture. His son told how he was canny enough to buy a carved oak chest believed to have been made for the Rev. Thomas Swift, grandfather of Jonathan Swift, when he bought their estate from one of the Swift descendants in 1874. It is now in Goodrich church.

George's son Harold Charles was a very different man, having no desire to follow his father into business and Parliament. 'H.C.' was born in 1860 into a moneyed background, but from an early age he wanted to experience work with his hands. When he was at Eton he joined the carpentry club, and for the rest of his life he was an ardent and talented craftsman. Many of his pieces still belong to his descendants, and they display workmanship of the highest order. His particular interest was early oak furniture, and while still a student he had already developed an eye for authentic pieces in unlikely situations. He seems to have spent much of his time when in Herefordshire visiting remote farmhouses buying up old chests and cupboards.

The Moffatts had a different philosophy with regard to furnishing Goodrich Court. It became a private house again, not a home for a famous collection. Some Meyrick pieces fitted with the decor that the Moffatts had in mind and they were still in the house when Harold had a photographic record made in 1928.[2]

The Goodrich Court estate was put up for sale again in May 1884, when it was advertised in the *Times* as consisting of 670 acres, with a rental roll of £1,100 per annum. In the event, it was not sold but remained in Harold Moffatt's ownership. The 1884 sale particulars show only one major change to the building

Fig. 120   A cupboard once owned by Sir Samuel

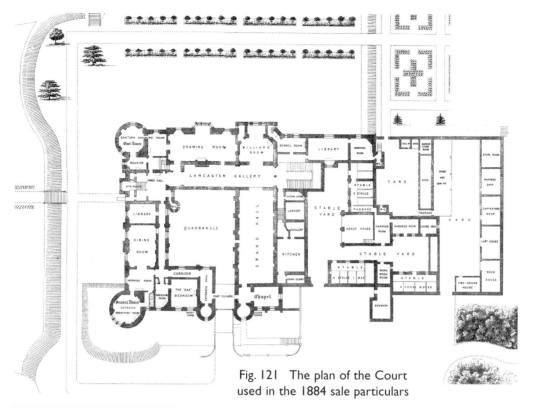

Fig. 121   The plan of the Court
used in the 1884 sale particulars

Fig. 122   The drawing room as illustrated in the 1884 sale particulars

Fig. 123   The Armoury as illustrated in the 1884 sale particulars

since the 1869 sale particulars had been drawn up—the Armoury had been shortened by some 18 feet or about one-fifth at the eastern end, to make room for a major new gallery running north-south, called the Lancaster Gallery. A large new staircase at the southern end of the gallery completed the transformation. The Armoury was now called the Grand Hall, and it had lost its gallery where Sir Samuel's display cases had once stood.

For the next twenty years or so the builders were regular visitors at the Court. One of the problems with the site was that the stables and other outbuildings occupied a prime plot of land. Hence, the decision was taken to remove all the ancillary buildings away from the Court—the noise from the stables was not really what a gentleman wanted next to his library anyway. The replacement red-brick stables are a familiar sight to anyone who takes the Goodrich road from the Monmouth gatehouse turning on the A40. Built around three sides of a square, they include living accommodation for the servants, and abut a large walled vegetable garden.

At very much the same time as the new stables were being built, the Moffatt family made a philanthropic gesture to the people of Goodrich. Demolishing one of the cottages they owned near Ye Hostelrie, they built a Reading Room for the use of the parishioners. It was built of red bricks in an elegant Tudorbethan style, and to all

Fig. 124   The stables as rebuilt by the Moffat family

intents and purposes it looks like the house of a prosperous villager. In only one respect can the buildings be said to have had unfortunate consequences—the use of red brick has been used as an excuse for allowing other brick buildings in what is traditionally a stone building area. To celebrate the centenary of the provision of the Reading Room for the village it was donated by the family to the people of Goodrich as a village hall. Although a large room has been added at the back, the frontage still looks as it did when Harold Moffatt provided it, and it is one of the handsomest village halls in the area.

The scene was now set for a major building project at the Court itself. Along with the stables and workrooms, Sir Samuel's brew tower was demolished. A final indignity was visited on the poor Armoury—it was converted to two storeys, the lower floor becoming the new kitchen, larder and pantry. Next to it, the original chapel was made into two store rooms. One of the problems with the original Armoury was that it was poorly lit, and had not been designed as the great hall of a

Fig. 125   Goodrich Village Hall

245

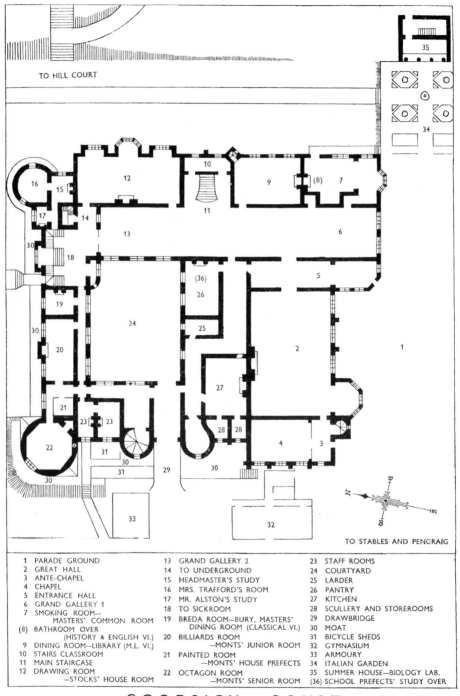

TO HILL COURT

TO STABLES AND PENCRAIG

1 PARADE GROUND	13 GRAND GALLERY 2	23 STAFF ROOMS
2 GREAT HALL	14 TO UNDERGROUND	24 COURTYARD
3 ANTE-CHAPEL	15 HEADMASTER'S STUDY	25 LARDER
4 CHAPEL	16 MRS. TRAFFORD'S ROOM	26 PANTRY
5 ENTRANCE HALL	17 MR. ALSTON'S STUDY	27 KITCHEN
6 GRAND GALLERY 1	18 TO SICKROOM	28 SCULLERY AND STOREROOMS
7 SMOKING ROOM—	19 BREDA ROOM—BURY, MASTERS'	29 DRAWBRIDGE
MASTERS' COMMON ROOM	DINING ROOM (CLASSICAL VI.)	30 MOAT
(8) BATHROOM OVER	20 BILLIARDS ROOM	31 BICYCLE SHEDS
(HISTORY & ENGLISH VI.)	—MONTS' JUNIOR ROOM	32 GYMNASIUM
9 DINING ROOM—LIBRARY (M.L. VI.)	21 PAINTED ROOM	33 ARMOURY
10 STAIRS CLASSROOM	—MONTS' HOUSE PREFECTS	34 ITALIAN GARDEN
11 MAIN STAIRCASE	22 OCTAGON ROOM	35 SUMMER HOUSE—BIOLOGY LAB.
12 DRAWING ROOM	—MONTS' SENIOR ROOM	(36) SCHOOL PREFECTS' STUDY OVER
—STOCKS' HOUSE ROOM		

GOODRICH COURT

Fig. 126   Plan of Goodrich Court in the 1940s

castle, the banqueting hall (now the drawing room) fulfilling that function in Sir Samuel's day. So Harold Moffatt set out to reconstruct a grand medieval hall, complete with hammer beam roof and minstrel's gallery.[3] It was designed by Henry Prothero of Cheltenham in 1888,[4] the hall replacing the service rooms to the south of the Armoury, and was lit from the south by large windows including a great oriel window. A new chapel led from it, double the size of the original. It was probably while the original chapel was being changed that the tombstone of Sextus Valerius Genialis found its way into the collection of Lord Bathurst at Cirencester, who later donated it to the Corinium Museum.

The hastilude chamber was replaced by a new grand staircase, having served as a billiard room since Sir Samuel's death. The Lancaster Gallery was lengthened still further and called the Grand Gallery, and a third entrance was built between it and the new Great Hall. The other rooms on the side of the Court overlooking Goodrich Castle to the east were remodelled. All in all, the living accommodation was perhaps three or four times the floor area of Sir Samuel's home—if one excludes the Armoury.

During the internal alterations at the Court, many of the rooms were remodelled, and the fixtures moved about. The linenfold panelling had been removed from Sir Gelly's chamber, possibly even before Sir Samuel's death according to Strong, and used to panel the walls of the Breda room. The Corinthian columns from either side of the door in the chamber were moved to the Breda room too, and the lower part of the overmantel was installed over the fireplace. The new Great Hall was enhanced further. Harold Moffatt designed and carved an enormous new overmantel in honour of the coronation of Edward VII, and a large organ was installed in the minstrels' gallery. Moffatt's energy was prodigious, as he published *The Church Plate of Herefordshire* with Stanhope in 1903.

The flat gardens overlooking the castle had been termed the 'tilt ground'. The southern half was remodelled as more formal gardens with flower beds while the Meyricks still owned the Court. In 1889 Harold Moffatt decided to have iron gates made to separate the new entrance forecourt from the garden. Also designed by Henry Prothero, they were manufactured by W. Letheren & Sons of the Vulcan Iron Works at Cheltenham.[5] These gates have a curious later history. The story is that they were sold to a dealer in 1949 who altered the '1889' on the gates to '1689', then sold them to an American who was unaware of their true age. At this time just after World War II many public buildings in London were without their railings. One such was the College of Arms in Queen Victoria Street, which had been damaged by bombing. The

College was given the garden gates to replace their originals, and there was great rejoicing when the gates were officially presented by the American ambassador Mr. Winthrop Aldrich in May 1956. The gates are still there today.

The formal gardens at the court were further enhanced in 1902 by a stone-built garden house which also survives, and ornamental flights of steps. The view of the Court from Goodrich Castle with its formal gardens and gravel walks was a favourite subject for postcards. Over the place where Sir Samuel's spring is located stands a small building—now dangerously dilapidated—sometimes called an ice house. Older inhabitants of Goodrich recall the lawnmower drawn by the same pony which was used to take firewood right into the Great Hall.

Fig. 127 The original design for the gates now at the College of Arms

Needless to say the Goodrich Court grounds were often in demand by local organisations for fêtes and similar events. Further public spirit was shown during World War I, when Goodrich Court was used as a convalescent home for soldiers from Australia recovering from wounds sustained in the hostilities. Harold Moffatt had four children, Cecil, and three girls Dorothy, Ruby and Phyllis. Cecil would in due course have succeeded his father to the estate but in 1916 he died childless, and the Goodrich Court estate descended to Dorothy, who had married into the Trafford family in 1907. The Traffords owned Hill Court, a beautiful house which was visible from the windows of Goodrich Court, across the Wye in the parish of Walford.

The Second World War was a watershed for so many houses and estates in Britain, but for a few years some had a new lease of life as schools and institutions were evacuated from the south and east of England. In May 1940, the headmaster of Felsted School was given forty-eight hours to evacuate the school and move from Essex to a

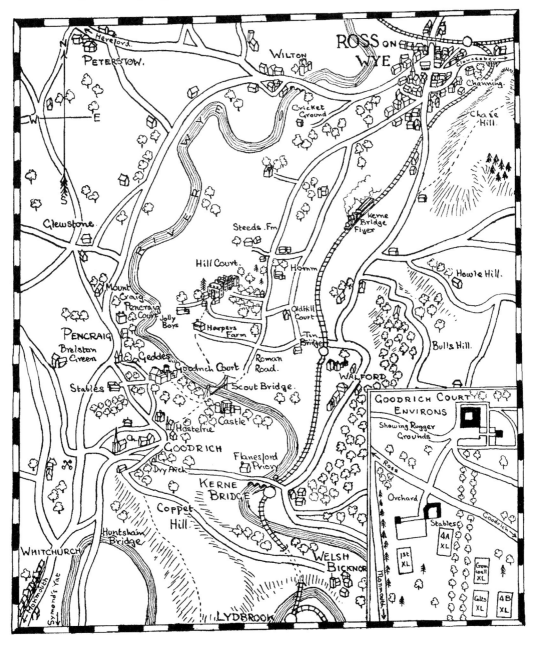

Fig. 128   Plan of the area when the Court was used by Felsted School

safer location. There must have been considerable negotiation behind the scenes before this, because just a fortnight after the last lesson in Essex on 28 May the boys were back behind their desks in Herefordshire. Felsted school is an ancient foundation dating from 1564 and at the time of the evacuation it had four hundred pupils.[6]

Dorothy Trafford had given over three of her houses for the use of Felsted's senior school: Goodrich Court, Hill Court and Pencraig Court, the latter a smaller house near to Goodrich Court. The junior school was sited twenty miles from Goodrich, at Canon Frome Court, the only building which was in any way suitable for the purpose. Although it was not too difficult for boys from Pencraig to attend their lessons which were all held at Goodrich Court, those in Hill Court over the other side of the river had more problems. The trip around by Kerne bridge was about three and a half miles, but this was brought down to one mile when a suspension bridge over the Wye was constructed by the boys. The bridge was reminiscent of those which cross Himalayan mountain streams, and with similar risks as the Wye can be very angry in winter. It was 167 feet long, and normally hung about 15 feet above the river, but when the river

Fig. 129   The suspension bridge over the Wye

flooded the footway was sometimes covered. Such a dangerous contraption would be inconceivable today, but there were no fatalities.

The chief problems at Goodrich Court were the lack of water, poor sanitary arrangements and a kitchen too small to cope with a large number of healthy appetites. Although the masters and their wives no doubt found the privations irksome, the years in Herefordshire made a great impression on the boys who experienced them. There were no rooms that could be used exclusively as classrooms, and many lessons took place on landings, in the Grand Gallery with people passing by, and even in a bathroom. The photographs taken at the time give a vivid flavour of the situation, and incidentally supply information on some of the rooms which were never otherwise photographed or illustrated in the sales particulars. One example is the octagon room, where Sir Samuel had pictures of medieval legends painted on the walls, and a piano with its case designed by Blore in one of the recesses. Unfortunately the paintings had been covered with protective screens, but enough can be seen to show how elegant the room must have been. The original wallpaper had a design of gold fleurs-de-lis on

Fig. 130 The Felsted boys in the Great Hall

pink, and although it is unlikely that it had survived for a hundred years the replacement gives a good idea of the effect. The boys were somewhat inconvenienced by the fact that a diesel engine for the electric lighting was located in the cellar underneath.

The Breda room was used by school societies when not required by classes or the masters, and it was remembered back in Felsted when a room where the boys held their society meetings was given the same name. The chapel at the Court was much too small to accommodate the boys *en masse*, and in general they joined in the normal services at the parish church of St. Giles, and held their special services there. The headmaster of Felsted was Canon K.J.F. Bickersteth, and one of the boys at least was inspired to follow in his footsteps and to become Bishop of Ramsbury. Fifty-five years after they had left the village, many Old Felstedians dug their hands deep into their pockets to support the Goodrich church spire appeal. The dedication service for the spire in January 2002 was taken by the same bishop, now retired.

Although much of the Goodrich Court furniture was put into storage for the duration of Felsted's occupation, there were enough pictures, tapestries and pieces of armour around to give the right impression. In some photographs of the time can be seen Meyrick pieces—the lectern designed by Blore which was evident in Shaw's drawing of the chapel can be seen in the new chapel, and a cupboard which Moffatt says was a Meyrick piece can be seen in the Breda room. The school moved back to Felsted in March 1945, and with their departure decisions about the future of the Court could no longer be postponed.

The death of Harold Moffatt's heir Cecil was mirrored by a similar tragedy in 1933 when Dorothy Trafford's elder son was killed in a car crash on his way to university. She had three remaining children: Cecily, Anne and John who were all destined to remain unmarried. Given the cost and difficulties of maintaining several large houses in the post-war period, she decided to try to sell Goodrich Court to an institutional buyer of some kind. There are stories that both Herefordshire County Council and London County Council had contemplated buying the Court but had been daunted by the cost of remodelling it to modern standards.

Having decided that Goodrich Court was no longer going to be occupied, Mrs. Trafford and the Moffatt relatives had a vast surplus of furniture, books and other items which they could not accommodate in their own homes. Accordingly, the best pieces were distributed around the family, and those no longer required were sold. The disposal started with a sale at Goodrich Court beginning on 26 August 1946, which lasted for four days.[7] The sale was conducted by a Hereford auctioneer, C.L. Marriott, when some 1,100 items went under the hammer. One of the items in the sale possibly dated to the Meyrick era—lot 451 was a stone font but as it was only 12 inches across it seems too small for that shown in Shaw's drawing. The first day was given over mostly to china and glass; the second to antique furniture much of which had obviously been collected by Harold Moffatt. There were lots consisting of old fireplace furniture and 'gothic' wall mirrors which may have been Sir Samuel's but were unattributed. None of the books, pictures or brasses sold on the third day seem to have been his, and of the miscellaneous furniture sold on the last day only the mahogany chest of drawers with lion-mask ring handles could be equated to 'a small chest of drawers mahogany with lion's head handles' in Sir Samuel's earlier inventory.

Mrs. Trafford had already disposed of some of her books at Hodgson's sale in London in July 1946,[8] and other good items were sent to Christie's London showrooms, where they were included in the sale of 17 October 1946.[9] In this sale it was claimed that the stained glass, alabaster plaques and a tapestry had belonged to Sir Samuel. In all there were about thirty pieces of the stained glass, much of it with military scenes or with armorials, dating from the mid sixteenth century of Swiss or German manufacture. Three of the alabaster plaques had made up a gothic retable of the fourteenth century Nottingham school, with scenes of the Resurrection, apostles and soldiers, and Christ and the Virgin.

Some Meyrick items from Goodrich Court survive in the possession of the Trafford family's relatives, while others were sold as part of the estate of Dorothy Trafford's son John, who had lived at Hill Court until he died in 1986.

The removal of books and the movement of furniture at the Court had exposed odd documents and pieces of paper. Sir James Mann had been invited by Mrs. Trafford to look around the Court in April 1946,[10] and he had found various armour sketches and heraldic scraps and cuttings from books by Sir Samuel,[11] and the documents concerning the despatch of the armour to the Art Treasures exhibition.[12]

The Court failed to sell, and for a while it sat empty, grass growing in the courtyard and an air of neglect overall. Mrs. Trafford took the decision to pull it down, much against the wishes of her daughters.[13] In June 1949 she sent Sir James Mann a mirror which had belonged to Sir Samuel, which had a miniature bust of Francis Douce attached at the bottom.[14] This had been presented to Sir Samuel by Lawrence Walker, Douce's executor.[15] Mann was invited to go do to Goodrich for one last look around, and she told him that Sotheby's was selling her famous virginal, which was no doubt the one made by Jacob Kirckmann, an eighteenth-century relative of Sir Samuel's friend Abraham Kirkmann. Also being sold by them was her armour, but it is uncertain whether there was any Meyrick armour.

On Wednesday, 24 August 1949 the first stage of the process of dismantling the Court was begun. Perry and Phillips, auctioneers from Bridgnorth in Shropshire conducted the sale.[16] Unfortunately all records of the sale were destroyed in a fire at their premises, and this has hampered research into the destination of the items sold. Certainly there was considerable interest in the many lots of antique woodwork which had been built into the Court by Sir Samuel and Harold Moffatt, with dealers coming from all over the country. There were 408 lots, which included such semi-structural items as doors and their framing. All the windows (with stone mullions) and floors were included, with a strict embargo on the removal of beams and joists which were *not* included with the floors. The purchasers had three weeks to remove their lots,

Fig. 131 The dismantling of the Court in progress, showing the roof of the Great Hall

Fig. 132   Breda room panels showing double eagle

which conjures up images of death-defying feats by the carpenters employed.

The prices fetched were in some cases derisory, for not only was Britain still labouring under post-war restrictions but few people had the money or the desire to embark on expensive building projects. Harold Moffatt's huge carved oak overmantel from the Great Hall made £50— somewhat less than £1,000 today— and the oak panelling there which was 10 feet high and ran for over 130 feet made only £350. The huge hammer beam roof fetched £200, but the purchaser did not get his money's worth. When he could not take it down, it was decided to pull out the walls and hope that it survived the fall, but it was smashed to pieces.[17]

Surprisingly, the antique overmantels did not make particularly good prices, and many of the buyers were attracted to the solid oak floorboards and panelling instead. There was some dealer interest in the Breda room, but in the end it was knocked down for £285 to a young man who had been charged by his wife with buying some furniture for their new home.[18] She was somewhat disconcerted with his purchase, particularly as he had to find someone to help him to dismantle the room. Most of the linen-fold panelling and the decorative panels found a home in a beautiful Carolean manor house in Surrey, where they remain to this day. The Corinthian door columns originally in Sir Gelly's chamber moved on with the not-so-young man to his next house. The ceiling of the Breda room proved to be more difficult to accommodate in an old building, and after a number of years in storage it was sold to one of the dealers who had been at the original Goodrich Court sale. Since then it has been lost to sight.

In Goodrich Court, the changes in the function of rooms over the years had had some curious consequences: the servants' hall boasted a carved marble mantlepiece surmounted by a finely carved oak overmantel, with the stained glass figures by Willement of William and Aylmer de Valence in the windows; one of the bathrooms had a very handsome carved mantelpiece with a coat of arms and figures of a saint and a knight of armour in the recesses. Many local people have small items from Goodrich Court, such as the clock from the entrance tower, or some panelling, or a bell. A linenfold-panelled lobby to Harold Moffatt's smoking room was sold at auction in 2002, having stood in a barn for over fifty years. Some linenfold panelling and two brass chandeliers were given to Goodrich church by the family.

There is a persistent story that Goodrich Court was dismantled and shipped to America, but the truth is much sadder. After pieces of any value had been sold the stone could be carted away at so much a ton. Iron girders had been used in the extensions of the Moffatt era, and took some pulling down. A local man who witnessed the demolition said that the building groaned like a wounded animal—a common if spinechilling phenomenon. There are still some iron girders lying on the site of the actual building, which is now a nature reserve. The Misses Trafford had a bungalow built on the old tennis court and lived there for a number of years, but that and the formal garden are now in other hands, the summer house being let for holiday accommodation. The woodland has

Fig. 133 Detail of carved column originally in Sir Gelly's room

reclaimed the rest of the gardens, and the sea of trees is all the visitors to Goodrich Castle can see of the site of Sir Samuel's 'new castle' on the Wyc. His creation had lasted just a hundred and twenty years.

Appendix   The Meyrick Ancestry

Sir Samuel's first certain ancestor in the Meyrick line was his great-grandfather James Meyrick (3) of Eyton and Lucton who died in 1749, whose eldest son was James Meyrick (4) who went to Lucton school and then set up the army agency business in London. James Meyrick (4) had two sons by his first wife: James Meyrick (5) and John Meyrick, Sir Samuel's father.

Sir Samuel's own version of his ancestry was as follows:

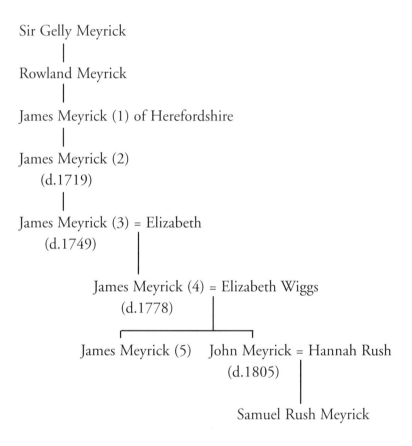

Sir Gelly Meyrick
|
Rowland Meyrick
|
James Meyrick (1) of Herefordshire
|
James Meyrick (2)
(d.1719)
|
James Meyrick (3) = Elizabeth
(d.1749)

James Meyrick (4) = Elizabeth Wiggs
(d.1778)

James Meyrick (5)   John Meyrick = Hannah Rush
(d.1805)

Samuel Rush Meyrick

James (3)'s will was proved at the Prerogative Court of Canterbury (PCC) on 23 October 1749, when his wife Elizabeth, his eldest son James, his other son Thomas, and his married daughter Margaret Simmons were mentioned. James (4)'s will was proved at the PCC on 6 May 1778, and in it he left £50 to his sister Margaret Simmons. James (3) and James (4) can therefore be definitely said to be father and son, but all the rest of the descent prior to James (3) is at best unproven.

One of the reasons that Sir Samuel found his earlier ancestors so difficult to trace is that the parish registers of Lucton for the seventeenth and early eighteenth centuries are fragmentary and in a very poor condition. The yearly transcripts of the registers which should have been sent to the Bishop of Hereford are missing or indecipherable in large part. The chapel at Lucton seems to have gone through a period of delapidation at this time, and the parishioners were sometimes forced to use other churches. The Meyrick family in the area used a very limited set of forenames which adds to the confusion.

When Sir Samuel started his genealogical researches he was convinced that his ancestors must have been gentlemen, and so would have had their wills proved in the PCC. As the only such will from the Lucton area was that of James Meyrick (3), he first took it into his head that his ancestors had come from Knighton where there had been a family of wealthy mercers called Meyrick whose wills had been proved in the PCC. After Sir Gelly Meyrick became a desirable ancestor the Knighton connection was dropped in favour of a descent from Sir Gelly's son Rowland.

According to Sir Samuel's submission to the College of Arms, James Meyrick (3) who died in 1749 was the son of another, James Meyrick (2), whose will was proved at Hereford in 1719. He had no proof of this, nor that a John Meyrick whose will was proved in 1720 was the son of James (2), though he was correct in the latter assumption. On the basis of this he concocted a spurious family tree, which is still perpetuated today. He cannot be blamed for his misinterpretation of a very involved situation, but he was guilty of deliberate falsehood in calling James (2) an 'esquire' when he was in fact a poor tailor whose effects were worth only six guineas on his death—about £600 today.

He also thought that the John who died in 1720 was married to Elizabeth (née Edwards), whereas in reality Elizabeth was John's mother. This was because Sir Samuel had made an elementary mistake in assuming that the Benjamin Palmer designated as a 'brother-in-law' by John Meyrick in his will had the modern meaning, whereas in fact it meant 'step-brother'. There are a series of deeds in Herefordshire Record Office which in conjunction with parish registers and the will of Elizabeth's brother Stephen makes it clear that Elizabeth Edwards married three times.

By her first husband John Prosser of Lucton, a weaver, she had a son John and daughters Mary and Elizabeth; by her second husband William Palmer also a weaver of Lucton she had a son Benjamin and a son Stephen who died in infancy; and by her third husband James Meyrick (2) she had John Meyrick who was baptised at Aymestrey in 1693 and who died in 1720. James (2) had another son James but not by Elizabeth Edwards, whom Sir Samuel co-opted as his great-grandfather James (3) who died in 1749. This James did have a son James, but the latter was a weaver in Covenhope or Connop in Lucton in 1759. He could not thus have been Sir Samuel's grandfather James (4) who was an army agent in London at the same date. The links Sir Samuel had proposed between Rowland Meyrick, James (1) and James (2) have no supporting evidence at all.

This still leaves the problem of Sir Samuel's ancestry unsolved. His great-grand-father James Meyrick (3) who died in 1749 was married by licence on 5 May 1716 to Elizabeth Laintoll at Presteigne, a market town a few miles away across the border in Wales. As they both came from Lucton this seems rather odd, but perhaps their parents disapproved. Their children were Sir Samuel's grandfather James (4) who was baptised on 4 June 1718, Margaret baptised 18 April 1719 and Thomas baptised 27 December 1722.

Sir Samuel claimed that his great-grandfather James Meyrick (3) was a captain in the army, but the regular army do not appear to have a James Meyrick as an officer at this time. He could, however, have been in the militia. Sir Samuel may have made the assumption based on the will John Pierrepoint, the founder of Lucton School, who left mourning rings to Roger Meyrick and a Captain Meyrick in his will dated 1707.

Roger Meyrick was a respected and fairly well-off local yeoman. He was a church-warden; as his property was fairly large he was entitled to one of the better pews in Lucton church and in 1710 he was affluent enough to make a loan of £30. On 1 April 1676 a marriage licence was granted to Roger Meyrick and Margaret Dodd, both of Croft which was near to Lucton. They had a son James, who was baptised at Lucton on 16 September 1682. Margaret was buried at Lucton on 12 August 1716, but Roger did not follow her until July 1730. It would seem quite feasible that their son James would name his first daughter in memory of his dead mother, and so this James is a possible candidate for James (3). Roger, his wife and an unnamed son appear as tenant to the impropriator of tithes of Eyton in 1692 and 1693 when they took crops from the Quaker John Bach to the value of the tithes he owed but would not pay.

Almost certainly Roger was the second eldest son of Thomas Meyrick, a fairly affluent weaver of Lucton who died in 1668 leaving eight children: Thomas, Roger, Mary, Margery, James, William, John and Elinor, the last four then being under age. Thomas Meyrick had only lately come into Lucton, as he is not shown in the Hearth Tax for 1665 or the Herefordshire Militia Assessments of 1663, though many smaller leaseholders would not have appeared in the latter. A Thomas Meyrick is shown with one hearth in Burrington, which was the home of a Meyrick family where the name Roger, otherwise uncommon in the Meyrick family, is also found in conjunction with the name Thomas. Even if it is not possible to prove which one of Thomas's sons was the father of James Meyrick (3), it seems quite possible that Thomas was his grandfather. With four children of full age, Thomas must have been about fifty, and therefore born *circa* 1618. Rowland Meyrick's children who were born around this time are all known, and do not include a Thomas of the right age. Rowland's sister had married into the wealthy Vaughan family, and her son and grandson were prominent men in seventeenth century politics. It is hardly credible that any of their Meyrick cousins would be living in obscurity in Lucton.

From the handwriting on James Meyrick (3)'s will it is possible to confirm his marriage licence, and to tie him to various other documents. He was churchwarden at Lucton in the early 1720s and he was the executor of the will of Elizabeth Meyrick, late of Kingsland, whose husband John had wanted their 'cousin' James Meyrick of Lucton to be her executor and his sole beneficiary. Elizabeth obviously resented this, and got her own back on James by purchasing numerous annuities which would cease on her death, and which would reduce the value of the estate. Having made the will in 1728 she died worth only £2 in 1743 when James Meyrick claimed the value of various poor bits of furniture he had 'lent' to her.

There are other pieces of evidence concerning the Meyricks in Lucton. A James Meyrick of Lucton was entitled to vote in the 1722 election for Herefordshire, and did so. An inquiry was held on 9 April 1722 at the Royal Oak in Leominster into which tithes were payable in Lucton. A number of Meyricks made depositions about the matter: two John Meyricks gave evidence, one aged about 65 from Shirlheath in Kingsland who said that tithes had never been paid on clover, hops, flax or hemp, and that about fifty years before his brother living in Lucton held lands indirectly from the Wigmore family. Elizabeth Meyrick (née Edwards) also gave evidence, as did James Meyrick yeoman of Lucton aged forty-four years and above, who had signed his name as a witness to a lease of the tithes in 1709.

Sir Samuel's ancestry will have to remain in obscurity until further evidence comes to light. The verdict of 'not proved' given by the York Herald against his descent from Sir Gelly Meyrick still stands.

Glossary

(See also illustration overleaf)

Armet	A close-fitting helmet where the weight is taken by the body and not the head, unlike earlier helmets
Carbine	A light, short musket often used by cavalry
Casque	An open helmet
Chanfron	The plate headpiece for a horse
Cuirassier	An armoured cavalryman wearing wearing a 'cuirass' or heavy breastplate and backplate, of the seventeenth century
Demi-suit	A suit for the upper body only
Garde bras	A piece of armour protecting the arm
Gisarme	*see* Guisarmier
Glaive	A weapon with a long blade set on the end of a staff
Grande garde mentonne	A grande guard is a large re-inforcement to the left shoulder for tilt armours, designed to protect the left side of the upper body where most of the force of the lance would be taken. A mentoniérre was a moulded piece of armour which attached to the breastplate and came up to the level of the ears, this grand garde would have come up to the ears
Guisarmier	A soldier carrying the guisarme or bill, where on the end of a staff there was a three-sided implement: a spike on the top, a curved cutting hook on one side and a short spike on the other. Typically used by the infantry in the fifteenth and sixteenth centuries
Halberd	A weapon with an axe-like head balanced by a fluke, carried on the end of a staff, topped with a spike
Polygar	A warrior from Hindustan
Ranseur	A weapon with a pointed blade set on the end of a staff, the blade lying between two upward curving blades
Solleret	Foot armour
Spetum	A weapon with a pointed blade set on the end of a staff, the blade sometimes lying between two upward curving blades
Target	A circular shield carried on foot
Tilting carousel	Target(s) rotating on a pole for practice for the tilt

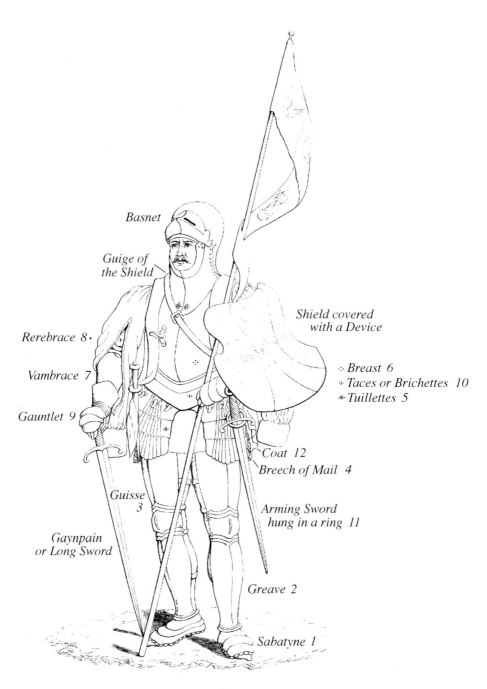

Basnet

Guige of
the Shield

Shield covered
with a Device

Rerebrace 8

Vambrace 7

∴ Breast 6
⸪ Taces or Brichettes 10
⸪ Tuillettes 5

Gauntlet 9

Coat 12
Breech of Mail 4

Guisse
3

Arming Sword
hung in a ring 11

Gaynpain
or Long Sword

Greave 2

Sabatyne 1

Manner and Order of putting on the different parts of Armour, from a letter dated 10 Oct. 1821
and addressed to Henry Ellis, Secretary of the Society of Antiquaries, published in *Archaeologia*

Select Bibliography

Ackermann, R.	*Loyal Volunteers of London & environs Infantry & Cavalry ... 1799*
Anon	*A List of the Chiefs, Officers ... of the Honourable Artillery Company*, 1789 *et* subs
Anon	*Felsted in Herefordshire*, n.d.
Anstruther, I.	*The Knight and the Umbrella*, 1963
Ashdown, C.H.	*British & Foreign Arms and Armour*, 1909
Aylmer, G. & Tiller, J.	*Hereford Cathedral - a History 2000*, p325
Bailey, H. & Barker Cryer. N.	*History of Freemasonry in the Province of Surrey*, 1970
Blair, C.	*European Armour*, 1979
Blair, C.	*The Meyrick Society 1890-1990* (privately pub. for the Society)
Bodleian Library	*The Douce Legacy* (Exhibition Catalogue), 1984
Borg, A.	Two Studies in the *History of the Tower Armouries*, 1976
Boutell, C.	*Arms and Armour*, 1905
Caygill, M. & Cherry, J.	*A.W. Franks*, 1997
Chapman, C.	*Marriage Laws, Rites, Records & Customs*, 1996
Chapman, C.	*Ecclesiastical Courts, Officials & Records*, 1997
de Cosson, Baron & Burge, W.	*A Catalogue of the Exhibition of Ancient Helmets and Examples of Mail*, 1881, reprinted in facsimile 1985
Cotman, J.S.	*Sepulchral Brasses*, 1839
Cox, G.V.	*Recollections of Oxford*, 1868 edition
Cripps-Day, F.H.	*A Record of Armour Sales 1881-1924*
Crofton Croker, T.	*A Walk from London to Fulham*, 1856
Evans, J.A.	*History of the Society of Antiquaries*, 1956
Eyre Evans, G.	*Lampeter*, 1905
Faraday, M.A. (ed)	*Herefordshire Militia Assessments of 1663*, 1972
Feret, C.	*Fulham Old & New*, 1900
Fishwick, H.	*History of the Parish of Rochdale*, 1889
Fosbroke, T.	*Archaeological Encyclopaedia*, 1825 & 1840
Fosbroke, T.	*The Wye Tour*, 1838
Foster, G.J.	*Doctors' Commons: Its Courts and Registries ...*, 1869
Glover, R.	*Britain at Bay - Defences against Bonaparte*, 1973
Guest, R. & John, A.	*Lady Charlotte*, 1989
Guy, A.	*Economy and Discipline - officership and administration in the British Army 1714-63*, 1985
Guy, A.	*Regimental Agency in the British Standing Army 1717-1763*, Bulletin of John Rylands Uni. Lib.

Hall, Mr. & Mrs. S.C.	*The Book of South Wales, the Wye and the Coast,* 1861
Hardie, M.	*English Coloured Books,* 1990 (reprint)
Hargrove, E.	*Anecdotes of Archery,* 1792
Hewitt, J.	*Ancient Armour & Weapons,* 1855 reprint 1996
Hodgkin, R.H.	*Six Centuries of an Oxford College,* 1949
Howcroft, G.B.	*George Shaw of St. Chad's Saddleworth,* Saddleworth Hist. Soc., 1972
Hughes, P. & Hurley, H.	*The Story of Ross,* 1999
Ireland, S.	*Picturesque Views of Wye,* 1797
Johnson, E.	*Sir Walter Scott - The Great Unknown,* 1970
Lacy, M.	'Students of Armour', unpublished PhD thesis, 1999
Laking, G.	*A Record of European Arms & Armour,* 5 vols, 1922
Leather, E.	*The Folklore of Herefordshire,* 1912
Little, B.	*The Story of Lucton School 1708-1958,* 1958
Mann, Sir James	*European Arms and Armour,* Wallace Collection Catalogues, 1962
McGarvie, M.	*The Meyricks of Bush,* privately published, 1988
Meller, H.	'Architectural History of Goodrich Court ..,' *TWNFC,* Vol. XLII, 1976-8, pp.175-185, & *TWNFC,* 1977, Vol. XLII Part 2 p.178
Meyrick, S.R. & Smith C.H.	*The Costume of the Original Inhabitants of the British Islands and adjacent coasts of the Baltic ... from the Earliest Periods to the Sixth Century,* 1815
Moffatt, C.H.	*Illustrated Description of some of the Furniture at Goodrich Court,* Oxford, 1928
Namier, L. & Brooke, J.	*The House of Commons 1754-1790,* 1964
Nash, C.	*The Goodrich Court Guide Hereford,* 1845
Nash-Williams, V.E.	*The Early Christian monuments of Wales,* 1950
Nichols, J.	*Literary History of the 18th Century,* Vol. 8, 1858
Phillips, B.	*Peterwell,* 1983
Planché, J.R.	*A Cyclopaedia of Costume or Dictionary of Dress,* 1876 (which contains illustrations of many tiems from the Meyrick collection) *Introduction to the Catalogue of Armour and Miscellaneous Objects of Art known as the Meyrick Collection,* Exhibited at South Kensington Museum 1869
Planché, J.R.	*Recollections and Reflections,* 1901 edition
Planché, J.R.	*History of British Costume,* 1836
Raikes, R.	*The History of the Honourable Artillery Company,* 1878
Raynor, K.	*Aide-Memoire to the Military Sciences,* 1853
Robinson, C.	*Manors & Mansions of Herefordshire,* 1873

Schom, A.	*Countdown to Battle 1803-1805*
Shaw, H.	*Specimens of Ancient Furniture,* 1836
Shaw, W.A.	*Knights of England,* 1906
Skelton, J.	*Engraved Illustrations of the Armour .., at Goodrich Court,* 1830 & 1854
Smith, C. Hamilton	*Selections of the Ancient Costume of Great Britain and Ireland from the Seventh to the Sixteenth Century,* 1814
Smith, C. Roach	*Retrospections Social and Archaeological,* 1883
Squibb, G.D.	*A History of Advocates and Doctors of Law,* 1977
Squibb, G.D.	*The High Court of Chivalry,* 1959
Stone, L. (ed)	*The University in Society,* 1972
Strong, G.	*Handbook to Ross and Archenfield,* 1863
Sutherland & Mitchell (eds)	*History of Oxford in the 18th Century,* 1986
Thorne, J.	*Handbook to the Environs of London,* 1876 facsimile edition 1983
Tisdall, J.	*Joshua Cristall,* 1996
Twamley, L.	*An Autumn Ramble on the Wye,* 1839
Wainwright, C.	*The Romantic Interior,* 1989
Weinreb & Hibbert	*The London Encyclopedia,* 1983
Westwood	*Lapidarum Walliae,* 1876-9
Wilson, D.M.	*The Forgotten Collector: Augustus Wollaston Franks ...,* 1984
Yarwood, D.(ed)	*Ancient Costumes of Great Britain and Ireland,* reprint 1989

Manuscript Sources

There are collections of Sir Samuel's letters and manuscript material by him or relating to him in the repositories noted below. Some other references are given in the endnotes.

Beinecke Library, Yale University
Letters to T.J. Pettigrew [Osborn Shelves Pettigrew]

Bodleian Library
Letters to Francis Douce [see catalogue of Western manuscripts]
Letters to Sir Thomas Phillipps [Phillipps-Robinson letters]
Letters to Joseph Skelton [MS Top Oxon b.80]

British Library
Journal of a Tour through part of England [Add 28802]
    & northWales in the summer of 1821
    by Llewellyn Meyrick Esq
The Meyrickian Museum [Add 28803]

Cambridge University Library
Edward Blore account books [Add 3925, 3927, 3955, 3956]

Cardiff Central Library
Letters to Angharad Llwyd [Doc 3.105]
Letters to John B. Nichols [Doc 4.189]
The Chronicle of the Princes of Wales by Caradoc [Doc 4.484]
   of Llangarran Abbey (MS copy)

Chetham's Library
Letters to Rev. Robert Raines [Raines Collection E.5.6]

College of Arms
Letters to T.W. King and other material [T.W. King Heraldic Miscellanies]

Hereford Library
Cambrian Eccentricities [914.29]
Goodrich Castle MS - history & measured plans [942.44 LPC 960]

Huntington Library

Letter to Planché	[MSS JP 1-279]
Meyrick's copy of Strutt's *Regal & Ecclesiatical Antiquities* with manuscript notes	[rare book 32462]

National Library of Scotland

Letters to Sir Walter Scott	[MSS 3893 to 3903]

National Library of Wales

Letters to Rev. T. Maurice and T.J. Pettigrew	[MS 6655C]
Letters to Rev. Walter Davies	[MS 1807E]
Letters to Abraham Kirkmann	[MS 6656C]
Letters to Rev. Walter Davies	[MS 1807E]
Llewellyn—an Historic Play in Five Acts	[MS 1233C]
Collecteana de Rebus Celticis	[MS 386C]
The British Genealogist	[MS 12689C]
Antient History of the Britons	[MS 178D]

Queen's College Library

Catalogue of the Names of the Sheriffs of North and South Wales	[Ref 410]
Catalogue of Paintings, Plate, Linen, etc.	[Ref 406]

Royal Armouries Library

Goodrich Court building account books	[AR6/1: I-275, I.401.1, I.401.2]
Goodrich Court Visitors' Books	[AR6/1 I-275]
Letters & drawings [see endnotes]	[AR6/2]

Southampton University Library

Letters to John C. Isaac	[MS 139 A5 53]
Report on Tower Armouries 1821	[WP1/685/21]

Wallace Collection

Box entitled Meyrick Collection containing among other items:

Journal of 1823 German Tour (Samuel Meyrick)	[item 1]
Journal of 1823 German Tour (Llewellyn Meyrick)	[item 2]
Llewellyn Meyrick sketchbook	[item 5]
Bound volume of drawings by Samuel Meyrick, some possibly for a third volume of engravings of the Meyrick collection by Skelton	[Ref. 701]

Published Works

Main Works

The History and Antiquities of the County of Cardigan; publ. 1808 and 1810 by Longman; 1907 by Davies & Co. Brecon; Facsimile edition 2000

The Costume of the original inhabitants of the British Islands from the earliest periods to the sixth century, to which is added that of the Gothic nations on the Western coast of the Baltic, the ancestors of the Anglo-Saxons and the Anglo-Danes (with Charles Hamilton Smith); publ. 1815 by Havell; reprinted 1818; facsimile edition 1989 Bracken Books

A Critical Inquiry into Antient Armour, as it existed in Europe, but particularly in England, from the Norman Conquest to the reign of King Charles II; publ. 1824 by Jennings; revised edition publ. 1842 by Bohn

Engraved Illustrations of antient Arms and Armour, from the collection at Goodrich Court from the drawings, and with the descriptions of Dr. Meyrick by J. Skelton; publ. in parts from 1826, usually dated 1830; 2nd edition by Bohn 1854

Abbildung und Beschribung von alten Waffen und R̜stungen welche in der Sammlung von L. M. zu Goodrich-Court aufgestellt sind; translated and published with an abridged text by Fincke of Berlin 1836

Heraldic Visitations of Wales and Part of the Marches, between the years 1586 and 1613, under he authority of Clarencieux and Norroy ... by Lewis Dwnn transcribed from the original manuscripts, and edited, with numerous explanatory notes by Sir Samuel Rush Meyrick; publ. by Rees, Llandovery, 1846 for Welsh Manuscripts Society

Collaborations

J. Carter	*Specimens of the ancient sculpture & painting now remaining in England from the earliest period to the reign of Henry VIII ... with notes by ... Sir Samuel Rush Meyrick*; 1838 edition publ. by Bohn
J.C. Cotman	*Engravings of Sepulchral Brasses in Norfolk and Suffolk ... with notes by Sir Samuel Rush Meyrick* (& others) second edition 1839; publ. by Bohn
H. Shaw	*Specimens of Ancient Furniture* drawn from existing authorities with descriptions by Sir Samuel Rush Meyrick 1836; publ. by Pickering
	Ancient plate & furniture from the colleges of Oxford & the Ashmolean Museum; publ. 1837 Pickering

Other Publications
The Analyst

Year	Page	
1834	22-28	Rudhall, Herefordshire
1835	73-84	Kentchurch Court, Herefordshire
1836	3-28, 243-266	Historical Memoranda of Wigmore Castle, Herefordshire

Archaeologia

Vol.	Page	
XVIII	442	Crosier bought in France (plate)
XIX	120-45	Observations on body armour
XIX	209-240	Observations on ancient military garments
XIX	336-352	The Lorica Catena of the Romans
XX	484-495	The tomb of Sir John Chandos (plate)
XX	496-514	The mode of putting on armour (plate)
XXI	445-449	The deed of gift to Abbey of Ystrad Marcholl
XXI	542	A British cup discovered in Flintshire (engraving)
XXI	549	The Queen of James 2nd's coffin plate
XXII	59-105	The history of hand firearms
XXII	106-113	Henry VIIIs armour (15 plates)
XXII	106-113	Sir Gelly Meyricke & the Cadiz booty
XXII	414-416	An ancient sword
XXII	417	The Great Seal of the Court of Pembroke
XXIII	92-97	Two British shields ... at Goodrich Court (plate)
XXIII	317-322	A pair of candlesticks & a pyx (plate)
XXXI	238-248	On a De Mauley effigy from York Minster (plate)

Archaeologia Cambrensis

1847	298-314	Inscription at Llanvair Waterdine, Shropshire
1848	13-29	On the state of the Druidic Religion in Britain, during the residence of the Romans

Transactions of the British Archaeological Association

Vol.	Page	
I	139-141	On a piece of chainmail
Ib	346	On the curved rail in Llanvair Waterdine church
Ib	390	On pagan religion in this country
II	343	On monument of Sextus Valerius Genialis
III	126	On a spur found at Fakenham

Cambrian Quarterly

Year	Page	L: letter; R: review; A: article
1830	143-5	L: On ancient inscribed stone from Tregaron & painted glass
1830	277-284	L: Re kinghts of Royal Oak & list of Welsh JPs in 1620
1830	484	L: Questions re meaning of Welsh words & place names
1831	27-8	L: Praising Planché's costume of Richard III & spread of Gelert legend

1831	133-5	L: History of Mongomery castle & inventory of arms & armour
1831	221-5	R: Skeltons Engraved Illustrations, short description of Goosrich court [SRM?]
1831	277-9	L: Re contemporary description of Owain Glyndwr & his armour
1832	16-24	L: Re Harleian MS 3859, a list of fabulous Welsh genealogies
1832	144-56	A: Irish mythology, Helio- & Lunar-Arkite worship, monuments
1832	248	L: On Prince of Wales motto Ich dien
1832	311-323	A: Irish mythology continued
1832	389-397	L: Corrections, Dwnn genealogies
1832	397-398	L: More about Ich dien
1833	115	L: Re cromlech at Newcourt, Pembs & his 1820 sketch of it
1833	119-20	L: Re busts of helmeted heads on the battlements of Caernarvon castle
1833	120-1	L: Reply re his error in Irish mythology, frontispiece of his Costume is wrong
1833	244-56	A: On the ancient money of Britain & Ireland
1833	272-4	L: On the course of Offa's Dyke in Herefordshire
1833	321-327	A: On the Roman gold mines at Pumpsaint, account written for him

Gentleman's Magazine

Vol.	Year	Page	L: letter; R: review; A: article; O: obituary
92-i	1822	307-309	L: Reply to review of Observations on Military Garments in *Archaeologia*
92-i	1822	386	A: Clambowe family
92-ii	1822	515-516	L: 'The Mermaid'
93-i	1823	112-113	L: 'Derivation of "Hundred"; The Merricks'
93-i	1823	393-394	L: 'Reginald de Breos, Lord of Brecon'
93-ii	1823	425-428 533-536	R: Parts 1 & 2 of review of *Critical Inquiry into Antient Armour*
94-i	1824	39-40 44-6	L: Reply to Parts 1 & 2 of review R: Part 3 of review of *Critical Inquiry*
94-i	1824	298	L: 'Curious Seal'
94-i	1824	387-8	L: Praising Kemble's King John for its accurate costume
94-i	1824	398-400	L: 'Druidical Woods, Groves, & Stone Structures; Etymology of Druid–Kit's Coty House, &c'
94-ii	1824	226	L: report on Sir John Mericks letter from Russia
94-ii	1824	256-7	R: Of Skelton's *Illustrations of the Antiquities of Oxfordshire*
94-ii	1824	389	L: Re armour query & double representation of events
94-ii	1824	483-4	L: Re Brônsted's Greek & Roman armour
95-i	1825	7-8	L: 'On the Religion of the Druids'
95-i	1825	53	R: James Robinson Planché's *Dramatic Costume*
95-i	1825	111-113	A: 'On the Religion of the Druids [conclusion]'
95-i	1825	224	L: 'Gipsy's Prophecy'
95-i	1825	246-247	R: *Delineations of Gloucestershire*
95-i	1825	329-330	R: *Graphic Illustrations of Warwickshire*
95-i	1825	403-7	L: On the Mericke family

95-i	1825	430-431	R: John Neale and John Le Keux, *Original Views of Churches*
95-i	1825	471	O: Owen Putland Meyrick
95-ii	1825	98, 386	L: Responses to his query re. the Bloundevill Family
95-ii	1825	351-2	R: Review of Blore's *Monumental Remains*
95-ii	1825	387-391	A: The Cosmogony of the Tahiteans
95-ii	1825	413-4	L: Criticism of a *History of Chivalry of Grenada plates*
95-ii	1825	482	A: Notes on an ancient helmet recently discovered
96-i	1826	65	R: No. 1 of Skelton's Engraved Illustrations advertised
96-i	1826	318-9	L: Re. Pacino, and extolling *Engraved Illustrations*
96-ii	1826	195-6	L: Lack of consultation with him re. Tower Armoury
96-ii	1826	391-2	A: Cowey Stakes
96-ii	1826	393-397 583-587	L: Kingsland Church & Evans of Eyton Hall
97-i	1827	195-196	L: Re work in Tower: Horse Armoury & obstruction by staff
97-i	1827	482	N: A Note on the word 'Sul'
98-i	1828	6-8, 103-4	L: About existence of Druidism & Helio-Arkite worship
99-i	1829	25-9	L: Replies from N.H. Nicolas & Meyrick to criticism from 'A clerk of Oxenforde'
99-i	1829	202-5	L: Re Welsh MS genealogy owned by Edward Evans of Eyton Hall
99-ii	1829	401	L: Note on a 15th-century brass hook
CII	1832	303	L: Re. cloth-yard arrows
CII	1832	599-601	L: Re. Articles of the Finsbury Archers
CIII-i	1833	504-5	A: The course of Offa's Dyke in Herefordshire
NS 5	1836	245-253	'Catalogue of the Doucean Museum'
NS 5	1836	378-384	'Catalogue of the Doucean Museum cont.'
NS 5	1836	585-590	'Catalogue of the Doucean Museum cont.'
NS 6	1836	158-160	'Catalogue of the Doucean Museum cont.'
NS 6	1836	378-384	'Catalogue of the Doucean Museum cont.'
NS 6	1836	492-494	'Catalogue of the Doucean Museum cont.'
NS 11	1839	68-72	R: *The Mabinogion*, pt 1
NS 12	1839	390-2	R: *The Mabinogion*, pt 2
NS 11	1839	393-396	R: An Essay on the Neo-Druidic Heresy of Britannia , pt 1
NS 12	1839	390-392	R: *Gwaith Lewis Glyn Cothi*
NS 12	1839	392-393 507-509	R: Albert Schulz's *An Essay on the Influence of Welsh Tradition upon the Literature of Germany, France, and Scandinavia*
NS 17	1842	169-174	cont.

The Graphic and Historical Illustrator

Apr	1834	353-354	Remarks on Burlesque Tournaments

Other

A Lecture on the Conduct which the Jews have experienced from the Christians delivered at the Mechanics' Institute, Leominster, Herefordshire ... October 1844; published by Wemyss

This list is not exhaustive, and a number of journals such as *The Retrospective Review* published articles anonymously.

References

Abbreviations used

BL   British Library
BLG   Burke's Landed Gentry,
    first edition,1838
BM   British Museum
Bod   Bodleian Library
CA King   T.W. King Heraldic Miscellany,
    College of Arms, London
CCL   Cardiff Central Library
ChCh   Christ Church College Archives,
    Oxford
Chet   Chetham's Library, Manchester
CUL   Cambridge University Library
DNB   *Dictionary of National Biography*
Douce   Douce MSS, Bodleian Library,
    Oxford
DRO   Dorset Record Office
DWB   *Dictionary of Welsh Biography, 1959*
GloucL   Gloucester Library
GL   Guildhall Library, London
GM   *Gentleman's Magazine*
GRO   Gloucester Record Office
HAN   Herefordshire Archaeological
    News, Woolhope Club
HFRO   Hammersmith & Fulham
    Record Office
HL   Hereford Library

HRO   Herefordshire Record Office
LMA   London Metropolitan Archives
NLS   National Library of Scotland
NLW   National Library of Wales,
    Aberystwyth
PCC   Prerogative Court of Canterbury
PRO   Public Record Office, Kew
QC   Queen's College, Oxford
RAL   Armouries Library, Leeds
RCHM   Royal Commission for Historic
    Monuments
RIBA   Royal Institute of British
    Architects
Royal   Royal Archives, Windsor
SA   Society of Antiquaries Library
SUL   Southampton University Library
TWNFC   *Transactions of the Woolhope Naturalists'*
    Field Club
V&A DPD   Victoria & Albert Museum,
    Dept. Prints & Drawings
V&A MA   Victoria & Albert Museum,
    Museum Archives
WA   Westminster Archives
WC   Wallace Collection Archives, London
WRO   Warwickshire Record Office

Chapter 1 Early Years

1. GM 1778
2. BLG
3. *Retrospective Review*, Vol 2, New Series 1828 p.223
4. CA King Vol 19 f3
5. See Appendix A for the Meyrick ancestry
6. Little, *The Story of Lucton School*
7. HRO Records of Lucton School BD13/15
8. *The Calcrafts of Rempstone* DRO
9. DRO Ryder of Rempstone D/RWR/X2
10. Phillips, *Peterwell*, Gomer Press 1983
11. Robinson, *Manors & Mansions of Herefordshire*
12. Namier & Brook, *The House of Commons 1754-1790*, 1964
13. £1,360,000 today. Guy, *Regimental Agency in the British Standing Army 1717-1763*
14. DRO D/RWR/X11 Account Book 1760-4

15. £2,000,000 today
16. *Town & Country Magazine*, Oct 1769, p.1
17. Guy, *op. cit.*, p.38
18. In 1766, James Meyrick was still in the business of selling commissions, this time for an American Lieut. Col. Josiah Martin, for £3,500 North Carolina Martin Papers Add. MSS XVI 41361 ff162-3
19. PRO WO55 p139
20. PRO WO55 p267
21. PRO WO55 p139 15 Dec 1757 & WO55 p.267, 26 Jan 1758
22. DRO D.86.X.13
23. Guy, *op. cit.*, p.429
24. *Survey of London*, St. Margaret Westminster
25. *ibid.*
26. Guy, *op. cit.*, p.46
27. Annual Register 1781, p.255
28. PRO PCC will proved 6 May 1778

29. In 1902
30. NLW MSS 6655C f9 to Rev. T. Maurice
31. Royal Society records
32. Guy, *op. cit.*, p.429. Morse had the distinction of living at No. 11 Downing Street from 1778-9
33. CCL Doc 3.105 f12 to Angharad Lloyd 6 Feb. 1823
34. WA Acc 331 Marriage settlement Oct 1787
35. Said during the trial of Lord Melville in April, 1806
36. Bod Douce MSS d27 f157 3 Oct 1831

Chapter 2 An Extraordinary Boy
1. £650,000 today
2. WA Acc 331 Marriage Settlement dated 28 April
3. GL MS3787 Draft will of Dec 1775
4. NLW MS 13132E f197 Letter to Cymdeithas Cymreigyddion y Fenni, 8 Sep 1837
5. Somerset Archive & Record Service: Bath Turnpike Trust records D/T/ba/62
6. *GM* lx. p960 June 1790
7. PCC Susannah Rush's will proved 17 June 1790
8. *Survey of London*, St. Margarets Westminster p.15
9. WA Registers of St Margarets, Westminster
10. *ibid.*
11. CA King Vol 19 f77
12. Weinreb & Hibbert *The London Encyclopedia*
13. Bowack, quoted in Feret *Fulham Old & New* Vol I, p.87
14. Feret, *Fulham Old and New*, p.90 et subs.
15. Crofton Croker, *A Walk from London to Fulham* p.165
16. £175,000 today
17. PCC Samuel Rush's will was proved 16 May 1787
18. Croker, *op cit.*, p.167
19. Thorne, *Handbook to the Environs of London* p.225
20. PRO C12/1718/10 3 Nov 1791
21. £450,000 today
22. *Biographical Dictionary of British Architects 1660-1840*
23. Feret, *op cit.*, p.155-6
24. GL A 1.3 no. 24
25. NLW MSS 6655C f6 [Rev. T. Maurice] 30 Jan 1815
26. WC Meyrick collection

27. *DNB*
28. CCL Dec 4.189 f27 19 Mar 1832
29. The Holophusicon had exhibited items brought back from Cook's voyages, and this may be the origin of some of these in the Meyrick collection
30. *A List of the Chiefs, Officers [..] of the Honourable Artillery Company* (1789 et subs)
31. BL Add MS 28801 Collections on Archery
32. *ibid.;* Hargrove, *Anecdotes of Archery*, 1792 York
33. Ackermann, *Loyal Volunteers of London & Environs Infantry & Cavalry ... 1799*
34. Published London 1798
35. Feret *op. cit.* Vol 2 p.152
36. HFRO PAF/1/5 Fulham Vestry Minutes
37. Feret *op. cit.* Vol 3
38. Raikes, *The History of the Honourable Artillery Co.* Vol II, pp.214-7
39. Feret *op. cit.* Vol 2 p.151
40. Nottinghamshire Archives DD/P/6/12/26/1-22
41. Meyrick, *Critical Inquiry into Antient Armour*, index
42. BL Add MS 28803
43. Feret *op. cit.* and Faulkner, *Historical Account of Fulham* derived from Weever's *Funeral Monuments*
44. PRO correspondence with Earl Cornwalllis
45. QC Archives
46. Lawrence Stone (ed.), *The University in Society*
47. R.H. Hodgkin, *Six Centuries of an Oxford College*, p.152
48. *ibid.*, p.154
49. Cox, *Recollections of Oxford*, pp.27-8
50. *University Life in Eighteenth Century Oxford* p.2
51. QC Archives Entrance Book, Table Dues Book, Batells Book
52. Stone (ed.), *op. cit.*, p.46
53. Hodgkin, *op. cit.*, p.155
54. Sutherland & Mitchell (eds.), *The History of the University of Oxford* Vol V, The Eighteenth Century, p.33
55. *ibid.*, p.335
56. Douce MSS d28 f106 20 Mar 1833

Chapter 3 The Welsh Connection
1. RAL AR 6/2. This is a curious cache of very intimate documents preserved by Sir

Samuel

2. NLW Parish Register of Llanfihangel y Creuddyn

3. Chapman, *Marriage Laws, Rites, Records & Customs*, p.17

4. NLW Castle Hill MS 856, Marriage settlement of James Parry & Eliz Morgan, 8 May 1777

5. NLW Castle Hill, MS 852 Copy of Will of David Parry, 24 March 1760

6. RAL AR 6/2 1g to Wm. Donaldson Esq. dated Forest Hall 1 Dec. 1803

7. NLW Great Sessions 4 Apr. 1778, f21 7 Mar. 38 Geo III (1797)

8. *ibid.*, report of inquest enclosed

9. *ibid.* The records are unclear as to the actual sentence carried out

10. NLW Llidiardau Miscellaneous Box 14/9/17

11. RAL AR 6/2

12. *ibid.* William to Samuel 17 Oct 1803

13. *ibid.* Samuel to William 23 October 1803

14. PRO Will proved 29 Jan 1806

15. PRO Will proved 17 June 1790

16. A. Schom, *Countdown to Battle 1803-1805*

17. R. Glover, *Britain at Bay - Defences against Bonaparte*, p.43

18. PRO WO 13/134, Pay Lists 25 Dec 1803 to 24 Dec 1804

19. PRO WO 13/134 & 135, Pay Lists 25 Dec 1803 to 24 Dec 1805

20, PRO WO5/106 Militia Marching Orders, p.441

21. *ibid.*, p.443

22. WA Register of St. Margaret's Westminster

23. Information from Chelsea Rate books (courtesy Claude Blair)

24. Weinreb & Hibbert, *The London Encyclopaedia*

25. RAL AR 6/2 ll

26. His memorial tablet says 52

27. Feret, *Fulham Old & New*, Vol 1, p.255

28. BL 822. b29, Catalogue of John Meyrick's Sale

29. Feret, *op. cit.*, Vol 1, p.213

30. Bod Mus Bibl III 617

31. Item 1371 was a Book of Hours which was also damaged in the wreck

32. NLW MSS 6655C f5 28 Jul 1813

33. PRO IR26/107

34. Equivalent to £2.7m

35. Deed, Private Collection

36. *London Gazette*, p.467

37. House of Lords Record Office HL/PO/PB/1/1807/47G3s2n208

38. Feret, *op. cit.*,Vol 2, p.154

39. RAL AR 6/2 Letter to Samuel from there 25 Aug. 1814

40. Deed, Private Collection

41. CCL Doc 3.105 f9, To Angharad Llwyd 16 Dec. 1822

42. Sutherland & Mitchell, (eds.), *The History of the University of Oxford* Vol V, The Eighteenth Century, pp.481-491

43. *GM*, 1817, ii p.200

Chapter 4 The Young Antiquary

1. Location unknown

2. Meyrick, *The History and Antiquities of the County of Cardigan*, 1st ed., 1808

3. NLW MSS 6655C f1 27 Apr 1807

4. NLW MS 12689C bought at Sotheby's ex Quaritch, Nov. 1966

5. NLW MS 12690C bought at Sotheby's ex Quaritch Nov 1966

6. NLW MS 386C bought 5 Nov 1918

7. QC Library Book 410

8. Location unknown

9. Bod MS Don 89 letter to Simcoe 17 Oct. 1807

10. NLW ex 936 Carr *History of Cellan*

11. Meyrick, *The History and Antiquities of the County of Cardigan*, 1907 ed., p.224

12. Eyre Evans, *Lampeter*, 1905

13. Bod MS Don 89 f137-8 17 Oct. 1807

14. NLW MS 6656C f85

15. Meyrick, *The History and Antiquities of the County of Cardigan*, 1907 ed, p.224

16. Nash-Williams, *Early Christian Monuments of Wales*, 1950 pp.104-6

17. Westwood, *Lapidarum Walliae 1876-9*, pl.38

18. NLW MS 1326C f33-6

19. Bod, Film of Longman archives 2581 d.847, Commission Books b1 pp.387-8, 396

20. NLW MS 1326C f33-6

21. Evans, *op. cit.*

22. NLW MS 6655C f2 to Rev Maurice 10 Feb. 1810

23. NLW MS 6655C f3 to Rev Maurice 14 Feb. 1810

24. NLW MS 1233 C

25. NLW MS 6655C f3 to Rev Maurice 14 Feb. 1810

26. NLW MS 93 B The inscription to 'Sire Remi' is difficult to read
27. HL Cambrian Eccentricities 914.29
28. *ibid.*, p.206
29. NLW MSS 6655C f4, 30 March 1812
30. NLW MSS 178-180D
31. Catalogue of Library sale lot no. 1376
32. *GM*, 1815, pt 2, pp.102-3; Beever, *Memorials of Old Chelsea*, p.348
33. LMA ACC/478/56
34. QC Library Item 406
35. CCL MS 4.189 f6 14 May 1810
36. Chapman, *Ecclesiastical Courts, Officials & Records*
37. Squibb, *The High Court of Chivalry*, p.133
38. Foster, *Doctors' Commons: Its Courts and Registries*, p.5 et subs
39. Squibb, *History of the College of Advocates*, pp.69-71
40. Douce MSS d24 f21 3 Mar 1822
41. Chapman, *op. cit.*, .p45
42. Doctors' Commons records are in Lambeth Palace library and the PRO
43. PRO Doctors' Commons Treasurers' Book letter, 18 Feb. 1824
44. Lambeth Palace Lib Fee Book DC18
45. Blair, *The Meyrick Society 1890-1990*, pp.20-21
46. Lambeth Palace Library DC12
47. NLW MSS 6655C f5 to Rev. Maurice
48. CCL Doc 3.105 f11 to Angharad Llwyd, 14 Jan. 1823
49. Devon Record Office 152M/C1812/OH22 8 Sep. 1812

Chapter 5 The Master Works

1. *DNB*
2. K. Raynor quoting Smith's article in *Aide-Memoire to the Military Sciences*, Vol I, 1853
3. CA King Vol 19 f479, 29 Jan 1842
4. Hardie, *English Coloured Books*, p.90
5. NLW MSS 6655C f5 28th July 1813
6. Yale Univ. Lib BAC A N45
7. Yarwood (ed.), *Ancient Costumes of Great Britain and Ireland*, Bracken Books, 1989
8. NLW MSS 6655C f6 no addressee 30 Jan 1815
9. BL Add MSS 28803 purchased at Sothebys, 24 July 1871
10. This chairback had been exhibited at the Society of Antiquaries
11. SA Minute Book Nov. 1808 - Jul 1811
12. Evans, *A History of the Society of Antiquaries*, p.214

13. *ibid.*, p.237
14. SA Minute Book for December 1811
15. Evans, *op. cit.*, p.245 et subs
16. 12 Nov 1827
17. GloucL Fosbroke Letters 8208 1260 Walford, 18 Dec. 1828
18. Evans, *op. cit.*, Appendix C
19. When the President was absent a cocked hat represented him
20. GM March 1836 p.246
21. Bod MSS Montague d.18 f80
22. Douce MSS d22 23 Dec. 1815
23. Bod, *The Douce Legacy*, Exhibition Catalogue 1984
24. Douce MSS e.31
25. Douce MSS e.34 & e.35
26. Nichols, *Literary History of the 18th Century*, Vol. 8, 1858. pp.660-3
27. *The Douce Legacy*, pp.130-139
28. About £2.5 million equivalent
29. Douce MSS d28 f168
30. *Survey of London*, Volume on College of Arms, p.94
31. CCL letters to Angharad Llwyd
32. NLW MS 6656C f19, 1 Oct. 1839
33. Kirkmann family history from current members of the family
34. Now at Browsholme Hall, Clitheroe
35. Planché, *Recollections and Reflections*, pp.36-7
36. *DNB*
37. *DNB*
38. Bailey & Barker Cryer, *History of Freemasonry in the Province of Surrey*. There may be an underlying thread of freemasonry to Sir Samuel's friendships which has not been investigated
39. NLW MS 6655C f22 to Pettigrew, 3 Feb. 1831
40. NLW MSS 6655C f13-f15 to Pettigrew, 1826

Chapter 6 An Acknowledged Expert

1. Planché, *Introduction to the Catalogue of Armour and Miscellaneous Objects of Art known as the Meyrick Collection. Exhibited at South Kensington Museum 1869*
2. CCL MS 4.189 f15 SRM to J.B. Nichols, 28 Sep. 1824
3. Meyrick Society archives. Unsigned, but identified by handwriting
4. WC Box 7610 Typescript of Colnaghi catalogue
5. WC Box 7610 Black and white photographs of scrapbook in private collection

6. Meyrick Society archives
7. WC A334
8. Norman, *Wallace Collection European Armour supplement*, 1986
9. Weinreb, *The London Encyclopedia*
10. Douce, d23 f17
11. Planché, R*ecollections & Reflections*, p.158
12. Borg, *Two Studies in the History of the Tower Armouries*
13. RAL AR 6/2 Letter from Samuel to Tower Authorities 1827
14. Douce MSS d23 f215, 3 Oct. 1820
15. Skelton, *Engraved Illustrations*, p.ix
16. Douce MSS d24 f10, 15 Feb. 1822
17. *GM* Vol 93-i, Jan. 1823, p.98
18. V&A DPD Pressmark 0.7.e 8964.A-m
19. NLW MSS 6655C ff 13-15 1826
20. Hardie, *English Coloured Books*, p.155
21. *GM* Vol 93-ii, pp.425-428, 533-536 and Vol 94-i, pp.44-46
22. V&A DPD Pressmark O.7.e Acc. No. 7921.1-20
23. RAL Box AR6/1 I-275 Sale Hodgson Nov. 21 1946 lot 451
24. NLS MS 3892 f69
25. NLS MS 3892 f125
26. NLS MS 3892 ff 85 & 125
27. NLS MS 3893 f7
28. NLS MS 3893 f47 24 Aug. 1821
29. S. Kensington Exhib. Catalogue 1869, p.80, item 1068
30. NLS MS 3893 f185, £800 worth
31. NLS MS 3894 f1
32. NLS MS 3895 f131-2
33. In the Scott letters there was much discussion about 'Andrea Ferrara', his identity, and why there are so many swords with his name in Scotland.
34. CCL Doc 3.105 f8 letter to Angharad Llwyd
35. NLS MS 3899 f263-4

Chapter 7 A Search for Home

1. BL Add. MS 28802
2. Bod MS Don 89 f141
3. *Antiquaries Journal*, Vol XIII, pp.152-154 pl. XXI
4. The tickets are in the journal. The garden still exists for public enjoyment
5. *DWB* p.593
6. Maxwell Fraser, 'Angharad Llwyd - Antiquary & Eisteddfodwr' in *Country Quest*, Aug. 1968, pp.8-10
7. CCL MS 3.105 1831 to 1830s, others in NLW
8. NLW MS 1807E f934, Letter to Rev. Walter Davies Manavon Monts
9. CCL Doc 3.105 f3, 12 Feb. 1822
10. As the votes cast were public knowledge, Samuel may not have wanted to risk Nicholl's displeasure. In a letter to Sir Walter Scott, NLS MS 3893 f47, Samuel alleges that he has voted for Scott's friend, Heber
11. CCL Doc 3.105 f4b, 11 Apr. 1822, Llanstefan, south of Carmarthen
12. CCL Doc 3.105 f6, 16 May 1822
13. Douce MSS d24 f89, 16 Oct. 1822
14. CCL Doc 3.105 f8, 25 Oct. 1822
15. CCL Doc 3.105 f9, 16 Dec. 1822
16. Leather, *The Folklore of Herefordshire*, p.xv
17. Douce MSS d24 f149, 12 April 1823
18. Hughes & Hurley, *The Story of Ross*, p.111
19. Ireland, *Picturesque Views of the Wye*, 1797
20. Hereford Museum
21. Tisdall, *Joshua Cristall*, p.38
22. CCL Doc 3.105 f33 to Angharad Llwyd, April 1828
23. Bod MS Top Oxon b.80 f97, 27 Aug. 1824
24. NLS MS 3895 ff 131-132, 30 Dec. 1824
25. CA King Vol 12 f129
26. CCL Doc 3.105 f25, 27 Mar. 1825
27. Duncumb, *Collections toward a History of the County of Hereford, Hundred of Wormelow*, p.88
28. NLW MS 6656C f3, 15 Apr. 1824
29. NLW MSS 6655C f6, 30 Jan. 1815
30. CCL Doc 3.105 f8, 25 Oct. 1822
31. WC Meyrick Collection
32. Fosbroke, *Encyclopaedia of Antiquities*, 1840, p.902
33. *Archaeologia*, Vol XXIII, pp.317-33
34. Douce MSS d24 f197, 3 Dec. 1823
35. Meyrick, *Critical Inquiry*, 1824, Vol 3, pp.142-145
36. *ibid.*, pp.141-142
37. Meyrick, *Critical Inquiry*, 1842
38. *ibid.*
39. NLW MS 6656C f2. 4 Aug. 1824
40. Douce MSS e.67 Collecta 1811 to 1823
41. NLW MS 6656C f3, 15 Apr. 1824
42. Bod MS Top Oxon b.80 f97
43. NLW MS 1562C
44. NLW MS 6656C f8
45. CCL Doc 4.189 ff 12-14. *GM*, Sep. 1824, pp.256-7

46. Bod MS Top Oxon b.80 f103, 20 Oct. 1824
47. Douce MSS d25 f144, 16 Jan. 1826.
    Prospectus in Douce's own copy now in
    the Bodleian s.839
48. *GM*, Jan. 1826, p.65
49. Bod inside Douce's copy s.839
50. CCL Doc 4.189 f17, 3 Apr. 1826
51. *GM*, April 1826 pp318-9
52. NLS MS 3903 f183, 21 Nov. 1826
53. Bod MS Top Oxon b.80 f123, 9 Jan. 1826
54. Douce MSS d28 f170, 28 Oct. 1833
55. Aylmer & Tiller, *Hereford Cathedral - a History*,
    p.325
56. *ibid.*, pp.259-265
57. Hereford Cathedral Lib. Chapter Act Book
    Nov. 1814 -Nov. 1834, pp.262-3
58. Photocopy of letter in Hereford Cathedral
    library
59. Hereford Cathedral Lib. Chapter Act Book
    Nov. 1814 -Nov. 1834, pp.289, 290, 302
60. V&A DPD Blore Acc. No. 8748 Pressmark
    A.265
61. CCL Doc 4.189 f26, 30 Dec. 1830
62. SUL WP1/685/21, 28 Nov. 1821
63. Douce MSS d24 f4, 28 Jan. 1822
64. PRO WO44/301, Ordnance in-letters
    bundle 2. Thanks to Claude Blair for
    pointing out these letters
65. *GM*, Aug. 1826, p.159
66. *GM*, Sep. 1826, pp.125-6
67. RAL Box AR 6/2 item 5
68. *ibid.*
69. *GM*, Mar. 1827, pp.195-6
70. *GM*, 1829 (ii), p.629
71. PRO WO44/301 ordnance in-letters bundle
    2
72. RAL Box AR 6/2 item 5
73. NLW MS 6655C f24, 6 July 1831
74. Bod MS Top Oxon b.80 f127
75. CCL Doc 3.105 f30
76. Bod MS Top Oxon b.80 f133
77. NLW MS 6656C f9
78. Hereford Museum Cat. 3021-3026: NLW MS
    6656C f9, 9 Apr. 1828
79. RAL I.275
80. Douce MSS d26 f100, 28 Mar. 1828
81. *GM*, May 1828, p.463
82. CCL Doc 3.105 f34, 12 Mar 1830
83. Royal Ref. RA GEO/23524
84. By courtesy of Claude Blair Letter dated
    Wed 2 Mar. [1831]
85. Anon., *The Analyst*, 1835, pp.26-28
86. Laking, in his *The Armoury of Windsor Castle*,
    p.xii, said he could find no mention of it
    at Windsor before 1852
87. NLW MS 6655C f23, June 1831
88. NLW MS 6655C f24, 6 July 1831
89. NLW MS 6655C f25, 10 July 1831

Chapter 8 Building the Court
1. Private Collection 134. Modern equivalent
   £300,000
2. Private Collection Numerous deeds
3. RIBA library SD91/1-6
4. CCL Doc 3.105 f33 to Angharad Llwyd April
   1828
5. HRO Quarter Sessions QSR 117 & 118
6. GloucsL Fosbroke letters 8208
7. *ibid.*, f255
8. *ibid.*, f276
9. *TWNFC*, 1870, p.84
10. Douce MSS d28 f28, 18 April 1832
11. HRO BF16/48
12. RAL Refs I.401.1, I.401.2. CUL Add 3925,
    Add 3927
13. CUL Add 3955 & 3955
14. CUL add 3927 p.51
15. RAL I.401.1
16. RAL I.401.2
17. V&A DPD Pressmark A.268 Ref. No. 8743.1-
    45
18. RAL AR6/1 I-275
19. 1869 Sales Particulars
20. RCHM
21. GloucL Fosbroke letters 8308 f294
22. Wye Tour 1845; Goodrich Court Guide
23. Douce MSS d28 f168
24. NLW MS 6655C f29
25. HL Goodrich Court Sale Particulars
26. NLW MS 6655C f28, Mar. 1832
27. Private Collection Deed 449
28. NLW MSS 6655C f17, Aug. 1830
29. Planché, *Recollections and Reflections*, p.162
30. NLW MSS 6655C f20, undated
31. Douce MSS d27 f183
32. £500,000 today
33. Private Collection Deeds 374, 211
34. Ibid. Deeds 143, 224, 230, 353
35. Douce MSS d27 f166
36. *Hereford Times*, 1 June 1831
37. Sir Walter Scott describes in his journal
    being given a demonstration of the
    technique at Allanton in May 1829, but
    regarded Steuart as 'a sad coxcomb' as a
    result of the success of the book
38. NLW MSS 6655C f20, Jan. 1831

39. NLW MSS 6655C f28
40. NLW MSS 6655C f29
41. CA King Vol 19 f313
42. Douce MSS d28 f96
43. RAL AR6/2
44. NLW MS 6656C f10, 20 Nov. 1832
45. Meller, *TWNFC* 1977, Vol. XLII, Part 2, p.178
46. NLW MSS 6656C f13
47. Gwent RO D361 F/P 4.67
48. BL Add 52413

Chapter 9 Triumph and Tragedy
1. NLW MS 6655C f20 dated by context
2. RAL AR 6/2 f10 to Pettigrew
3. Chet Raines correspondence ref. E.5.6 2/4/1846
4. RAL AR 6/2 f11, 23 May 1831
5. Douce MSS d28 f96, 1 Feb. 1833
6. Published in McGarvie, *The Meyricks of Bush*, p.71
7. Held 5 Nov 1831. Report in *Hereford Journal*
8. RAL AR6/1 I-275
9. Douce MSS e.33; Maxim & Opinions, p.40
10. Douce MSS d27 f149, 2 Sep. 1831
11. Douce MSS d27 f155, 20 Sep. 1831
12. Douce MSS d26 f237, 19 June 1829
13. NLW MS 6655C f25 to Pettigrew 10 July 1831 from Windsor Castle
14. *ibid.*
15. NLW MS 6655C f26
16. Douce d28 f216, 26 Dec. 1833
17. The portrait was exhibited at the Royal Academy in 1826, now in Torre Abbey
18. Johnson, *Sir Walter Scott - The Great Unknown*, Vol 1, p.637
19. NLW MS 6655C f26, 20 Jan. 1832
20. RAL copy of WO44/301
21. Shaw, *Knights of England*, Vol 2, p.332
22. The pills were probably calomel, or mercurous chloride
23. NLW MSS 6655C f27 to ff 34
24. Private Collection, 24 Apr. 1832
25. Douce MSS d28 f28, 18 Apr. 1832
26. Private Collection Doc 333
27. PRO Death Duty Registers IR26/107
28. *ibid.* £2.6m equivalent
29. SUL MS139 A5 182
30. Wainwright, *The Romantic Interior*, p.264, 15 July 1833
31. NLW MS 6655C, 23 June 1833
32. SUL MS 139 A5 53.

33. Douce MSS d28 f168, 21 Oct. 1833
34. NLW MS 6655C f36, 23 June 1833
35. HRO J12/IV/6, 7 Nov. 1839
36. HRO J12/IV/6, 7 Nov. 1839
37. Douce MSS d28 f168, 21 Oct. 1833
38. RAL AR6/1 I-275 Visitors' Book
39. Douce MSS d28 f242, 21 Jan. 1834
40. Douce MSS d28 f96, 1 Feb. 1833
41. HRO Q/Ros/8
42. Bod MS Eng Hist c.149, Frederic Madden's diary for 1834
43. Letters to *Hereford Times* 5 May 1866 onwards
44. *Hereford Journal* report
45. *ibid.*
46. RAL AR6/2 Loose papers
47. PRO AO2/57 p203
48. *The Douce Legacy*
49. *ibid.*
50. PRO PROB10/5462 C-G
51. Nash, *The Goodrich Court Guide*, Hereford 1845
52. *The Analyst*, pp.22-28
53. *ibid.*, pp.73-84
54. *ibid.*, pp.2-28, pp.243-266
55. Douce MSS d27 f32
56. RAL Box AR6/1 I-275 Visitors Book 1831-5, p.129
57. Burges bequeathed some items from the Meyrick Collection to the British Museum. BM Accession Books July 1874, Aug. 1881.
58. See de Cosson & Burges, *Catalogue of Exhibition of Ancient Helmets & Examples of Mail*
59. Meyrick Soc letter dated 17 Nov 1834
60. RAL AR6/2 letter to Pettigrew, 7 Dec. 1835
61. Bod Phillipps-Robinson letters e.372 f75
62. Letter recently printed in *Ross Gazette*, sent 6 Jan. 1836
63. RAL AR 6/2 Letter to Pettigrew, 23 Feb. 1837
64. Meyrick Society document
65. CA King Vol 19 f313. He was in fact a commoner
66. Nash, *Goodrich Court Guide*, 1845, p.12
67. Bod MS Top Oxon b.80 f133
68. RAL AR6/2 Letter from Martin to Richard Cotton dated 11 Aug. 1837
69. CA King Vol 10
70. HL Trial of Coward vs Wellington Hereford Assizes Aug 1836
71. CA King Vol 19

72. Meyrick Society archives. Note in pencil in margin of document
73. CCL MS 4.189 f15, 28 Sep. 1824
74. *Hereford Journal*, 4 Aug. 1836
75. HL. Trial of Coward vs Wellington Hereford Assizes Aug. 1836
76. Bod MS Top Oxon b.80 f127 to Joseph Skelton, 7 Aug. 1826
77. NLS MS 3903 f183 to Sir Walter Scott, 21 Nov. 1826
78. HRO Colwall parish register
79. Bod MS Top Oxon b.80 f133 5 Oct. 1827
80. College of Arms King. Vol 19
81. RAL AR6/2 Letter from Francis Martin to Richard Cotton, 11 Aug. 1837
82. *ibid.*
83. NLW 6656C f13 20 Nov 1837
84. RAL AR6/2 Letter from Francis Martin to Richard Cotton, 11 Aug. 1837
85. *ibid.*
86. ChCh Collections Book LIB.5, p.42
87. NLW MS 6655C f33, 18 July 1832
88. ChCh Archives Battels Book xc363
89. £21,000 today
90. *The Times*, 17 Apr. 1860

Chapter 10 The Goodrich court Experience
1. This chapter has been written for a visit in 1845. Material has been taken (and intermingled) from the following sources, except where otherwise noted: Louisa Twamley, *An Autumn Ramble on the Wye*, 1839, pp.108-111. College of Arms T.W. King, *Heraldic Miscellany*, Vol 19, f313. Thomas Fosbroke, *The Wye Tour*, 1848, pp.51-77. Charles Nash, *The Goodrich Court Guide*, 1845. Mr. & Mrs. S.C. Hall, *The Book of South Wales, the Wye and the Coast*, 1861. Samuel Meyrick, 'The Catalogue of the Doucean Museum', *GM*, Feb. to Dec. 1836. Henry Shaw, *Specimens of Ancient Furniture*, 1836. Joseph Skelton, *Engraved Illustrations of the Armour at Goodrich*
2. NLW MS 6656C f13, Nov. 1837
3. Sir Samuel deliberately made his visitors wait so they had time to admire the knocker. George Strong, *Handbook to Ross and Archenfield*, 1863, p.61
4. Plate 21
5. Skelton, *Engraved Illustrations*
6. Rich was also in Egypt and travelled widely in the Middle East
7. In the BM Acc. Ref. 1878 Nov 11-1/579, 580. Bought from estate of E.J. Andrews RAL AR 6/2
8. South Kensington Catalogue of Meyrick Collection, item 1238
9. *GM*, Vol 95-ii, Nov. 1825, pp.387-391
10. CA King Vol 19 f277
11. NLW MS 6656C f26, 18 May 1840, 'Jones the carpenter has made a body and arms for the head of Edward 2nd'
12. 'Viator' Hastilude Chamber, Goodrich Court in *The Analyst*, 6 Aug. 1834, pp.110-111
13. A sort of helmet
14. Part of the horse armour
15. CA King Vol 19 f461, 10 May 1841
16. CA King Vol 19 f281
17. Private Collection of cards
18. Nash says 1822 - it was 19 July 1821
19. Anstruther, *The Knight and the Umbrella*, 1963; Geoffrey Bles, pp.5-9
20. NLS MS 3893 f47
21. *Times* 13 July 1821
22. Perhaps £25,000 today
23. Blair, *European Armour*, pp.170-178
24. Meyrick, *Critical Inquiry*, Vol 3, pp.82-83
25. *ibid.*
26. *ibid.*, Vol 2, p.266 Plate LXIII standing figure
27. *ibid.*, Vol 2, p.271 Plate LXIV figure on left
28. *ibid.*, Vol 2, p.285 Plate LXV
29. *ibid.*, Vol 2, p.288 Plate LXVI
30. *ibid.*, Vol 3, p.5 Plate LXVII
31. *ibid.*, Vol 3, p.63
32. *ibid.*, Vol 3, pp.4-5 Plate LXVII. Wallace Coll A62. Now dated to 1590-1600 and made at Greenwich
33. WC A989
34. Letter recently printed in *Ross Gazette*, Jan. 1836
35. Now in the Wallace Collection A407
36. Now in National Museum of Wales TGARN/1 and TGARN/2.
37. Douce MSS d28 f216
38. *GM*, Jun 1837, p/584
39. NLW MS 6656C f64 & f69. Now in Corinium museum
40. V&A DPD Pressmark A.268 Acc. No. 8743.10
41. BM Acc. Ref. 1878 November 11-1/1
42. BM Acc. Ref. 1878 November 11-1/2

43. Douce MSS d28 f114
44. RAL Box AR6/1 I-275 Clerk of Works Cash Book
45. RAL Box AR6/1 I-275 Clerk of Works Expenses Book
46. *Archaeologia*, Vol XXXI, pp.238-248
47. BM Acc. Ref. 1878 November 11-1/3
48. The coins are now in the Ashmolean Museum
49. CA King Vol 19 ff 253-273, passim
50. Now in the Wallace Collection
51. Now in the Wallace Collection
52. Plate 24
53. Plate 28
54. CA King Vol 19, Fifth Excursion, Aug. 23 1841
55. CA King Vol 19, f467
56. These may be the chairs sold at Goodrich Court, 26 Aug. 1946 lots 369-372
57. They have been copied and engraved by Callot
58. SUL J.C. Isaac MS 139 A5 53/193-6
59. Probably on his mother's side
60. The location of these portraits is unknown
61. Douce MSS d27 f18, 8 Mar. 1830. Coke Smyth is best known for his scenes of Canadian life
62. Some of these names are taken from the 1869 Sales Particulars
63. This may be the piano sold at Goodrich Court, 27 Aug. 1946, lot 420
64. Bought from Swabey, according to a letter to J.C. Isaac. Some were bought in Germany, however
65. Letter to *The Analyst*, 7 July 1834, pp.22-28
66. BL Add MSS 34192 f1
67. Possibly that in the BM Acc. Ref. 1878 November 11-1/106
68. BM Acc. Ref. 1878 November 11-1/105
69. Now in a private collection
70. RAL Box AR 6/1 Heiton Book entry for Jan. 3/10 1830

Chapter 11 A True Welshman
1. Preface to *History & Antiquities of .. Cardigan.* Lots 370, 371& 1046 in his library sale
2. NLW Caerwys MS 1562C to Angharad Llwyd, 27 June 1825
3. CCL Doc 3.105 f2, 1 Dec. 1821
4. Douce MSS d24 f95, 14 Nov. 1822
5. *DWB*
6. Sale Catalogue
7. Guest & John, *Lady Charlotte*, p.96

8. Many other important personalities have had to be omitted
9. The *Mabinogion* is Lady Charlotte's translation and transcription of medieval copies of earlier Welsh poems and romances
10. Letter from Hartshorne to Albert Way, 8 Dec. 1837 (courtesy C. Blair). Possibly 'pyrgological' = pyrological, to do with fire
11. Letter from Sir Samuel to Hartshorne, 5 Dec. 1837 (courtesy C. Blair)
12. NLW MS 6656C ff67 & 74, Sep. & Oct. 1843
13. *DWB*
14. NLW Lady Charlotte Guest Journal Vol X 1835-37
15. NLW MS 13132E f196
16. NLW MS 13132E f197
17. NLW Lady Charlotte Guest Journal Vol X 1835-37
18. The spelling until the Halls changed it to Llanover
19. NLW MS 6656C f12 3 Nov 1837. The uniform may have been that of High Sheriff or of Deputy Lieutenant
20. Maxwell Fraser, 'Lady Llanover & her Circle', *Journal of NLW*, pp.171-188
21. *ibid.*
22. *Monmouthshire Beacon* report
23. NLW Lady Charlotte Guest Journal Vol X 1835-37
24. *Monmouthshire Beacon* report
25. NLW MS 1807E Rev. Walter Davies f930, 17 Nov. 1837
26. NLW MS 1807E f931, 9 Dec. 1837
27. *ibid.*
28. NLW MS 13487C p.4. 25 Aug. 1837
29. NLW MS 131-C
30. NLW MS 13960E 51-63
31. CA King Vol 19, ff543-581
32. NLW MS 1807E f932, 19 Jan. 1838
33. NLW MS 6656C f15, 27 Feb. 1838
34. SUL MS 139 A5 53/187, 21 Sep. 1838
35. Cotman, *Sepulchral Brasses*, Vol 2, p.7 mistake is in *Critical Inquiry*, Vol 2, pl.xxxviii
36. Weinreb, *London Encyclopaedia*
37. Steventon was near Acton
38. Anstruther, *The Knight and the Umbrella*, p.63
39. Lot 1328 in the sale of his library
40. Anstruther, *op. cit.*
41. Quoted in McGarvie
42. RAL AR 6/2
43. *Archaeologia*, Vol XX, pp.496-514

44. HRO L24/34, 7 Feb. 1839
45. HRO BF16/22, 9 Sep. 1829
46. SUL MS 139 A5 53/189, 28 Apr. 1839
47. Letter from Hartshorne to Albert Way, 17 Oct. 1840 (courtesy C. Blair)
48. Letter from Hartshorne to Albert Way, 24 May 1838 (courtesy C. Blair)
49. Letter from Hartshorne to Albert Way, 17 Oct. 1840 (courtesy C. Blair)
50. CA King Vol.12, f143, 26 May 1841
51. BL Add 56396 f22
52. Died suddenly 10 Aug. 1838, Nathaniel Morgan journal
53. HRO J12/IV/6, 7 Nov. 1839
54. NLW MS 6598E f77 to Traherne, 10 Dec. 1840
55. Letter to Hartshorne, 27 July 1840 (courtesy of C. Blair). The Llandaff Charters are a collection of early ecclesiastical land deeds
56. *DWB*
57. *GM*, Mar 1839, pp.202-5
58. *GM*, Apr. 1839, pp.303-4
59. NLW MS 1807E f933, 27 Mar. 1840
60. RAL AR 6/2 2a
61. Nash, *Goodrich Court Guide*, p.14
62. Bod Philipps-Robinson letters c.417 f136
63. *The National Review*, 1910, pp.646-652
64. Bod Phillipps-Robinson letters e.372 f75
65. NLW MS 1807E f934, 1 May 1840
66. Joseph Morris of St. Johns Hill Shrewsbury & William Watkin Edward Wynne (1801-80)
67. NLW MS 1807E f935, 20 July 1840
68. CA King Vol 19
69. Saddleworth Museum H/HOW/GS/60(22), 7 Aug. 1845
70. Howcroft, *George Shaw of St. Chad's Saddleworth*, Saddleworth Hist. Soc.
71. CA King Vol 17 f411, Oct. 1 1845
72. Tighwick, *History of the Parish of Rochdale*, pp.214-5
73. CA King Vol 17 f411, Oct. 1 1845. It is odd that Raines should have expected Sir Samuel to act like Sir Pertinax Macsycophant or Shakespeare's jack-in-office Dogberry
74. Quoted in *Lancashire*, magazine of Lancs FHS, Vol 9, No 3, 1988
75. Chet Raines Collection ref. E.5.6. 7 Apr. 1843
76. C.. Richardson, *Studies from Old English Mansions ...*, 1848, IV
77. Introduction to *Dwnn* p.xxxii
78. NLW MS 1807E f936, 22 Mar. 1841
79. Bod Phillipps-Robinson letters d.129 f204 & 205, 27 Dec. 1841
80. Bod Phillipps-Robinson letters c.493 ff 9-15
81. NLW MS 1636E 1637E letters in Sir Samuel's own copy of *Dwnn*
82. *ibid.*

Chapter 12 An Indian Summer ... and Fall
1. NLW MS6656C f26, 18 May 1840
2. SUL MS 139 A5 53/196A
3. CA King Vol 19 f461, 10 May 1841
4. CA King Vol 12 f139, 22 May 1841
5. Anvil in BM Acc. Reg. 1879 Mar 3-5/1
6. RAL AR6/2 unnumbered copy of agreements
7. Deeds 123, 294, 327, 356, 357 Private Collection
8. NLW MS 6656C f33, 1 Mar. 1841
9. CA King Vol 19. Now 'Charlton'
10. Strong, *Handbook to Ross and Archenfield* 1863, p.81
11. Deeds 103, 104 Private Collection
12. HRO AW87
13. Lowe, Field meeting to Goodrich, HAN 72 (2001) pp.25-37
14. Nash, *Goodrich Court Guide*
15. CA King Vol 14 f31, 2 Apr. 1844
16. NLW MS 6656C f70, 3 Nov. 1843
17. Deeds 200a, 214 Private Collection
18. Copy at Ye Hostelrie
19. Strong, *Handbook to Ross and Archenfield*, 1863, p.80
20. Chet Raines Collection E.5.6, 3 Jan. 1846
21. RAL AR 6/2
22. CA King Vol 19
23. RAL AR 6/2, 30 Apr. 1842
24. Bod Phillipps-Robinson letters b.144 f158, 28 June 1842
25. Deed 449 Private Collection
26. Chet Raines Collection E.5.6, 7 April 1843
27. RAL AR 6/2, 27 May 1843
28. RAL AR 6/2, 4 June 1843
29. CA King Vol 19 f481, 7 Dec. 1843
30. *ibid.*
31. HL Herefordshire Pamphlets 296
32. NLW MS 6656C f72, 28 Nov. 1843
33. RAL AR 6/2 to Pettigrew, 11 Apr. 1831
34. CA King Vol 19 f490, 22 Dec. 1845
35. CA King Vol 19 f499, 12 Mar. 1846
36. Chet Raines Collection E.5.6, 6 Nov. 1846

37. *GM*, Jan 1828, pp.6-8; Feb 1828, pp.103-4
38. Pettigrew, *History of Egyptian Mummies and an account of the Worship & Embalming of the Sacred Animals*, 1834
39. Chet Raines Collection E.5.6, 6 Nov. 1846
40. BL Add 56230 f69, 1 Jul. 1844
41. CA King Vol 14 f15
42. Fairclough, 'A Gothic-revival Ewer and dish from Goodrich Court' in *Amgueddfa*, Autumn 1992
43. CA King Vol 14 f15, 27 Nov. 1844
44. SA MS 857/7 MS Coll of C.R. Smith 1845
45. RAL AR 6/2, 1 Nov. 1845
46. Issue of Saturday, 8 Aug.
47. RAL AR6/1 I-275, 21 June 1843 to 12 June 1847
48. In March 1872 Sir Samuel's Welsh harp was apparently in the keeping of Lady Llanover when Mr. Leslie from Kensington Museum came to see it with a view to it being exhibited there. NLW Dolaucothi corr. L2580
49. SA MS 857/8 MS Coll C R S 1846
50. Bod Phillipps-Robinson Letters e.380 f149v-150, 26 Dec. 1846
51. NLW MS 13487C Cardiganshire notes, Vol VII Rev. George Eyre Evans
52. NLW MS 6656C f72, 28 Nov. 1843
53. CA King Vol 19 f521, 26 May 1847
54. NLW Cambrian Association letters 18 Aug. 1847
55. *Archaeologia Cambrensis*, Vol 1, pp.351-371
56. NLW Llidiardau Corr Box 14/6/1-186, 26 Apr. 1847
57. Deed 86 Private Collection
58. CA King Vol 19 f525, 21 Oct. 1847
59. NLW MS 6656C f90, 15 Jan. 1848
60. Meyrick Society, letter to King, 9 Feb. 1848
61. NLW MS 6656C f93, 10 Mar. 1848
62. RAL AR 6/2, 11 Mar. 1848
63. CA King Vol 19 f531, 17 Mar. 1848
64. CA King Vol 19 f535, 24 Mar. 1848
65. CA King Vol 19 f577, 19 July 1848
66. Strong *Handbook to Ross and Archenfield* p.62

Chapter 13 The Meyrick Heritage

1. PRO IR26/1810
2. Hereford Lib H.L. Davies Coll H Vol 50, 238
3. RAL Box AR6/1 I-275
4. Wright, *Wanderings of an Antiquary*, 1854 p.3
5. Printed in Carter's edition of the poem printed in 1857
6. Saucer showing Goodrich Court kindly given to the author by T. Carey
7. WC Meyrick collection box
8. Planché, *Recollections and Reflections*, pp.363-366
9. *ibid.*, pp.365-6
10. Laking, *The Armoury of Windsor Castle*, pp.236-40
11. *ibid.*, pp.201. Now in the Wallace Collection
12. Planché, *Recollections and Reflections*, p.434
13. HRO A.W.H. Meyrick's account book with J. Preece
14. *ibid.* About £40,000 today
15. Deeds 138, 139, 254, 292, 334, 435 Private Collection
16. Deed 335 Private Collection
17. V&A File MA11/M1972 30543 Bruce Seton to Henry Cole, Aug. 1868
18. V&A Coles Diary, quoted in McGarvie
19. *Hereford Times* reprint from the *Builder*, 26 Dec. 1868
20. V&A MA File MA11/M1972 No.1381, 8 Feb. 1872
21. V&A MA File MA11/M1972 Minute Paper No 12, 14 Jan. 1871 and No. 1275, 14 Jan. 1871
22. V&A MA File MA11/M1972 Note
23. V&A MA File MA11/M1972 Minute sheet 266
24. Goodrich parish registers & census information
25. BL add 34192 f1

Chapter 14 The Fate of the Treasures

1. Mann, *Wallace Collection Catalogue - European Arms and Armour 1962*, p.xvii
2. *ibid.*, pp.xiii-xxxi
3. Norman, in the 1986 Supplement to Mann *op. cit.* says 600,000 francs
4. WRO CR1886/Box 834/12 Pratt to Warwick, 19 Mar. 1873
5. WRO CR1886/Box 834/14 Pratt to Warwick, Sep. 1873
6. WRO CR1886/Box 834/14-16, 19 Sep. 1873
7. WRO CR1886/Box 789/82 Pratt to Warwick, 30 June 1875
8. *ibid.*
9. WRO CR1886/Box 789/90 Pratt to Warwick, 10 Nov. 1875
10. WRO CR1886/Box 789/82 Pratt to Warwick, 30 June 1875

11. WRO CR1886/Box 789/97 Pratt to Warwick, 22 Mar. 1876
12. WRO CR1886/Box 789/98 Pratt to Warwick, 11 Apr. 1876
13. *The Times*, 19 Mar. 1878. p.6
14. An expert catalogue of the arms & armour was made for Eastnor in 1962
15. Item c.14 in the same catalogue
16. Lacy, 'Students of Armour', unpublished PhD thesis 1999
17. Information from Blair, *The Meyrick Society 1890-1990*, printed for the Society
18. BL Add Mss 40678-40684
19. BL Add Mss 40682 pl. XXIX
20. Material from a full account of Laking in Lacy, *Students of Armour, op. cit.*
21. Information from Blair, *The Meyrick Society 1890-1990*
22. Now in the Bodleian Library
23. Now in a private collection
24. Now displayed at Torre Abbey, Torquay
25. Wilson, *The Forgotten Collector*, Caygill & Cherry, *A.W. Franks*
26. *ibid.*, p.41
27. BM Acc. Ref. 1879 Mar 3-5/1 purchased from Wm Wareham collection
28. BM Acc. Ref. 1878 Nov 11-1/48 Meyrick
29. *ibid.*, Nov 11-1/178 Meyrick
30. *ibid.*, Nov 11-1/72 Meyrick
31. *ibid.*, Nov 11-1/3 Meyrick
32. *ibid.*, Nov 11-1/85 Meyrick
33. *ibid.*, Nov 11-1/379 Meyrick
34. *ibid.*, Nov 11-1/381-580 Meyrick
35. *ibid.*, Nov 11-1/450 Meyrick; Skelton, pl.88 fig.17, pl.143 fig.2
36. *ibid.*, Nov 11-1/581-629 Meyrick
37. *ibid.*, Nov 11-1/590 Meyrick
38. *ibid.*, Nov 11-1/653-686 Meyrick
39. *ibid.*, Nov 11-1/33 Meyrick. Douce 6
40. *ibid.*, Nov 11-1/34 & 35 Meyrick. Douce 48 & 47
41. *ibid.*, Nov 11-1/42 Meyrick. Douce 73

Chapter 15 Goodrich Court

1. HRO Hill Court Collection F8
2. Moffatt, *Illustrated Description of some of the Furniture at Goodrich Court*
3. Meller, 'Architectural History of Goodrich Court, *TWNFC*, Vol XLII, 1976-8, pp.175-185
4. Meller, 'Note on Goodrich Court', *TWNFC*
5. T*he Building News*, 7 June 1889
6. Anon., *Felsted in Herefordshire*, n.d.
7. HL Catalogue of sale fplc 728.8
8. RAL I.275 I.87
9. *ibid.*
10. *ibid.*
11. *ibid.*
12. WC Meyrick Collection box
13. Pers. comm. from Cecily Trafford
14. TAL I.275 I.87
15. GM Doucean Museum item 76
16. Sale Catalogue with some prices in author's possession
17 Pers. comm. from Cecily Trafford
18 Pers. comm. from the purchaser

Appendix A Meyrick Ancestry

1. HRO Marr. Licences, 24 Feb. 1741 Margaret Meyrick of Lucton & William Symmons of Kingsland
2. CCL Doc 3.105 f9 to Angharad Llwyd, 16 Dec. 1822
3. HRO will proved 4 Apr. 1719
4. HRO will proved 28 Feb. 1720/1
5. HRO G39/1/1/13
6. HRO G39/1/1/10-40
7. HRO dated 2 Apr 1717. Stephen was the son of William of Cleobury, Shrops.
8. Married Harris
9. Married Griffiths
10. HRO BTs bap. 17 May 1685
11. HRO BTs bap. 20 Apr. 1689 bur 16 Aug 1689
12. A James Meyrick and his wife Jane or Janet had children baptised at Aymestrey: Jane, 1679; Eleanor 1683; James 1685. Aymestrey BTs say April 1686 for James' baptism. Jane died 1689
13. HRO Lucton Parish Registers and BTs
14. HRO Lucton pew judgement
15. HRO G39/1/1/11, 26 May 1710
16. HRO Marriage Licences 1663-73
17. His will has not been found
18. HRO A85/1A Friends Suffering Book
19. HRO Hearth Tax
20. Faraday, *Herefordshire Militia Assessments of 1663*, Camden 1972
21. John Meyrick of Kingsland's will proved 12 Aug. 1727, but his widow was Maria
22. HL fplc 324.242 Copy of Poll Book for Herefordshire, 28 Mar. 1722
23. PRO E134/8Geo1/East5
24. This would make James' birth date from 1678, 6 years too early for him to be the son of Roger

Index